A FRAGRANCE OF OPPRESSION

TURNING POINT Christian Worldview Series
Marvin Olasky, General Editor

A FRAGRANCE OF OPPRESSION

*The Church and
Its Persecutors*

Herbert Schlossberg

CROSSWAY BOOKS • WHEATON, ILLINOIS
A DIVISION OF GOOD NEWS PUBLISHERS

Library of Congress Cataloging-in-Publication Data
Schlossberg, Herbert.
    A fragrance of oppression : the church and its persecutors /
Herbert Schlossberg.
        p.   cm. — (The Turning point Christian worldview series)
    Includes bibliographical references and indexes.
    1. Persecution—History—20th century. 2. Church history—
1945- 3. Church and state. I. Title. II. Series.
BR1601.2.S39 1991   272'.9—dc20   91-13621
ISBN 0-89107-626-3

99		98		97		96		95		94		93		92		91
15	14	13	12	11	10	9	8	7	6	5	4	3	2	1

TABLE OF

CONTENTS

P R E F A C E

On a treadmill you maneuver your legs but you do not move. In writing this book I have had the opposite problem. I have tried to make the material hold still long enough to analyze it, but it keeps shifting. First, what used to be called the eastern bloc collapsed as I began writing. Then, after I had finished the chapters on Islam, the Arab world split apart in a war—with the West, but also between its own members. The outcome of both these dramas is still unknown. Meanwhile, I have done a lot of rewriting to try to bring things up to date. In a sense, that is a task doomed to failure. Months will elapse between the finishing of the book and its appearance in print and much more may change in that time—not to mention the greater time until the last reader has read it. I will have to ask the reader's indulgence not to judge too harshly the author's failure to know something that you, now reading, know perfectly well.

Still, the corrections I have had to make because of these changes have been almost entirely superficial—modifying a present to a past tense, bringing an event up to date, and the like. None of the major conclusions I had reached before these momentous events have needed to be changed. My guess is that the inevitable march of historical events in the coming months and years, although I cannot predict them and am likely to be as surprised as everyone else, will not require fundamental revision of the conclusions. The reason is that this is not a book of current events, nor even a history. Rather, I have tried to see the patterns that occur as the church suffers persecution in this or that region, this or that period, and draw inferences from those patterns. I believe we can learn from such patterns and do things differently than if we had remained ignorant of them. To the extent I have been accurate in ascertaining their meaning, this work should be useful for a long time to come.

The Soviet Union—to use one prominent example—is a very different place, a much more humane place, than when I first began learning about the church there. But we cannot know that these changes are permanent. And even if they are, it would be surprising if analogous circumstances did not pop up elsewhere. Have we seen the last of an ideologically-driven totalitarian regime bent on crushing the resistance of all opposition? Not likely. Nor is it likely that when such a regime surfaces the church will be confronted by strategems that are completely new. It seems likely, rather, that future tyrants will imitate predecessors or at least stumble accidentally on similar techniques of oppression.

If some readers, at least, find useful the lessons drawn from the experience of the church in other places the efforts of the author and sponsors will be amply repaid.

Some obligations are gratifying to discharge, and that is the case in publicly thanking those who have helped give this book what merit it has. Howard and Roberta Ahmanson and Marvin Olasky were behind the project from the start and made it possible. Marvin Olasky, Terry Schlossberg, Kent Hill, Anita Deyneka, Patrick Sookhdeo, Marsh Moyle and George Otis, Jr. made many valuable suggestions and saved me from errors of fact and judgment—some of them, at any rate—proving that friendship, not to mention matrimony, is useful as well as pleasurable.

I am also grateful to Daniel Kyanda for making available to me his valuable thesis on the persecution of the church in Africa, a subject on which it has proven difficult to obtain information.

For we do *not* want you to be ignorant, brethren, of the affliction we experienced in Asia; for we were so utterly, unbearably crushed that we despaired of life itself. . . . But thanks be to God, who in Christ always leads us in triumph, and through us spreads the fragrance of the knowledge of him everywhere. For we are the aroma of Christ to God. . . .

2 Corinthians 1:8; 2:14,15a

A FRAGRANCE OF OPPRESSION:
THE CHURCH AND ITS PERSECUTORS

PERSECUTION AND CIVIL RIGHTS IN THE TWENTIETH CENTURY

*P**ersecution.* The word has a sinister ring to it, even if we're not sure exactly what is meant by it. To some it may call to mind the Roman Colosseum with hungry lions set loose on Christians. Others may think of dungeons or labor camps, arrests in the middle of the night, beatings in police stations, perhaps worse.

People living in free countries may think the subject is somewhat academic for them, a serious concern only for those living in other parts of the world. Or now that the communist world has entered a state of collapse, and elsewhere, too, democratic forces have been advancing at the expense of authoritarian regimes, it may seem as if the subject is losing its importance.

But that would be a serious mistake. When Jesus spoke to His disciples on this point He told them that just as He was being persecuted, so would they (John 15:20). And the entire history of the church has substantiated the interpretation that He was not speaking only of disciples in His own generation.

Taking the long view, then, we need to consider not the immediate trends which are often misleading in helping us discern what we should expect, but rather the Biblical principles which inform the church on this subject, and also the historical material that shows us how those principles are actually worked out in time and space. Thus, the two themes this book treats on the subject of persecution are *the-*

ology and *history*. But we are not going to treat them in an abstract and detached way. Rather we'll be looking at flesh-and-blood people in concrete situations. We'll see what persecution means to those who are suffering and to those who are causing the suffering.

Most important we'll want to understand what it all means to us, the followers of Christ who may be far from the situations of persecution. Are there principles we should learn that will help us prepare for a future that may be less peaceful than we have known in the past? Are there things we could and should be doing for those who are suffering now? Are there ways an understanding of persecution can help us be more faithful disciples of Christ in whatever situation we might find ourselves?

Let's begin by meeting a few people who have known persecution firsthand and see if by their experience we can come to a better understanding of what this subject is all about.

ALEXANDER OGORODNIKOV[1]

As a teenager Alexander Ogorodnikov, a convinced communist, became a leader in the Komsomol, which is the Russian name for the Young Communist League. He once went to church while holding that position in order, he says, to see "the funeral of Orthodoxy." But then something happened that he didn't expect. His Komsomol position gave him access to literature that the ordinary Soviet citizen is denied. He took a particular interest in some of the classic Russian books, especially those of the nineteenth-century novelist Dostoyevsky. To his surprise this brought him into contact with Christian faith, which he began to understand for the first time. He now says about his conversion: "Dostoyevsky reached my heart." In comparison he came to find Marxism vulgar and inhuman. At the time he was studying in the philosophical faculty of Moscow University. When he began to criticize Lenin's view of materialism, the authorities expelled him from the university. Ogorodnikov's conversion to Christian faith came suddenly when he realized he had been fooled by the party line. He then went to a university at Sverdlovsk in the Ural mountain area.

When he became a Christian he realized he knew nothing about his faith. He began reading the Bible, and everything began looking different than it had. He learned that Christians have to consider society's needs as well as their own, but how to work that out in the Soviet

Union? He not only was impressed by his own ignorance, but also knew nobody who thought as he did. He was completely isolated.

In order to break out of his isolation, Ogorodnikov began hitch-hiking across the Soviet Union in order to meet people. His key contact came in Leningrad when he met another believer on the street. They spoke about matters of the spirit, and the two of them were later to establish the Moscow Christian Seminar. In 1974 they began breaking bread together and praying. It didn't take the KGB (the secret police) long to find out about these activities, and they took the position that this was a new form of political opposition, even though there was no political component to what Ogorodnikov and his friends were doing. What was "new" about it was that there was no organization—no committees, no officers, no agenda. Since it had no head, the KGB found it difficult to close it down. They couldn't penetrate the informality of this non-organization.

Ogorodnikov and his friends now called their meeting the Christian Seminar. There were perhaps a dozen of them, all members of the Russian Orthodox Church. They wanted to regenerate the church and create a new reality, a new community. Or rather, numerous new communities. The objective was to set up groups like theirs all over the Soviet Union. By 1977 they had identified about 300 people across the country.

They communicated with one another by using couriers. As Ogorodnikov now tells it, it would have been stupid to do it any other way, since all their telephones were tapped and the mail was routinely opened by the authorities. Nevertheless, the KGB seemed willing to let them continue until the group began writing papers. These papers were written for their own edification, but found their way into the stream of communications that the Russians call *samizdat*, or self-publishing. (They use typewriters with a number of sheets of carbon paper to prepare these documents and pass them around from hand to hand. Those who get the fourth or fifth carbon sheet from a manual typewriter are doing well to be able to read the faint tracings.)

When these papers began circulating, the KGB called the seminar members in for questioning one by one, and before long the entire Moscow seminar had been put behind bars. They charged Ogorodnikov with "anti-party activities" and sentenced him to seven years in a severe regime labor camp. This is the worst kind, with very hard labor and grossly insufficient food. In the camp he went on repeated hunger strikes for the right to have a Bible; once he didn't eat anything for ten days straight. He describes the pain in his abdomen by making tearing motions with his hands. The guards always ended up force-feeding him through a tube in his nose. When I asked him why the guards cared if he died, Ogorodnikov explained that the Soviet authorities are obsessed with what the West hears about people like him; they know they can't keep it a secret. "They can persecute only in the shadows," he explains. He finally did get a Bible, but was allowed to keep it only six months.

The punishment cells were kept in the 40s Fahrenheit, and the guards allowed the prisoners to wear only a thin garment. He was constantly beaten for not cooperating. One time his fellow prisoners in the punishment cells supported him with loud clamoring when the guards tore his hand-made cross out of his mouth, where he put it to try to keep it from them. The response was a dose of tear gas for the whole cell block.

After Ogorodnikov finished serving his time, the authorities gave him another five-year sentence for being uncooperative. The amnesty of 1987, in the third year of *glasnost*, finally caught up with him, and he was released in February of that year, having served eight and one-half years of exceedingly harsh time in the labor camp, including 689 days on hunger strike.

ALLEN YUAN[2]

When the Chinese communists won the civil war in 1949 and took over the country, Allen Yuan was pastor of a church in Beijing. He had become a Christian some seventeen years earlier through the influence of two Christian teachers at the YMCA in that city. In 1950 the government made it mandatory for the churches to join the Three-self Patriotic Movement, an organization it had set up as a means of controlling them. Eleven churches in Beijing refused to do this, including Yuan's. They would not recognize the leadership of the Three-Self organization, many of whom were Marxists or were otherwise opposed to the historic Christian faith. But the main problem was that the Three-Self Movement put the spiritual power of the church under the control of the temporal power of the state. This made the church a tool of the state rather than a tool of the Holy Spirit, and Yuan could not see how he could be a part of it and still serve God.

The regime said this refusal to join the Three-Self Patriotic Movement was an anti-revolutionary act. Beginning in 1955 the pastors who did not join went to prison. Yuan's turn came in the latter part of 1958. At forty-four years of age, he was one of the youngest of his group to be taken; the head of the government's Religious Affairs Bureau wanted to give him some time to think it over while he was locking up the other pastors. By then Yuan and his wife were caring for six children as well as his mother.

In addition to the political charges, the government also accused him of cheating his flock and pocketing the money. There was no lawyer, no defense, and no jury. Yuan and another pastor were sentenced to life imprisonment; others received sentences from fifteen to twenty years. From 1958 to 1965 Yuan was in prison in Beijing making socks and plastic shoes. He could receive one visitor a month for twenty minutes. When the prison became too full, they moved him to a reform camp up north, near the Soviet border. This camp held about two thousand prisoners, all living in one big building. On winter nights it got down to about 40 degrees Fahrenheit. The prisoners did farm work nine hours a day, with one day off every two weeks. At night they were required to study politics for two hours and then listen to more politics on the radio.

The hardships included serious food shortages. Guards would abuse the prisoners without being disciplined. Officials accused Yuan of being an American spy because they said he had a foreign religion. And also a Japanese spy because the chapel of which he had been pastor was begun by Japanese missionaries. These charges were carried back to Beijing and made his wife's lot even harder.

Yuan never despaired and never doubted God's love. He fully expected to be in prison for the rest of his life. But when Deng Xiao Ping came to power he released all prisoners over the age of sixty who had been in prison for more than twenty years. Yuan fell into that category, and he finally was sent home after twenty-one years as a prisoner. When he arrived at the railroad station in Beijing his family walked right by him; they didn't recognize him.

CHARLES MENDIES[3]

Nepal is the only officially Hindu country in the world. Occupying mountainous terrain between India and Tibet, it is known to outsiders chiefly for its trekking opportunities. Nepal is a kingdom that remained closed to all outside influence until less than forty years ago. Since that time a flourishing Christian community has existed in the country, even though some of its activities are contrary to Nepalese law.

Charles Mendies, although still in his early thirties, has been active in village evangelism for many years. He and his wife Susan have in addition to their own three sons more than fifty orphans living with them in their family compound, children who likely would be dead if the Mendies family had not taken them in. For several years he has been in and out of jail for short periods on charges relating to his activities for the church. Susan also spent time in jail during one of her pregnancies. Their pastor, Susan's brother-in-law, was jailed for a time without trial and told that if he did not leave the country his imprisonment would continue for a long time. He went back to his native India, along with his family, and is now conducting a ministry with Nepalese in that country.

The official status of Hinduism has led to laws that make Christian ministry almost impossible. It is not illegal to be a Christian, but it is illegal for a Hindu to *become* a Christian. This is a crime punishable by a year in jail. When the convert emerges from jail his conversion is nullified; hence if he goes to church he is liable for another jail term. Those who convert others are sentenced to six years imprisonment. This is not a healthy environment for an evangelist. Foreign protests were effective for some time in keeping Mendies and a few others—mostly those who lived in the capital, Kathmandu—from serving long sentences. Few foreigners venture far into the sparsely-settled and mountainous countryside from there.

In the fall of 1989 in an outlying village the police raided a church, severely beat the pastor and several members, and dragged them to a Hindu temple, forcing many of them to bow before an idol. This followed a period of increasing pressure on the Christians in many villages. Mendies immediately met with a number of other Christian leaders in Kathmandu to discuss how to meet this challenge. Shortly thereafter the police picked him up. He had been convicted of preaching Christianity several years earlier, the supreme court had affirmed his six-year sentence, and now his freedom came to an end. In 1990, however, he was freed along with other Christians when the pro-democracy demonstrations almost brought down the government. The draft constitution that has been recently circulated apparently provides some relief for the religious oppression, but the guarantees are tenuous and subject to interpretations. And Hinduism remains the established state religion.

ALBAJAR BARANI[4]

The status of Christians in the Islamic world varies widely from country to country. That is true even within a particular region. In Morocco, for example, it is virtually impossible for Christian citizens to live openly as followers of Christ. In Egypt, by contrast, there is a long-standing Christian community in the Coptic Church, and there are also evangelical groups that operate more or less openly. But there is considerable pressure brought on them, pressure that ebbs or flows depending on the fluctuation of both political fortunes and the fervor of the dominant Islamic community.

Albajar Barani traveled to Egypt along with a fellow Moroccan Christian in order to attend a training program for Christian workers. Late one night they were suddenly dragged to the police station along with their two Tunisian roommates. The four were not allowed to eat or sleep for three days and three nights while they were questioned, and they were beaten numerous times. The favorite method was to strike them repeatedly on the soles of their feet with sticks and then make them run in place on their bruised and swollen feet.

They spent the next six months in Torah prison in Cairo, under persistent pressure to convert to Islam. One of the Tunisians was put in a cell with members of the Moslim Brotherhood and could have been killed. Nobody on the outside knew what had happened to these men for two months. Then they were able to get word to the outside, and friends began to mount a worldwide publicity campaign. This had many fits and starts, and the men were going downhill with the heat, hunger and thirst of prison life. For the first two months they could not shave, bathe or brush their teeth. They had only small quantities of beans and rice to eat, and this was full of worms and other insects. There was no furniture; they slept on the stone floor.

Friends on the outside eventually provided them with a lawyer, and they were allowed into an Egyptian courtroom to plead their case. This proved fruitless. In the end it was political pressure from other countries on the Egyptian government that got them released.

RIGHTS AND THE MODERN AGE

Religious persecution has to be considered in the context of all violations of human rights. Many people regard the twentieth century as the golden age of human rights because there is such widespread concern about these issues. Here is the way a recent book by former U.S. Congressman Robert F. Drinan begins:

> Across the world a new gospel is echoing in the hearts of men and women—the good news that their human rights are recognized and somehow guaranteed by the law of nations. It is a rather recent realization among the oppressed of the world. But since this novel idea was first promoted in the Charter of the United Nations (1945) it has entered the consciousness of humankind and has become one of the great driving forces of the modern world.
>
> The concept that the protection of the fundamental human rights of every person transcends local and national law is an earth-shaking idea like the abolition of slavery, the phasing out of colonialism, and the abolition of apartheid.[5]

It's hard to imagine how a Jesuit priest like Drinan could make so many errors in one short passage on a subject like this. Apart from his uncritical hailing of something he calls a "new gospel" (replacing the "old" one?), Drinan has lost sight of the fact that there may be no century in which human rights have been as flagrantly violated as ours. Nor does he recognize that human rights concerns are not modern at all, but rather are ancient, as a consideration of the documents of his own church could have persuaded him.

The Old Testament documents are not the first we have concerning human rights, but they have been the most influential. And they do it in the light of the same definition that Drinan uses: they say that people have rights that transcend human statutes. The Pentateuch quotes the Lord in this way: "Follow justice and justice alone, so that you may live and possess the land that the Lord your God is giving you" (Deuteronomy 16:20). Moreover the Old Testament portrays God as being enraged when these rights are trampled on and the people suffer injustice. "'Because of the oppression of the weak and the groaning of the needy, I will now arise,' says the Lord. 'I will protect them from those who malign them'" (Psalm 12:5).

If Drinan is mistaken concerning the novelty of the human rights talk of the twentieth century, he is even more wrong in failing to recognize the depths of the failure of our century in protecting human rights. Apart from the wars that have caused so much suffering, governments in the twentieth century have by and large repudiated the notion that human statutes are to be subject to higher law, which means that politicians do not see themselves as being subject to an authority beyond the political process. This is even true in places where the human rights record is relatively good. The fruits of this disregard for Law beyond the laws have been especially bitter in powerful and lawless governments like that of the Nazis, and for almost all Marxist-Leninist regimes. Estimates of those murdered by Stalinism in the Soviet Union alone begin at around twenty million and go on up to more than double that figure, and some of the high numbers are now coming from Soviet sources.

Most of the human rights violations in the present age are little known. They take place in small countries that are not well covered in the press because they play little role in the big stories connected with the struggle between East and West—and are therefore of little interest to journalists. Sometimes those who control the media are sympathetic to the regimes that commit human rights violations, and thus are little inclined to follow up on reports of repression. Even religious groups are sometimes driven by ideological ideas that blind them to the realities of those whose plight ought logically to move them deeply.

The foregoing paragraphs are intended to show that although the persecution of Christians has a force and meaning peculiar to Christian faith (and that is the perspective that dominates in this book), it also is connected intimately with the larger historical context. The human rights movement occupies something close to center stage, and so does wholesale violation of human rights. Both are connected with the persecution story we are examining here, and thus we have to consider both of them.

This makes our story more puzzling in some ways, but truer to the complexity of human history. Does it make sense in the light of the later history of the Soviet Union (when the church leadership underwent wholesale murder) that for a short time after the Bolshevik revolution triumphed in Russia in 1917 the Russian Orthodox Church had *more* freedom than it had enjoyed under the Tsars? And yet that is the case.[6]

TAKING ACCOUNT OF CHANGE

That example from the early history of the Soviet Union illustrates another inescapable fact of all forms of oppression, including religious persecution: they ebb and flow. That is especially important to keep in mind now because of the momentous events that have taken place recently in the Soviet Union and eastern Europe. We tend to view change as something that brings a new fixed situation into being, so that we might think that persecution is a thing of the past in the U.S.S.R. But the record suggests otherwise. The 1920s and '30s were a disaster for the churches in the Soviet Union. By the time World War II began, it was questionable if the church could even survive. But the early war successes of the Germans were so overwhelming and the Soviet people so little inclined to fight for the continuation of Stalin's rule that government policy changed. In order to bring the church into the struggle on the side of the government, Stalin made concessions that gave reasonable basis for believing the bad old days were over, and there was a revival of the Russian Orthodox Church.[7] After the war, his need for the church ended, and Stalin renewed the repression that the war had interrupted.[8]

In the history of human rights in the Soviet Union, the transition from the Stalin period to that of Khrushchev is usually regarded as merciful change for the better. But that was not true of the history of the church. Khrushchev launched a disastrous repression, with more than half the evangelical churches forcibly closed during his tenure. By 1965 there were only eight thousand Orthodox churches open in the whole country, which was about one-third the number that were in use at the start of the campaign in 1959.[9] The repression continued and even worsened in the Brezhnev years.

We now have another thaw in the Soviet Union, one that in some ways has been more fundamental than any before it. Can we say the problem of religious repression has finally ended in the Soviet Union? Not if we are wise. It is not only the history of the Soviet Union that should make us wary of a statement such as that. It is the whole history of the persecution of the church. The early centuries under the Roman Empire, for example, saw not one persecution but many. The repression might flower in one region of the Empire for a time and then die down while it sprang up elsewhere. At various times and places Christians might have been tempted to think that finally the persecution of the church had become a thing of the past, but that never happened.[10] There are also disquieting signs that *glasnost* is not as all-pervasive as western observers think. Ordinary Soviet citizens are noticeably less enthusiastic than foreigners about what is happening in their country. And, five years into the *glasnost* era,

Christians are still being murdered in KGB-planned operations, a fact that is almost completely absent from newspapers in the West.

If we are to take the long view, then, we should avoid focusing unduly on the dips and surges in the persecutions. It is only in this way that we can avoid both despair and naive optimism, and understand better the forces that drive the persecutions and give them their meaning. Perhaps a useful metaphor for understanding this process is that of an ocean. There are very great variations in the height of the sea at a given place. From low to high tide there may be many feet of difference. And in rough seas the distance from the height of the crest to the trough may also be very large. Still there is such a thing as *sea level*. People whose business requires them to know about such things must consider all the variations without losing sight of the *norm* that is represented by the idea of sea level. The fluctuations are expected, and someone who wants to understand the movement of the seas must do so while accounting for the changes. This is not a static conception, just as history is not a static conception.

Similarly, when we see persecution reaching a fever pitch in one place or recede in another we should not forget to look at the big picture. We're going to look at peaks and troughs, but we're going to do it in the context of the sea level of persecution, a sort of constant that stands behind the fluctuations. I believe the writer of the book of Hebrews intended to convey something like this when he instructed the early church to stand fast in the faith in the midst of persecutions, and he held up as their examples the experience of the ancient Hebrew prophets (Hebrews 11:32—12:12). Evidently he considered the intervening millennium or two of small import in the constant fact that God's people can always expect to be persecuted.

That constant should give us the motivation to understand the phenomenon better, to see how the historical events confirm and illustrate the Biblical teachings, to prepare better for what could befall any of us, and to see how we can help Christians everywhere who are suffering for their faith.

A word about the scope of this book before we continue: We are going to be considering the persecution of the Christian church by outside forces, whether governmental or otherwise. There is a long unhappy chapter yet to be written about relationships between Orthodox, Catholic and Protestant, and even within each of those groups, but that is outside our present task.

THE PERSECUTION OF CHRISTIANS BY ISLAM

WHAT IS THE PROBLEM?

Since some experts have denied or minimized the existence of the problem we are dealing with in this chapter, perhaps the best way to begin is to give a few concrete examples of it. In a later chapter we'll consider who is denying the problem and why.

•Indonesia—in which Islam is predominant—rules the territory of East Timor after having taken it over militarily in 1975. But it's having trouble pacifying its conquest. The Roman Catholic bishop of East Timor, Carlos Filipe Belo, has accused the Suharto government of great brutality, including torture. And he characterizes as "lying propaganda" government assertions that the abuses do not exist. He had to smuggle his statement out of the country because foreigners are not permitted to visit East Timor. Muslims have made many threats against his life. Indonesian authorities regard East Timor as Islamic territory.[1]

•In 1987 there was serious rioting in Nigeria. The ruler, Gen. Ibrahim Babangida, led the country into the Organization of the Islamic Conference, which delighted the 50 percent of the country's Muslims but caused foreboding among the 35 percent who are Christians. (These figures are disputed; it's hard to get accurate statistics in Nigeria.)[2] The violence began March 6 after a Christian revival meeting took place in an Islamic college town. Anti-Christian riots spread to several other cities in the Muslim north of the country. Gen. Babangida, a Muslim, declared that the riots were part of a coup d'état by "an ambitious group of mindless power-seekers."[3]

•The government of Malaysia has embarked on a gradual program of Islamization, evidently in response to a resurgence of Islamic fervor among much of the populace. It is trying to induce Islamic values into national life. The Muslim call to prayer is now heard over radio and television, which also carries Muslim evangelistic programming. Islamic civilization has become a compulsory course for students in the universities. There is much talk of introducing the Sharia, which is Islamic law. Increasingly Islamic life is being equated with nationalism, leaving non-Muslims in a kind of limbo. As part of its anti-colonial drive the government has been requiring strict adherence to the policy of the primacy of the Malay language. But *Malay* is synonymous with Muslim, just as other religions are almost exclusively associated with different nationality groups, such as the Chinese and the Indians. Legislation in several states makes it illegal to use certain words alleged to be Muslim in other religious literature on the grounds that it would confuse Muslim theology with that of other religions. Thus the Malay Bible cannot use the word for "gospel" or even "God" (Allah) because of this supposed confusion. As a result Christians may not distribute the Bible in the national language.[4]

•Turkey, which is formally a secular society, in recent years has stepped up harassment of Christians, apparently in order to head off conversions from the overwhelming Muslim majority. There have been church closings, arrests, beatings, death threats. Even foreigners have undergone this treatment notwithstanding the diplomatic risks.[5] In 1987, an evangelical congregation called the Istanbul International Fellowship, composed entirely of foreigners, was forced to disband in spite of repeated attempts to register in compliance with the law. The cases involving internationals were mostly dismissed. Evidently, there is some conflict between the authorities, with the police acting arbitrarily and courts hewing closer to the law. One report said the police were rearresting Christians who had previously had the cases against them dismissed.[6]

•Sudan was declared an Islamic republic in 1983, and the Sharia became the law of the land. Partly in consequence, the government began a campaign to pressure the Christian south of the country, the homeland of the Dinka tribe, to conform to the Sharia. In March of 1987 a disturbance erupted when twenty-five Dinka Christians were forced from an evening prayer service by an armed Muslim mob. A half dozen Christians lost their lives that evening, and dozens of homes were destroyed by fire. The next morning the Dinkas were boarding a train for evacuation from the town when hundreds of Muslims descended on the station. They heaped burning mattresses on the defenseless Dinkas, and shot, clubbed and mutilated others. According to a report by two Khartoum University professors, both Muslims, more than one thousand men, women and children lost their lives.[7]

The north of Sudan, exercising the preponderance of governmental power, has followed a policy of forcing the Christians of the south to convert. A brutal civil war has been part of the process, and the resulting starvation has been a weapon in these conversions. If you want to eat, embrace Islam. This activity has been bankrolled by Saudi Arabia, although famine relief from western nations has been diverted into the effort as well. The Roman Catholic bishops in Sudan put it this way: "The Sudanese government's plan to Arabize and Islamize the Southerners through absorption and assimilation is being realized." The weapons used in this struggle have been state controls on the Christian churches, arming tribal militias to fight as proxies of the government, the clever timing and placement of famine relief so as to effect conversions, and the manipulation of aid to displaced persons.

Many Christians expected these policies to end when autocratic President Gaafar Mohamed Nimeiri fell from power, but in spite of the election of 1986 the government has continued its Islamization policy. The Catholic Church which has about two million members has not received a permit to build a church for about twenty years, despite numerous applications. Muslim mosques are not required to have permits. The laws increasingly have been based on Islamic precepts. Flogging and amputation for theft are now common. One Italian Catholic priest was lashed for storing communion wine in his home.[8]

•Bangladesh banned a translation of the New Testament because it uses certain words that the law reserves for the exclusive use of Muslims. Official press releases say the action was taken because Muslims would take offense at such words in a Christian book. Some sources reported that the past two or three years have seen increased sensitivity to evangelism on the part of the government. The Bangladesh constitution guarantees freedom of religion.[9]

•A Baptist church in Bethlehem has been struck repeatedly by

the Muslim revival movement. It is surrounded by a high wall sur-
mounted with barbed wire. When someone suggested that the church
looked like a fortress, the pastor replied, "Perhaps more like a
prison." This church is composed entirely of people from Christian
backgrounds, although the pastor made no secret of his intention to
engage in evangelism among Muslims.[10]

FACTORS IN THE ISLAMIC RESURGENCE

Emmanuel Sivan reports walking through the streets of Cairo and
East Jerusalem in the early 1980s and seeing people buying fresh
reprints of six hundred-year-old books on *jihad* (holy war) from the
street vendors. He concluded from this that modern Islamic political
interests were busy mining the past for useful precedents.[11] But this
lively interest was a grass-roots phenomenon, not something directed
by politicians.

Although the resurgence of Muslim piety is a recent phenomenon, the condition of Christian life in Islamic countries has
always been a problem. At times it has been virtually impossible to
live in Muslim-dominated areas, at other times only difficult and pre-
carious. The last fifteen years have seen the difficulties take a turn for
the worse—much worse—even while Christians in other difficult
areas, such as China and Eastern Europe, have found their condition
easing, in some cases dramatically so. One reason for the change is
that the Organization of Petroleum Exporting Countries (OPEC) has
been able to exact cartel prices from the oil-consuming world. This
has made it impossible to treat Arabs as simply poor, backward and
powerless people whose wishes do not have to be taken seriously.
Even if they do not overtly threaten the oil supply of outsiders there
is a tacit threat. And the oil revenues mean there are enormous sums
of money in the hands of militant Muslims who have a consuming
missionary desire.

At the same time the Khomeini revolution in Iran has inflamed the
imaginations of millions of Muslims who are tired of the secular or
quasi-secular rule of the politicians and hunger for what they think is a
more authentic expression of their religion. When militant masses pressure their hesitant rulers toward militancy against the Christian minority, there is less counter-pressure from human rights groups on the
outside. It is one thing to press for human rights in poor, isolated

Romania; but against oil money and the influence it buys self-interest often wins out over principle.

One source of the resentment fueling the resurgence of Islam is the miserable failure of the modern Muslim countries to achieve much of value, not only in the eyes of foreign observers but also in their own eyes. They keep asking what went wrong. One of the answers on which there is widespread agreement is not that they have not become western enough, as many westerners and not a few Muslims believe, but that they have become too western, and in so doing have turned their backs on their own traditions. The prime examples for them are Turkey and Iran under the Shah. There the conscious westernization and along with it contempt for their own Islamic heritage led to both moral and economic failure. Or so many Muslims believe, and thus are motivated to recover their past.[12]

The massive return to Islam after the 1960s was largely born out of disillusionment with the alternatives. Western liberalism was seen as repressive and supportive of Israel; Nasser's Egyptian pan-Arab socialism had failed; there was nothing attractive about the Marxist-Leninist states. Most serious, the disastrous loss of the 1967 war with Israel had caused a catastrophic loss of morale. When Muslim preachers told people that their troubles came because they had turned their backs on Islam, that made sense to them. (The same psychological realities affected the Egyptian Copts as well, and they also experienced a massive return to the churches.) And the successes of the Egyptian army in the 1973 war, as contrasted with 1967, convinced many that they were on the right track, seeking their salvation in Islam.[13]

In Egypt the message of the Muslim Brotherhood in the early 1970s was that the country was in terrible shape and needed reform badly, and that Sharia law was the proper instrument of reform. This was the beginning of the alliance between President Sadat and the Muslim Brotherhood. The Brotherhood would support Sadat politically, and Sadat in turn would help the Brotherhood by bringing about the establishment of the Sharia. Hence the increasing pressure on the Christian minority.[14] (This alliance broke down later on, and the Brotherhood assassinated Sadat.)

It's interesting to see how analyses of the Egyptian religious scene by a secular-minded sociologist and a Coptic Christian apologist end up with similar conclusions. Nadia Ramsis Farah begins her book by pointing to the coincidental change in the personalities at the top of both state and church: Anwar Sadat became president in 1970, and Pope Shenouda III took over as head of the Coptic Church the next year. The stage for conflict was set when the Sadat government established Islam as a basic source of legislation in the new constitution and released most of the Muslim Brotherhood cadres who had been arrested by Nasser. Meanwhile Shenouda represented the younger, better educated clergy less inclined to follow submissively, people who were willing to have their demands voiced in the political arena. This made confrontation between church and state almost inevitable.[15]

Shawky Karas, writing from a Coptic perspective, highlights the reversal in political alliances with the coming to power of Sadat. The new president threw over Nasser's pan-Arab socialism with its close alliance to the Soviet Union in favor of ties with the West. This created the need for a delicate balancing act. For he needed the support of militant Islamic forces in order to offset the loss of leftist support. This required him to go along with the anti-Christian hysteria being whipped up by the religious leaders. Sadat had a genuine Muslim piety, but the political situation was probably paramount.[16] This interpretation does not vary significantly from Farah's, but Karas goes on then to deal with the religious elements as well, as she does not.

Karas believes the increasing pressure on the Copts in the 1940s had similar causes, being due to King Farouk's support for the Moslim Brotherhood, which in turn was motivated largely by his attempt to counter the opposition of the Wafd Party, a secular opposition group. Most of the Coptic politicians were in this Party. Karas also associates many cases of Islamic pressure in Egypt with the international scene; when there is conflict between Christians and Muslims any place in the world, there will be a "spillover" effect felt by the Egyptian Christians.[17]

The persecution of the church in Uganda also had connections with external affairs. Idi Amin's efforts to Islamize the country received strong backing from Saudi Arabia and Libya. He justified it with the claim that the Christian minority was enslaving the Islamic majority. In addition to the Arabs he was able to rely on the U.S.S.R. for political and military support.[18] This added a cold-war component to complicate the situation.

THE BACKGROUND OF THE PERSECUTION

The basic Islamic attitude toward people from other religions centers on the concept of the *dhimmi*, which defined the relationship for many centuries. *Dhimmi* status came from contracts between Mohammed and the Jewish and Christian tribes in Arabia in the seventh century. But the voluntary nature of the relationship ended after the prophet's death. The concept then became a framework for the subjugation and persecution of the non-Muslim peoples in areas where Islam dominated. It became the means whereby military conquest was transformed into civil domination and repression. The reason this was logically necessary was the assumption, first, that Islam was the only true religion; and second, that it required an amalgamation of all aspects of communal life, there being no distinction between religious and secular. This status of the inferiority of the *dhimmi* was a constant, even though the practical implications might vary with the ebb and flow of Muslim religious sensibilities over the centuries. Times of relaxation on the part of the Muslim authorities were matters of privilege, not of right, and they could change along with circumstances.

Aspects of the *dhimmi* status included discriminatory land taxation, which was intended to show that the *dhimmi* were no longer freeholders of land, but rather tenants. Also the *jizya* or poll tax. Sometimes this was paid with a humiliating ceremony in which the *dhimmi*, while paying the tax, were struck on the head or neck. These taxes sometimes led to a wave of conversions to Islam. The *jizya* itself was a piece of parchment worn on the wrist or some other part of the body which served as a receipt for the tax and which allowed the *dhimmi* to move to a different place. Without it they could be jailed. *Dhimmi* could not ride a "noble" animal like a horse or camel, but only a donkey. These restrictions were found in some places as late as the 1940s. At times the *dhimmi* had to have lower houses than others in town, or lower doors, so that they were forced to stoop to enter the house. Their houses were not protected against raiding and pillaging like Muslims' were, and sometimes the *dhimmi* built them like labyrinths on the inside to facilitate hiding. There were strict limitations on where they could live, and in many places on what clothes they could wear. They were forced to bow to Muslims, to speak in low voices, to move out of the way when Muslims passed them in the street.[19]

In Egypt the escalation of violence against the Christian community—called the Copts—became severe in the late 1970s and included deadly violence. Along with the violence came proposals for a drastic change in the legal status of the Christians. The Muslim Brotherhood argued that while nobody should be forced to become Muslim, the country should nevertheless abolish all institutions that stand between Islam and non-Muslims. This implies nothing less than the abolition of The Coptic Orthodox Church. Proposals included adopting the Sharia not only for the general administration of the country but also in such sensitive areas as family law. Thus even if Christians were not forced to become Muslims they would be required to live as if they had. Meanwhile, President Sadat was speaking darkly of links between the church and foreign powers, thus providing ammunition for charges that the Christians were unpatriotic collaborators with the nation's enemies. The times were made more difficult by widespread resentment of the long domination by Christians of the nation's intellectual and commercial life out of proportion to their numbers.

In such an atmosphere, the 1980 constitutional amendments struck like a dagger at the heightened sensibilities of the Christian community. For the first time in a century or more, the Copts' status as equals in Egyptian society was not guaranteed by law. The state could treat them as it saw fit. If it wished to apply the letter of the Islamic law the Copts would return to the status of *dhimmi*, which was supposed to have been eliminated forever in 1850.[20]

Of course, among Arab countries Egypt's policies, even the more repressive ones of recent years, are models of restraint. Many of these countries do not have a living memory of the long tradition of indigenous Christian communities that exists in Egypt. Rather they have small clandestine fellowships of evangelicals which the authorities repress whenever they are discovered. The police use not only threats and jail terms, but also have a softer approach in which they employ inducements for people to abjure Christianity. They might offer the passport that was refused, an ending of the continual surveillance, a certificate of good conduct that is needed to obtain employment.[21]

Islam obviously creates great fear among Christians when it is in control. It is a little-known fact that people fear it even when it supposedly is subjugated to others. When the centuries-old Ottoman Empire began breaking up late in the nineteenth century, Muslim rule was replaced by nominally Christian regimes. Then in 1908 Turkey was convulsed by a revolution that was the immediate cause of a missionary strategy conference to examine the new situation held at Lucknow,

India. One woman, attending the conference from Russia, reported the "astounding" fact that the Russian government, which was Christian, permitted the Muslims to proselytize among Christians, but did not allow the same privilege to non-Orthodox Christians. She said, moreover, that this was the same policy followed by the British government in Africa. Here is her assessment both of the reason for the Tsar's policy and the results:

> It seems to me that our government is afraid of arousing the Mohammedan part of the nation by any such unjust and harsh measures which it is not afraid to apply toward Russian sectarians [non-Orthodox Christians]. The effect of this policy is an encouragement to Islam; it allows it to be aggressive and spread. And it certainly does spread.[22]

In the Dutch East Indies a similar fear of Islam made the government more favorable to Muslims than to Christians. This was said to be proof to the natives of the superiority of Islam.[23] In India the Muslims were loyal to the British, so the government did nothing to offend them. In Sudan the British prohibited Christian meetings in the Muslim section for the same reason. And in Nigeria, ". . . British officials are afraid of them and have implicitly declared the superiority of Islam."[24]

RELIGIOUS SOURCES OF PERSECUTION BY ISLAM

Why is there so little religious freedom found in Muslim countries? The most likely place to seek an explanation is within the precepts of the religion. Islam regards itself as the fulfillment of Christianity and Judaism, God's final message to mankind. Whoever does not submit to the religion is not submissive to God's will and therefore liable to legitimate subjection. At times Muslim conquerors have allowed Jews or Christians to keep their faith—the Koran gives them special place as "people of the book"—but this privilege does not extend to anyone who desires to leave Islam. Apostasy is a grave sin, punishable by the death penalty. Westernized Moslems are very uncomfortable with this position. They do not like the rise of Muslim militancy.[25]

For Muslims religion cannot be separated from all other aspects of society because of the comprehensive, integrated nature of its conception of life. The division between public and private, state and society, that has become common in the West is unknown to Islam. As one scholar put it, "The state is only the political expression of an Islamic society."[26] Samuel Zwemer, the great missionary scholar of Islam, emphasized the same point. He described the word *Islam* as standing for *unity*: in religious conception, in political theory, and in the ideals of a civilization.[27] Thus for another religion to exist in the society—or worse, for someone to commit apostasy from his Islamic heritage—is not just a religious matter, but strikes at the very heart of their whole society and destroys its organic unity.

That means it is not only religious but also political when a Muslim becomes a Christian, inasmuch as a Muslim cannot conceive of a separation between the two. That is why King Hassan of Morocco, for example, is considered not only a political leader but also head of the Muslim state. One of his subjects who becomes a Christian, therefore, commits a political act as well as a religious one. There are also societal implications apart from the politics inasmuch as the convert is taken to have broken the implicit relationships with an extended family and community. One woman in Morocco was told by the police that she could be a Christian but only privately.[28] Apparently their idea was that private religion did not present the communal hazards of an open break with Islam, which was the glue of the society and the political structure.

Their intense preoccupation with Islam as a religion is the reason that many Muslim militants, to the surprise of westerners who hear of it, oppose pan-Arab nationalism; they see it as a substitute for religion. They were not enamored of Egypt's revered President Nasser, whom they saw as infected with western ideology—socialism and nationalism. Arabism, they came to think, was becoming a "surrogate religion," however useful it might be in accomplishing certain tasks. The fact that so many Christian Arabs were part of the movement only served to confirm them in this opinion.[29]

There is also a philosophy of history behind the Islamic hostility to others. Muslims believe there was a golden age in the past, one that relativizes and condemns other societies, including present-day Islamic societies with all their shortcomings. For Islam the model for the good was the perfect society established by the prophet Mohammed. Everything that has come since is tainted, and this affects their view of social change.

In Islam, the only legitimate change is change which results in the moral betterment of the Moslem community. The validity and quality of any structural variation of Muslim life is measured by its conformity to God's law and by the degree to which it is believed to direct the community back to that perfect model of existence created by the Prophet.[30]

What to outsiders seems to be a lack of interest in events of the present may be perfectly coherent in light of the Islamic historical sense, which is almost precisely the opposite of the Biblical, with its eschatological hopes for the future. Islam appears to be backward looking because in fact it looks backward. But its proponents regard that as a strength, not a weakness.[31] How is it that a religion can foster so much violence? *The Missing Religious Precept*, a Muslim manifesto, regards *jihad* as a religious precept, like fasting and praying, that the Muslim populace must adopt or be forced to adopt. *Jihad* acts against infidels and also against Muslims who don't conform to Islamic precepts, such as the assassinated Egyptian president, Anwar Sadat. The purpose is to enforce the Sharia in order to revitalize society. This teaching is not common in Islamic writings, but events show clearly that it strikes a deep chord in some Muslims.[32]

Although terrorism is a practical policy intended to accomplish certain ends, which is true any place it is used as a tactic, it is more than that. Terrorism seems to be rooted deep in the modern expression of Islam. It is not followed secretly and denied, as in most communist countries; rather it is openly proclaimed. Sheikh Abdullah Ghoshah, supreme judge of the Kingdom of Jordan, made this statement, which was published by the Islamic Research Academy following its conference in 1968:

> Jihad is legislated in order to be the means of propagating Islam. Consequently non-Muslims ought to embrace Islam either willingly or through wisdom and good advice or unwillingly through fight and jihad. War is the basis of the relationship between Muslims and their opponents unless there are justifiable reasons for peace, such as adopting Islam as their faith or making an agreement with them to keep peaceful. It is unlawful to give up jihad and adopt peace and weakness, unless the purpose of giving up is for preparation for further action whenever there is something weak among Muslims and their opponents are strong.[33]

Muammar Gaddafi, the Libyan ruler, put it this way in Rwanda in May 1985: "Africa must be Muslim. Christians are intruders in Africa and are agents of colonialism. We must wage a holy war so that Islam will spread in Africa." To westerners Gaddafi is a lunatic or a clown, but for millions of young Muslims he is a genius who communicates his vision for the spread of Islam to them. Still, Iran's Ayatollah Khomeini's vision was incomparably grander:

> Holy war means the conquest of all non-Muslim countries. Such a war may well be declared after the formation of an Islamic government worthy of that name, at the direction of the Imam . . . or under his orders. It will then be the duty of every able-bodied adult male to volunteer for this war of conquest, the final aim of which is to put Koranic law in power from one end of the earth to the other.[34]

On this issue the Shiite segment of Islam is much more dogmatic; among Sunni Muslims there is little support for *jihad* and in any case there is no office of Imam and therefore nobody with the authority to call for a holy war.

This chapter has dealt with religious factors in the Islamic persecutions of Christians, but there are other things for us to consider as well. To those we now turn.

T H R E E

THE ISLAMIC OFFENSIVE

SOCIAL AND PSYCHOLOGICAL FACTORS IN THE ISLAMIC PERSECUTION

Although it's important to consider the extra-religious factors in the Islamic persecutions, I do so with a distinct lack of enthusiasm for many such explanations I have seen. The Egyptian sociologist Nadia Farah, for example, devotes considerable attention to the causes of the inter-communal hostility in that country, but of all the reasons she advances none seem to have anything to do with religion. She uses the reductionism so typical of social science "explanations"—plenty of talk about "elites" and such, but nothing of the role of religious ideas and convictions. One suspects that the people about whom she writes, on whatever side, would hardly recognize the struggle she claims to be describing.[1]

Yet there is a paradox here, for in a number of countries in the Middle East and North Africa religious identities are emblems of communal membership and may have little to do with faith commitments. Israel is one of these places. In the system cemented into place during the Turkish administration of Palestine everyone was assumed to belong to a particular community, and the labels they gave these communities were Muslim, Jewish and Christian. So a member of the Greek Orthodox community, for example, is naturally called a "Christian," and no assumption is made about the nature of his faith.[2] That misleading terminology leads to much confusion. "Christian" is taken in a communal sense and therefore assumed to be almost synonymous with European countries and governments, and by extension western countries in general.

When the Ottoman empire was disintegrating in the last half of the nineteenth century it was thought to be suffering because of the actions of "Christian" countries. Russia moved in the late 1870s to separate Bulgaria, Romania, Serbia and Montenegro from the Empire. In 1881 France took Tunis and Greece took Thrace. Throughout Europe secret Armenian societies plotted separation from Turkey. After Turkey surrendered at the end of World War I the "Christian" countries ended the Ottoman Empire by dismembering it and leaving it only its ancient homeland in Asia Minor. Hence "Christian" was equated with being anti-Turkish.

Even before that the Sultan, observing that the European powers were not united on how to protect the Christian minority, had embarked on a program of deliberate massacre of the Christian Armenians in September 1895. Crowds of armed civilians joined the Turkish army in raping, pillaging, destroying and killing. Many were killed after being given a chance to deny Christ and save their lives. Something like 100,000 Armenians lost their lives at that time. Many more thousands were killed in further atrocities in 1909, 1914 and 1918.[3]

The communal issue is so central in those countries where it is applicable that it affects profoundly the way Christian churches conduct themselves. In Israel an Arab Baptist pastor told me in 1988 that he did not work with either Jews or Muslims. His evangelism was among the nominally Christian community of Arabs, those who had the communal identity as Christians but had not come to faith in Christ. He said that some years earlier he could and did visit Muslims for evangelism, but the Islamic revival had put an end to that. He now felt hostility everywhere he went and felt unable to speak to Muslims about Christ. He said the local mosque used to be empty at the hour of prayer; now it was packed. The flexibility he had formerly enjoyed in crossing the communal barrier was gone.[4] The communal aspect of this conflict explains why analyses of the situation are so often of little use. A book entitled *Muslim-Christian Conflicts*, for example, sheds little light on the issue of persecution because it deals largely with inter-communal conflicts between two political and cultural entities known respectively as Muslim and Christian. The book could have been written essentially as it now appears if these two names were not at their heart religions.[5]

Another analysis from a westernized Muslim perspective, also concludes that Islamic aggression has nothing to do with religion but rather is a manifestation of a psychological condition. Islam is not inherently terroristic, Amir Taheri says, any more than other religions, but Islamic terrorism presently exists because of the psychological pathology of people who are uncomfortable in the twentieth century and want to go back to a much earlier period of history.[6] He refuses to take seriously what many of the Muslim leaders say, and he relies on the kind of psychobabble that almost always trips analysts with a superior view of the subject.

Notwithstanding our criticism of Taheri, some psychological explanations that are based on obvious motives can be useful in helping us understand why people do things. John Laffin argues that much of the Islamic hostility to Christianity is based on serious blows to the pride of Islam. The Koran had described Muslims as the most noble of the human race, but in the modern period Islamic forces were everywhere thrown back. From the most feared nation on earth the Ottoman Empire had become *Turkey*—the "sick man of Europe," as it was called. And it was Europe, in most places regarded as "Christian Europe," that had brought this about. The scorn with which Islamic peoples were held was a terrible shock to a proud people. The response to this blow took the form of violent revival and nationalist movements in the nineteenth and twentieth centuries. Laffin cites a prominent Islamic scholar, Ronald Nettler, who believes that Arab nationalism is intended to revive Islamic supremacy throughout the world. Thus Islam, not Arabism, is the primary thing. As Nettler puts it: "The Arab response to Western hegemony is to a large degree formed by the feeling of having been overcome by a Christian West which all Muslims know is spiritually inferior to Islam, though temporarily superior physically."[7]

Persecution by Muslims is heightened by the intrusion of normal political tensions and rivalries. Many Copts believe the agitation in Egypt has been worsened by the fact that the sheiks inflaming the mobs to attack Christians were on the payroll of Libya's Gaddafi, who has had a running feud with Egypt for many years.[8] In October 1987 the government of Malaysia instituted a crackdown on Christian leaders that alarmed the church throughout the world. A leader in the Malaysian church points out that what was often missed was the fact that along with the Christian leaders the government also scooped up numerous others, including opposition politicians, leaders of public interest groups and Islamic fundamentalists. This all stemmed from a crisis in the United Malay National Organization, which is the dominant party both in the country and in the coalition government. As part of the same crisis the government removed several supreme court judges from office. This was a serious breach of civil rights, but regarding it simply as a crackdown on the Christian community would seriously distort the reality.[9]

Malaysia also illustrates the effects of communalism, in addition to the Arab examples we have already seen. To be a Malay is by definition to be a Muslim. And it also means to be a supporter of the UMNO party. Since all three major parties are racially based, politics is racial and therefore also religious. When a Muslim becomes a Christian one number is subtracted from the Muslim population; but it is also taken to mean that one number is subtracted from the Malay race and one from the UMNO Party.[10]

These hostilities take much of their meaning from the past, and aggrieved peoples can have long memories. The common term among militant Moslems to describe the West is "the Crusaders," and this shows the legacy of battles now five centuries and more in the past. Muslims commonly say their three enemies are Communists, Zionists and Crusaders, by which they mean Western "Christians."[11] And by extension, any Christians. Hatred and resentment conquer not only time but space, and we have reports that the Crusades are a present source of anti-Christian feeling thousands of miles away in Malaysia![12]

PERSECUTION FROM SOURCES OTHER THAN THE STATE

The example of President Sadat being pressed by political forces to follow policies harmful to the Christians of Egypt suggests that sources other than the state may be responsible for persecutions. Islamic militancy began making strong gains in Egypt in 1977, which was the year Sadat traveled to Israel to cement that historic rapprochement. This led to accelerating demands for the establishment of the Sharia in Egypt. The movement came to an end formally with the arrests at Sadat's death. But the case was dismissed against all but a small number of the *jihad* plotters because, it was said, the security police used torture. Little credence should be given to that explanation since this incident is the first time any arm of the government accused the security service of anything. The speculation in Egypt is that the extremist Islamic groups are so powerful that nobody wants to jeopardize his own safety by angering them, even to prosecute the assassins of the president.[13]

The unofficial nature of much of the persecution accounts in part for the tremendous variability between Arab countries in their reaction to Christians. In one place the hostility seems unremitting, while in a neighboring country with many similar characteristics there may be less repression. For reasons hard to identify the population may be more or less open to religious variation and dissent; in some places family and friends will offer less opposition to a conversion than in a neighboring country.[14]

The conventional generalization that Islam and government necessarily work hand-in-hand because of Islamic belief in the unitary nature of society needs to be qualified. One scholar notes that governments use Islam for their own purposes. If they use religious arguments, it is often because they believe they can score political points with them. "Thus, Islam may be invoked and exalted where needed in order to reinforce official ideology and not because of the specific values it represents."[15] Another scholar studying Islamic hate literature in Algeria noted continuing hostility between the writers and the central power of the state. In these cases it appeared that the religious arguments were used more to score against the government than to advance the cause of Islam.[16] In the Persian Gulf crisis of 1990 Saddam Hussein of Iraq, who had been viewed by militant Muslims with hostility and suspicion because of his dealings with "infidel" nations and his socialist ideology, began working overtime to reestablish his Muslim credentials. The Iraqi leader evidently was impressed by the political advantages of identifying himself with the Muslim masses of the Arab countries arrayed with the alliance against him. It was a performance worthy of Henry IV of France who in the early seventeenth century gave up the Protestantism that had animated his drive for the throne in order to be accepted as king. He is today chiefly known for this monument of political cynicism: "Paris is worth a Mass." Saddam Hussein and other leaders of the Islamic countries would know what he meant.

Of course, even when politics rather than religious fervor ignites the persecution against Christians, the victims may not be able to distinguish one kind of pain from the other. Still, for those in the countries of persecution and others on the outside trying to help them, it seems unnecessary to argue the proposition that it's better to know the true nature of your adversary than to mistake it for something else.

Not only does persecution against Christians sometimes take place without the participation of government; it can even come as a popular movement in which the government tries to protect the church against it. In Pakistan the government of Benazir Bhutto intervened in Islamabad to grant permission for the building of a local church, despite local opposition, after four thousand Christians marched in protest to get wider recognition of their plight. Early in 1989 construction was halted when an angry mob of Muslim students attacked the site. This was during the furor caused by the publication of Salman Rushdie's novel *The Satanic Verses*. Even with the backing of the national government it remains doubtful that the church ever will be built.[17]

The government of Nigeria, which has not proven to be especially friendly toward Christians, is in the process of enacting a new federal constitution, scheduled to go into effect after October 1992, which provides that non-Muslims will not be subject to any Sharia court. The purpose is to prevent the Muslim states from bringing Christians under Islamic law. But Muslim hardliners are not giving up the struggle to make Sharia apply to all Nigerians. Christian leaders expect the Muslims to keep pressing on this.[18]

CLAIMS OF TOLERATION

Seldom do the religions which persecute Christians admit to such policies. Most of them have political reasons to appear to fit in with the general abhorrence of oppression, and they have public relations programs of greater or lesser sophistication to handle damage control duties. The first line of defense in most cases is to cite constitutional guarantees of freedom of religion, evidently in the hopes that observers will be satisfied with such documentary evidence and not pay close attention to what actually happens. Some Islamic apologists take advantage of the fact that there is a certain resemblance between liberal Christian theology and the Moslem concept of God. The former emphasizes the humanity of Jesus in such a way as to lose the divinity. Moslem scholars point this out. A Church of Pakistan bishop notes that "Muslims rightly claim affinity between their own view and that of these 'radical' theologians," evidently in order to diminish the perceived gap between the two religions.[19]

One of the most energetic propaganda campaigns is conducted by the World Assembly of Muslim Youth, which is based in Riyadh,

Saudi Arabia. This organization publishes a series of pamphlets on various aspects of Islam, all designed to put the religion in the best possible light. The pamphlet on human rights gives the gist of their claim: *"There should be no coercion in the matter of faith."* "Along with the freedom of conviction and freedom of conscience Islam has given the right to the individual that his religious sentiments will be given due respect and nothing will be said or done which may encroach upon his right." "Every human-being is thereby related to all others and all become one community of brotherhood in their honourable and pleasant servitude to the most compassionate Lord of the Universe. In such a heavenly atmosphere the Islamic confession of the oneness of God stands dominant and central, and necessarily entails the concept of the oneness of humanity and the brotherhood of mankind." The tract goes on to quote verses from the Koran and defends principles of freedom from arbitrary arrest and imprisonment without due process of law, the right to protest against government tyranny, the right to free expression, freedom of association, freedom of conscience—all the wonderful things conspicuous by their absence in most Islamic countries.[20]

Islamic modernists, usually westernized, have pointed with pride to the complete equality and freedom that the minorities, such as Christians, enjoy in their countries, even though it usually wasn't true. This was partly because they had truly absorbed western values and partly because they were trying to put on the best face toward those they thought could help them. By the late sixties the radicals were singing a different tune, and that difference would finally turn into the anti-Christian rioting in the early 80s.[21]

Government spokesmen tend to be the most shameless of the Muslim apologists. Khan Bahadur Khan, Minister for Religious and Minority Affairs of Pakistan, told a religious liberty conference in London in 1989: ". . . human rights in Islam essentially emanate from freedom of conscience, ordained or presupposed in Koranic teachings. Koran ordains, 'Speak plain truth.' This is not possible without freedom of conscience."[22] As sickly as this looks in writing, it was even less convincing in person. This conference took place under the sponsorship of the International Religious Liberty Association. The IRLA is controlled by the Seventh-Day Adventists, which have long had an interest in religious liberty issues. There is no mystery about why government propagandists come to meetings like this to tell lies; that's their job. But it's hard to see how the IRLA could have thought its purpose was being served by inviting such people to its conference.

It is not only the politicians who make up stories about their religious freedom. We are treated to similar fantasies propagated by educated Muslims trying to persuade the West of the toleration of Islam. Here is one example:

> These non-Muslims [in Muslim countries] have a guaranteed right to their religious conviction, to profess and defend their own convictions and even to criticize Islam and engage in a dialogue with Muslims. Non-Muslims also have the right to regulate their private life, education, and family life by adopting their own family laws. If there is any rule in the *shariah* which they think religiously incompatible, they can be absolved from it.[23]

It is difficult to believe that this writer should not have known the falsity of his statement.

IS THERE HOPE THAT ISLAM WILL STOP PERSECUTING?

What are the prospects for the cessation of persecutions by militant Islam? First we should note that the bad reputation Islam has received because of its human rights record is well understood by Muslim leaders and is a matter of great concern. In late 1988 the first of a series of conferences was held in Jeddah, Saudi Arabia. Called by the Organization of the Islamic Conference (OIC), it was attended by officials of all forty-four Islamic countries. OIC Secretary-General Sharifuddin Pirzada set the tone: "Our faith is vilified, our culture sneered at, our difficulties magnified and our peoples, governments and institutions subjected to misrepresentation, ridicule and censure." Some speakers noted that Iraq had been partly responsible for this in its use of poison gas against Kurdish civilians. One mentioned reports of terrorism and massacres, slavery, chemical weapons and genocide. A member asked: "Why is it that Muslims are involved in so many terrible events? We can justly criticise the foreign media for exaggerating those happenings, but we cannot accuse it of inventing them."[24]

Are there cases in which predominantly Muslim countries do not indulge in such behavior? One interesting example we can use in considering this question is Senegal, whose experience shows that a country can be primarily Islamic while permitting religious freedom.

The Senegalese do it with something like a separation of church and state in spite of the fact that most commentators say this is not possible in Islam. The population in Senegal is 83 percent Muslim, 12 percent animist, and 5 percent Christian, and the government is "secular." Djibril Samb, a professor at the University of Dakar, calls this an Africanized brand of Islam.[25] But how do we get this "Africanized" kind of Islam? Given the record of Islam elsewhere in Africa, is the Senegalese experience capable of being applied elsewhere? One analyst points out that Senegal has embraced both the Sufi mystical tradition of otherworldliness and the worldly impulse that demands power. "The history of Islam in Senegal is one of a complex process of wavering between these two poles, in accordance with social, economic and political changes." The government of Senegal declares itself to be secular, but in the same breath says that that does not mean quite the same thing as in the French radical tradition. They have a policy which functions by gaining the friendship of the Muslim leadership through the granting of favors. The politicians' goal is to influence the elites of Islam by making themselves indispensable. The divided nature of Islam in Senegal makes it possible for the state to hold the upper hand.[26]

Given this set of circumstances, the Senegalese model does not seem promising for use elsewhere. In fact, one has to wonder how stable the situation in Senegal will remain, since its favorable aspects are based neither on firm constitutional provisions nor on any principles that undergird the kind of Islam they practice, but rather on a balance of power between competing factions of Islam which is exploited by the government. Will the normal vicissitudes that affect political fortunes almost everywhere turn against the present politicians and make alternative policies seem more attractive? Should the present regime falter, it is not difficult to imagine competing politicians successfully vying for attention by appealing to the same aggressive Islamic instincts that have proved so alluring elsewhere.

In some ways Indonesia is similar to Senegal. Eighty-five percent Muslim, it has evidently never had a strong movement to establish an Islamic state although, as the story at the beginning of the preceding chapter shows, its record is far from perfect. Denys Lombard analyzed the situation there and concluded that the reason for its relatively good record is, once again, the division of Muslims into two main camps. The *Santri* are the orthodox Muslims, usually urban, often merchants; they keep up with international Islam and are more modern, even egalitarian in some ways. The *Abangan* live mostly in the villages, mix their Islam with pre-Islamic rituals, and are less Islamicized.[27] There are reports that the church is alive and well in Indonesia.[28] The question is the extent to which it is really *Islam* that surrounds it and to what extent it is a primitive animism with a thin Islamic covering.

The Syrian model provides another potential paradigm. There about 13 percent of the people are Christians (some sources cite a lower figure), belonging chiefly to the Roman Catholic and several Orthodox national churches. There are also 25,000 Protestants. In addition to secular courts, Syria has separate religious courts for Muslims and Jews and for Catholic, Orthodox and Protestant Christians. Preaching is not censored, Bibles are available, and there is no problem getting permits to build or repair churches. Christians even have some access to state-run media. There is little contact between Christians and Muslims, and the Orthodox traditional churches show no desire to evangelize Muslims. One threat to this situation is that the Christian population is losing ground through emigration, partly because of close ties to the West.[29] And it can be questioned whether the non-evangelism stance of the Orthodox church means that its members and leaders are buying peace at the expense of a semi-Christian existence.

Syria also differs from most predominantly Islamic countries in that since 1973 it has not been officially Muslim. The constitution adopted that year specifies the religion of the president, but not of the country. So it is formally a secular state. There is no reason to assume that this is permanent; there was rioting on behalf of traditional Islam over the adoption of the new constitution. Moreover, the regime that came to power at that time was a revolutionary one whose program was informed by pan-Arab socialism which, as we have seen, is regarded with great suspicion by militant Muslims throughout the region. It is also a tyranny; the good treatment of Christians there is only relative, since no group is treated well. This hardly presents the vision of a golden future for Christians in the Islamic world. We also have informal reports suggesting that the legality of the Christian community in Syria has not protected it against surveillance and repression that exist beneath the surface.

In some respects the present Syrian situation resembles that of Turkey after the 1908 revolution. One missionary reported that the new leaders understood the contradictions between Islam and the changes they were making, but they did all they could to conceal this from the masses. The Young Turks met with bitter opposition from the religious leaders. The counter-revolution that took place in 1909 had as its watchword, "Honour to the Sheriat [Sharia]." It would likely have succeeded had it had better leadership, because the masses favored the call to the Sharia.[30] The Armenian massacres provide sufficient evidence for that. And even now when these Young Turks have been politically ascendent for more than three-quarters of a century Islamic thinking remains dominant among the masses, and the government and people together make things very difficult for Christians.

This suggests that an alteration in government policy apart from a fundamental shift in the cultural outlook of the people is going to be fragile at best, and in most cases illusory. If the masses remain devoted to Islam and Islam remains as hostile to non-adherents as it has been, tolerable situations can easily erupt into severe repression and even mass killings.

There are reports that a healthy church exists in Jordan, in which the Christian community is largely an Orthodox communal one, similar to those in Egypt and Syria. But here again the church's position is fragile, based as it is on the protection of a westernized king, the target of numerous assassination attempts. There is no way of telling how deeply the population accepts the existence of a Christian minority in their country, but it would be unwise to count on much depth, especially after King Hussein is gone. One missionary in Israel reports that the Arab *intifada* in that country has led to such hostility toward the Christians as well as the Jews that some Muslims are saying to Arab Christians: "Someday we're going to begin on Saturday and finish on Sunday," by which they mean they'll kill the Jews first (Saturday) and then the Christians (Sunday). This missionary says that when he served in Jordan Muslims there were saying the same thing.[31]

The record of Islamic countries in international human rights work does not bode well for the future. There are sixteen Muslim or Muslim-influenced governments that have not signed such pacts as the International Covenant on Economic, Social and Cultural Rights (1966), the International Covenant on Civil and Political Rights, and the Convention Against Torture and Other Cruel and Degrading Human Treatment or Punishment. Many have violated these agreements consistently. In 1990 twenty-four African governments collaborated to form a new organization called Islam in Africa in order to eliminate Christianity completely from the continent. The German periodical that reported this commented that if the twenty-four governments had collaborated toward the elimination of elephants, pandemonium would break loose in the rest of the world, but there has hardly been a peep from the conventional media.[32]

With all the repression, there are still concerns about human rights within the Muslim world. The Arab Organization for Human Rights has more than six hundred members in eighteen countries, but since no government would allow the organization to meet on its territory the founding meeting in 1983 had to be held in Cyprus. Four years later all the Arab states refused to allow the AOHR consultative status at the United Nations. Only Egypt and Sudan have permitted local chapters on their own territory.[33]

Amir Taheri, whose views we have already considered in another connection, believes that by 1986 the militant Muslims were on the way downhill. The call for Sharia was decisively rejected by the revolution in Sudan, but this was only the most dramatic example of the general rejection. No other country followed the Khomeini example, and even in Iran there is much that he wanted to do and could not accomplish due to widespread resistance. Taheri thinks that Muslim terrorism manifests many Marxist and fascist elements that have nothing to do with Islam. He is a westernizer who believes that salvation for the Muslim world will come from dropping the hatred and becoming like the West. He contends that it's possible to be a good Muslim while doing that.[34] Taheri writes as if he has never spoken to the people on the edge of the Christian-Muslim frontier, and there is an air of unreality to his book.

I see only a germ of hope in Taheri's argument. Or rather none at all in his argument, but perhaps some in what Taheri himself represents. As a westernized Muslim he has lost many of the habits of thinking and values that make Islam so dangerous. If westernization, which is another way of saying the veneer of a now thinly Christian civilization, affects large numbers of Muslims, it could change the aggressive impulses that now dominate the relations between Muslims and Christians. We have seen that the anti-Zionism of the Middle East and North Africa is capable of accommodating movements like Arab nationalism and socialism. And we have also seen how these trends have been resisted by many Muslims who recognize them as forms of secularization. In such cases the results have been complementary to Islamic aggression. But another form of "infection," like westernization, could work counter to it.

Meanwhile the realities vary considerably from Taheri's vision. The Soviet Union is shaping up as potentially the main hotspot of Islamic persecution of Christians. Six republics in the country have Muslim majorities. If they get rid of Moscow's domination, as they show every evidence of trying, and install Muslim leadership, will they allow the propagation of Christianity? It may turn out that Christians in those parts of the Soviet Union will look back with longing for the good old days when communist oppressors were in charge of their lands.

At the newly renamed Evangelical Christians/Baptists meeting in February 1990, there was great rejoicing at the new freedoms of the Baptists under the loosening of state power in the U.S.S.R. But a discordant note was struck by delegates representing regions with Muslim majorities. They spoke of the persecution that, if anything, is greater than when they only had to worry only about the communist regime. Many people fear for their lives, and there has been large-scale migration to other parts of the Soviet Union. One man reported that of his congregation only seven people remained. There were reports that Muslim mullahs were threatening to cut out the tongues of the Christians. The conference appealed for pastors to move into these Muslim regions where they are desperately needed, even at the risk of their lives.[35] This report is especially noteworthy because it comes from a mainline Protestant group in the U.S. that normally puts a rosier gloss on Soviet affairs than others think is warranted.

One Christian in the south central Asian part of the Soviet Union reports that a Tadzhik Muslim said to him: "I respect you, so I'll kill you with this knife so others can't torture you to death." People of German and Russian nationality are being advised to leave the region before the bloodbath.[36] So unstable are many of the Muslim lands that other geo-political events could unleash further devastation. A recent study on Islam concludes: "One thing is certain. The emergence of a revolutionary fundamentalist Egypt . . . will shake the Muslim and non-Muslim worlds even more than did the 1979 Iranian revolution."[37] The number of imaginable earth-shaking events of this nature is virtually unlimited—the Iraqi conquest of Kuwait occurred only a few months after those words were published.

The revolution in eastern Europe in late 1989 should have taught us what Christians ought to believe anyway: that the course of history brings many surprises. In September of that year, only weeks before the revolution began, I participated in an international consultation on the persecution of the church. Of the forty people in attendance, all specialists on the subject, not a single one mentioned the possibility that all our assumptions about the church in that part of the world were about to be overturned. Inasmuch as Christians believe that God—and not presidents, kings or ayatollahs—is the Lord of history, we should be imbued with the virtue of hope rather than being filled with dread about the future.

THE PERSECUTION OF CHRISTIANS BY OTHER RELIGIONS

The preceding two chapters have sought to demonstrate that the main religious sources of the persecution of Christians have been Islamic. If Muslims would cease persecuting the followers of Christ, perhaps 90 percent of the problem would be solved. But not all of it. This chapter suggests other areas of concern that comprise the remainder of the problem.

SOME ILLUSTRATIVE EXAMPLES

•Evangelical workers in India have suffered threats from a radical Hindu group called Rashtriya Swayamsevak Sangh (RSS). At least seven are said to be on a "hit list." One man was approached by several RSS members and asked for his address. "We want to see how you will burn." (This is taken very seriously in India, where burning alive is a common form of murder.) In October 1989 in the southern state of Tamil Nadu, RSS members killed an Indian pastor. They chased him with swords as he was returning from a church service on his bicycle and decapitated him. Four former convicts were arrested after being identified by eyewitnesses, but it appeared as if the police, who often side with the RSS, would not charge them with the crime. In fact the police asked the pastor's widow to sign a document which would dismiss charges against the men. She refused. RSS is not only calling for a return to traditional Hindu spirituality, but is also demanding abolition of the secular state and replacing it with a Hindu government.[1] It has conducted massive reconversion ceremonies, in an effort to entice Indians away from Christian faith. Hare Krishnas in the U.S. have been reported to be financing RSS activities, including about forty churches burned down in India.[2]

•An Indian army major, Mohan Rao, who converted to Christ, has been forced to undergo psychiatric treatment with large quantities of drugs. He was hospitalized for the second time in two years after requesting to be excused from a ceremony that included an animal sacrifice to the goddess Durga.[3]

•On November 12, 1989, in Bhaktapur, eight miles east of Kathmandu, the capital of Nepal, a church service had just ended when two police vans arrived. Officers arrested the forty people remaining in the church and hustled them off to jail. They were all forced to watch as their seventy-six-year-old pastor, Tir Bahadur Dewan, was badly beaten. The deputy superintendent of police then said to them: "The same fate will happen to you if you don't bow down to this Hindu idol and have the sign of the Tika smeared on your foreheads." Most of them went through the ceremony. The others remained in jail for ten days and then were released on bail. Pastor Dewan remained imprisoned for several months longer. This was said to be a departure from the past in its brutal attempt to get Christians to bow to the idols; in its venue, right next door to Kathmandu instead of in the hinterlands where it could be kept from westerners; and in its bold trumpeting by the government, instead of being kept hidden.

In 1988 the World Hindu Federation met in Kathmandu and declared the king and queen the "emperor and empress of the Hindu world." Queen Aishwarya by all accounts is the one who has taken this most seriously, and as a consequence there has been a noticeable pickup in the Hinduization campaign. Buddhists as well as Christians have suffered confiscation of property and beatings. Some analysts believe that the king has been concerned about the situation because the Christian church is the fastest growing group in the country. Even though it numbers only fifty thousand out of a population of eighteen million its fast growth undermines the status quo which is essential to an absolutist regime.[4]

Also Christians are unwilling to accept passively the current situation in a way to which Buddhism is predisposed. By that I mean that the quietism and acceptance of what is fated, a central feature of the

Buddhist mentality, is very different from the active participation including dissent from the established order that are implicit in such Biblical principles as stewardship, incarnation, the prophetic voice, evangelism and sanctification. The 1990 uprisings have improved the position of Christians, and a number were released from jail. But the new constitution retains the Hindu character of the state.

•In early 1990, Buddhists in Thailand, acting with the support of some government ministers, began putting new pressures on growing Christian churches. They focused their attention on active congregations with a lively sense of calling, leaving alone the more staid churches that were not growing.[5]

FACTORS IN THE HINDU RESURGENCE

Hinduism, which is a very different religion from Islam, nevertheless shows some of the same characteristics with respect to relations with Christianity. This is contrary to its general reputation. One Indian scholar subtitled his recent book on neo-Hinduism *A Missionary Religion*. He quotes a speaker at the World Congress on Hinduism that had been held at Allahabad. "Our mission in the West has been crowned with a fantastic success. Hinduism is now becoming the decisive World religion and the end of Christianity has come near. Within another generation there will be only two religions in the world, Islam and Hinduism."[6] Notwithstanding the exaggerated bravado there are objective reasons to pay close attention to what lies behind such statements. Johannes Aagaard of the University of Aarhus in Denmark explains why the most widespread views of the pacific nature of Hinduism are wrong: People normally consider only one brand of Hinduism, and the least prevalent one at that.

> The nature of Hinduism is normally described in connection with the liberal reformers, while the orthodox and aggressive Hinduism is neglected. Therefore, the whole nationalist and revivalist line is tuned down and the expansion and mission of Hinduism in its political and ideological dimension is not seen. The result is a complete caricature of Hinduism and its nature and mission, a caricature for which the scholars are to be made responsible. It is not a minor mistake, it is . . . bad research which has been fatal and is fatal for the understanding and praxis of the Indian Churches today.[7]

Hindu ideology encourages the persecution of Christians, and

Indian law assists in the process. The supreme court has concluded that the freedom of religion article in the constitution of India does not safeguard the right to try to convert others; to be the subject of a conversion attempt is an infringement on one's own religious freedom, even without any use of force, threat or illicit inducement to convert. This interpretation is especially serious because of the all-inclusive nature of the Hindu religion, which uncritically includes almost any set of beliefs within its own system. Thus tribal peoples, who are most often animist, have been artificially construed as part of Hinduism. And so have the untouchable masses, although they are not permitted to enter the Hindu temples. Thus it can be claimed by Hindus that when a tribal animist becomes a Christian, that is a case of the conversion of a Hindu. It is almost unheard of for tribal people to complain about conversions among tribals, but quite common for Hindus to do it, usually people with interests that might be threatened by the conversion of tribals.[8] Should this prohibition on attempts to convert others be enforced strictly, persecution in India could reach the extremes that have occurred in Nepal. Even if that doesn't happen, a relative tolerance could be at the expense of becoming a toothless kind of Christianity similar to the communal model in a few predominantly Muslim countries.

To the intrinsic appeal of its own features, Hinduism in India has added the potent force of nationalism of a peculiar kind. Rather than a nationalism based on territory, which it denounces, it has instead advocated *cultural* nationalism. Thus the identity of the country is said to be founded on Hinduism, which makes non-Hindus suspect— unpatriotic and perhaps traitorous. The nation is declared to be in danger from non-Hindus, who are associated with foreign threats. By raising this cry Hindu zealotry is rallied to the detriment of other religions.[9]

The connection between politics and religion, however it is raised, is not all contrived. When Christianity spread among the poor rural people in the nineteenth century, this threatened the hold of the few who held political and military power and therefore the de facto slave society. It did this by affirming the common humanity of all people. There are no "untouchables" in a Christian worldview. Although the caste system is expressly outlawed in modern India, it nevertheless exists in fact. The old slavery is now allied with the modern party system in Indian politics, and local politicians are no less powerful than their predecessors. They have been utterly opposed to Christian evangelism among poor Indians, including tribal animists. Some of the opposition known as "Hindu" is in reality the simple reaction of a political and economic power structure that sees the spread of Christian faith as likely to undermine that illicit power.[10]

Some analysts believe that the persecution by Hinduism in Nepal is to some extent similarly motivated. The rugged topography separating adjacent areas works against national feeling, and their theory is that the fragile unity would be undermined by religious divisiveness. This ties in with the long-standing xenophobia that kept Nepal closed to outside influences until a generation ago. Newspaper accounts tell of an international theological conspiracy. That may be why some arrests have gone beyond the law's prohibitions on converting others or preaching to Hindus, and have extended to arrests and beatings of Christians doing little beyond merely attending church services. There are further fears that Christianity serves to undermine the political and social order by challenging the divine nature of the king, who is regarded as a god, and also by challenging the caste system.[11]

CLAIMS OF TOLERATION

In a paper delivered in London in 1989 and entitled, "The Wonder of Nepal," Prem Bahadur Shakya, Patron of the Nepal Buddhist Society, said, "Perhaps in no other country is there such a degree of religious tolerance as one finds in Nepal. . . . There is complete freedom in our country to practice any kind of religion."[12] In the question and answer period afterwards I asked him why he neglected to mention all the Christians under indictment or serving time for practicing their faith, or the fact that numerous U.S. congressmen had signed a letter to the king several months earlier expressing concern about the lack of religious liberty in Nepal. His answer was unintelligible.[13]

HARASSMENT IN ISRAEL

In Israel, the government protects the liberties of both Christians and Muslims, but non-official orthodox Jewish groups target evangelical churches and ministries with opposition of various kinds. They are especially hard on groups which welcome Jews to Christian faith. One pastor in Jerusalem reports that members' pictures, names and addresses are plastered all over town, comparing them with the Ku Klux Klan. It has been claimed that they were supported by the

Palestine Liberation Organization, that they were exporting Jewish children to Germany and so on. Christians have been harassed on the telephone, and police, fire engines and commercial services have been called to their address. They have also been picketed. Demonstrations have been organized by an "anti-missionary" extremist organization called the Yad L'Achim, but more respectable groups have also participated, such as university people.[14]

A church in Tiberias on the Sea of Galilee that has been in existence for several years has undergone serious trouble from the Yad L'Achim. Started by an American businessmen and some friends, it met for a time in a rented room in a hotel. During services opponents would heave rocks through the windows, some of which struck worshipers. Finally the opposition ended the meetings in the hotel by setting it afire and seriously damaging it. When the church began meeting in the woods, their assailants went out there also and disrupted the services. The electronics business where many of the church members work has also been harassed. And the usual wild rumors have been spread all around the town. Still, the church carries on and gains both numbers and strength.[15]

The state of Christianity in Israel has been a source of encouragement for many believers in that country. There is now a national committee for evangelism, an inter-confessional fellowship, three magazines (one published for children), and a growing collection of churches and house churches. Yet the ultra-orthodox parties have been growing stronger, and from them emerges a possible threat to the peace of the liberties of the Jewish Christian church.[16] Another knowledgeable observer agrees with that assessment. From the mid-1960s to the mid-1980s some two hundred books and articles about Jesus were published in Israel. Some of the prejudice against Christianity died out with the older generation, and, as elsewhere, the secularity of modern life had left a spiritual vacuum among the young people. Many people are now intensely curious about Jesus, and some are saying: "Give us back the Jewish Jesus. He was ours before He was yours." Many are ready to discuss, even when not to acknowledge, His claims to divinity. Thus we have reason for hope that is more tangible than in the case in the Muslim world.[17]

THE TOTALITARIAN PERSECUTION OF THE CHURCH

IDEOLOGY AND TOTALITARIAN PERSECUTION

In the previous chapters we considered the persecution of the church by other religions. Now we begin a consideration of persecution by totalitarian governments—mostly Marxist-Leninist governments in the present world, but not exclusively. This distinction is useful but also artificial, and it should help our understanding of both if we consider why it is artificial.

The artificiality comes from the dual nature of both the persecuting religions and the persecuting totalitarian governments. In the first case, the persecuting religions are often backed by totalitarian regimes. And in the second, the totalitarian regimes that we consider in this chapter, for all their proud secularity, contain most of the trappings of religions; they have quasi-sacred writings, an ultimate loyalty, a theory of history, an ethic, a doctrine of last things, an epistemology, a metaphysic. Analyses of the religious nature of communism have become commonplace, and help us understand why there is such hostility toward Christianity. "It is quite clear," a French scholar has written, "that Communism (systematic humanism) and Christianity (systematic theism) are rigorously antithetical."[1] Most totalitarian regimes, whether communist or not, have similar characteristics. Here is a statement from the Nazi period to illustrate the point. It comes from Baldur von Schirach, leader of the Youth of the Reich, at a rally held in 1939:

> All of us who have taken part in the fighting period of our Movement and now are seeing the wonder of Germany's resurrection are inspired by the same religious feeling. . . . We serve God by being loyal to our Führer and doing our national duty. We are, therefore, a youth that believes in God, because we serve the Divine Law that is called Germany.[2]

We could find hundreds of such statements which regard the service of the totalitarian state or its leader as a religious duty. One scholar has concluded that the German persecution came naturally from two of its most important features, "its political nihilism and its ideological fanaticism."[3] In those two respects, and many more besides, communism is little different from Naziism. The Marxist-Leninist conviction that everything of the old structure must be swept aside in favor of the new society is a reflection of the same kind of nihilism the Nazis displayed. And the religious zeal with which communists accomplish this aim is if anything more evident than under the Nazis, especially the way in which the appeal stretches throughout the world, instead of being narrowly focused on one nationality.

At the same time the all-encompassing nature of the church and its beliefs is truly dangerous to the totalitarian ideal; paranoia is not all that makes the totalitarian state persecute the church. It is almost inevitable that communist regimes will strike at Christians. For Christianity stands as a refutation of the economic and social determinism that is part of the Marxist ideology. And Christians have a transcendent loyalty that relativizes everything that Communism teaches is absolute. The ideology, the party and the state are all relativized by the belief that there is a God above the flux of social and political systems, one who judges all human institutions and actions.

And even the final sanction the regime has for those who do not recognize its right to dominate the whole society—death—is for the Christian only semi-final; therefore the teaching and even the very existence of the church is a reproach and defiance of the regime, even when Christians are not strong or wise enough to recognize this. Many German Christians knew not only that the ethic of the Third Reich was wrong, but also that the nationalist rhetoric that put the German nation above everything else was wrong. They knew this

because the leader, the nation, and the power of the state are all relativized by a gospel that proclaims Jesus Christ as Lord.

HISTORY AND PERSECUTION

But ideology is not the only determinant of persecution. History is
another factor. By that I mean that the experiences of the past are
inherited by church and state, both of which are thereby influenced.
In the Soviet Union, for example, state control over the church did not
begin with the Bolshevik revolution, but was a feature of the Tsarist
system from the time of Peter the Great in the early eighteenth century.[4] Similarly, a recent analysis of church-state policy in communist
China concludes that four sources served as determinants. These are:
1) the tradition of state control of religion in imperial China, 2) the
neo-Enlightenment movement of the early 1920s, in which Chinese
intellectuals took over the idea current among some westerners that
all reality must be tested by science, a test they believed religion could
not survive, 3) Lenin's idea that religion was a force allied with impe-
rialism; this gained support not only among the Chinese communists,
but also in the ranks of their enemy, the Kuomintang of Chiang Kai-
shek during the short period they collaborated (1924-1927), and 4)
Mao's theory of contradictions.[5] Thus, according to this analysis,
three out of four determinants of Chinese communist policy come
from before the birth of Chinese Communism, and two of those do
not stem uniquely from the regime's ideology. Since totalitarian governments by definition concern themselves with every area of life, as
does Christian faith, we are not surprised to find numerous cases of
persecution directed against the church for reasons that appear to
have nothing to do with religion. In the Soviet Union, for example, a
perennial commitment of the regime has been to complete the
russification of the entire multi-national empire, especially in sensitive
areas such as the Ukraine which have resisted the encroachment of
Russian culture. This may be the best explanation for the fact that
Stalin forced the Eastern Catholic (Uniate) church out of existence (at
least officially), and also abolished the Ukrainian Orthodox Church
as a separate entity, merging it into the Russian Orthodox Church.
Since the Ukrainian churches were part of and reinforced the tradition of a separate national existence, their abolition was more closely
related to Soviet imperial ambitions than to anti-religious policy. Of
course abolition had the additional advantage of giving the authori-

ties the task of dominating the affairs of only one church in the Ukraine rather than three.[6]

SECRECY AND OPENNESS

These extra-religious motivations account in some measure for the varying ways totalitarian regimes persecute the church. Sometimes the persecution will be open and evidently unembarrassed, in other cases covert. In Burundi the restrictions on the church have been openly proclaimed. The policy promulgated in February 1985 was called "Rules for the Church in the form of a letter to the Provincial Governors from the Minister of the Interior," and prohibited unauthorized public meetings, religious meetings outside of regular worship services held only on Saturdays and Sundays (no services at mission posts, no prayer meetings, no retreats, and so on), and public displays of religious symbols without official authorization.[7]

State policy in Mozambique was also unambiguous and out in the open. The Ideological Department of the ruling party (Frelimo) held its Second National Conference on June 10, 1978, and adopted a resolution on religion summarized by Radio Mozambique as follows: "Noting that religious organisations propagate an anti-scientific culture, the conference decided that the ideological and political education of the members of the party and the population in general, constituted the most effective means of combating the massive influence exercised by religious organisations." But the activities of the state did not stop at resolutions. The Ideological Department created a network intended to supplant religious views with the official ideology. It divided the entire country into groups of several hundred people organized in villages, city streets or suburbs. Each cell held compulsory meetings. Cell members were required to sing songs, shout slogans, and discuss political speeches, all touting the Frelimo ideology, all directed explicitly against religion. Jorge Rebelo, the secretary of the Ideological Department, was quite open in giving the state's reason for this: "We are against religion and idealistic concepts because they are prejudicial to production. The religious person thinks that all he has, has been given by the Divine will. He is convinced that whether he works or not, God will send him his food if it is God's will, and if it is not God's will, then there will be no food." In 1978, when Rebelo wrote those words, it was evidently still possible for some people to assert seriously that Marxism-Leninism could assure a productive economy.[8]

In contrast Ethiopia determined to keep its anti-religious policy secret and either deny all instances of religious persecution or else to say they were aberrations whose perpetrators were investigated and punished. But a top secret document dated September 1982 and entitled *How to Root Out Religion* reached the outside. It originated in the Ethiopian Ministry of Information and National Guidance, and its aim was stated in the preface: "The major purpose of this analysis is the need to uproot and destroy completely the anti-revolutionary situation that is prevalent in religious practices." Part I contains a twelve-point program of specific actions to destabilize the churches. It includes turning monasteries into museums, confiscating religious literature, burning religious clothing, creating artificial shortages of such supplies as candles and wax, and encouraging the preaching of a gospel in which the message of Christ was equated with the building of socialism.[9]

THE CHURCH AS TOOL OF THE STATE

The totalitarian government does not regard religion solely as a detriment which it must put down by force. It also sees the church as a tool for the furtherance of state policy. When officials of Soviet churches confer with foreigners, the KGB does what it can to insure that the conversation echoes the themes of official Soviet propaganda. In fact the relations of the Orthodox Church with foreign churches is considered by the state as a part of Soviet foreign policy. Just as the Soviet state condemned the Hungarian uprising of 1956 and supported the Warsaw Pact invasion of Czechoslovakia in 1968 and the Soviet invasion of Afghanistan of 1979, the Orthodox Church did the same.[10] When the Russian Orthodox Church makes official statements concerning world peace, those statements always take the same position as Soviet foreign policy. The Soviet Peace Fund apparently receives 15 percent of the total receipts of the Orthodox Church, funds which are contributed by its adherents.[11]

Such efforts at neutralization and control are not limited to totalitarian governments that have already seized power. Even during the revolutionary phase, the budding totalitarians recognize the direction in which their real problems lie. In the Philippines the Marxist-Leninist New People's Army regards Christian ministries as among their most serious enemies. NPA propaganda is normally rejected by Christians, and so guerrilla fire is directed at church growth and expansion ministries. In the late 1980s some 150 church leaders were assassinated by the NPA.[12] Even when policy seems to reduce the pressure on the church that, too, may be related to state interests. Stalin's relaxation of the murderous attack on the church during World War II, under pressure of the German assault when Soviet citizens were welcoming the invaders, is the best known example of this in the Soviet Union,[13] but there are others. During its *glasnost*ian thaw the regime relaxed the long-standing ban on the church (and everybody else) engaging in charitable activity. Keston College (which has the most comprehensive research effort on religion in communist countries) speculates that as long as such activity is focused on people who are seriously ill in hospitals, mentally ill, the elderly and invalids—in other words, those who are not likely ever again to play a leading role in society—the regime has little to lose and the church can be used to compensate for the inability of the society to care for such people otherwise.[14]

This ability to manipulate the church, both in the open and covertly, suggests that the totalitarian regimes have become expert in understanding their adversary. There is considerable evidence that such is the case, beyond the fact that it is generally the intelligence services that have the responsibility for this task. Josef Tson, one of the most influential of Protestant pastors in Romania before he was forced to leave the country, talked to a number of communist officials whose job it was to neutralize the effects of organized religion, and he believes he learned some things about their methods that he has not seen published. These officials told him that they studied in detail the beliefs and practices, strengths and weaknesses of the different churches and individual leaders. They deal with four separate entities: the denominations, the local churches, the pastors, and selected individual believers. Tson believes you cannot understand what is happening by looking at this or that event; it is necessary to see the phenomenon of persecution by the government as a whole.[15]

DESTABILIZING THE CHURCH

In the Soviet Union, religious activities are formally governed by the 1929 statute enacted early in Stalin's rule and subsequently amended.[16] The totalitarian regimes all have somewhat different forms, but most of them follow the major features of the Soviet model. It is easy to state what the church is able to do in these countries, since its sole function is to administer the religious worship service. The list of what may not be done requires more explanation. Article 17 of the 1929 law puts it this way:

> Religious associations may not: (a) create mutual undertakings, or in general use property at their disposal other than for the satisfaction of religious needs; (b) give material support to their members; (c) organise special prayer or other meetings for children, young people and women, nor general Bible, literary, handicraft, work, catechetical and other similar meetings, groups, circles and departments, nor organise excursions and children's playgrounds, nor open libraries and reading rooms, nor organise sanatoria and medical help. Only books necessary for the performance of the relevant cult may be kept in the prayer buildings and premises.[17]

To anyone familiar with the Biblical basis of church life as well as the actual events of church history, the intent behind this list of prohibitions is plain. They might as well have put it this way: "We're going to let you hold worship services, and by so doing give the lie to claims that we do not permit religious liberty. But we are not going to allow an association of believers actually to behave as churches have been accustomed and as believers say the church ought to function." Still, the law is not the worst of the situation, since one intent of such laws is the desire to put the best face on the situation for outside consumption. This means that as bad as these laws tend to be, believers ordinarily do not enjoy such protection as they are supposed to afford. As we shall see the regime feels free to break even the bad laws it imposes.

One by-product of harassment by the regime is the increase of distrust within the church. Almost all totalitarian governments have agents in the church. Everyone knows this, and the believers often will say they know who the informers are. But they cannot be absolutely sure, and this is often a serious barrier to forming real unity and openness in the church. It is difficult to foster a sense of community with mutual trust when people are uncertain if their confidences will end up in a police file folder. The head of the Soviet Baptists before the 1990 reorganization was widely rumored to report to the KGB. When I asked one Baptist in Leningrad if he believed there was any truth to the rumor, he replied that he didn't know, there were people on both sides of the question.[18] He seemed to see nothing strange about this kind of disagreement in the church, but it's clear that the regime has been able to create a wonderful tactic for its destabilizing purposes.

When the remarkable group who made up the Moscow Christian Seminar was broken up in the late 1970s and went to prison, two of its members pleaded guilty. They gave information that the authorities found useful in further investigations, and in return were put into comfortable cells and given unusual privileges. Finally their sentences were suspended and they were freed. One of these men, Lev Regelson, reportedly engaged in a duel of wits with an interrogator, in which the officer pretended to be a secret Christian who wanted to help him, while Regelson pretended to believe him. Regelson got in over his head and the KGB man won the game, which is only to be expected of an amateur matching wits with a professional. Regelson had an interesting explanation for caving in: he said he would go to prison for the faith but not for human rights.[19] Of course, we're not in a position to know if he was just seeking to justify what he did or if he was genuinely confused. But it's clear what happens to a Christian community when some of its members betray others.

Similar events have taken place in Africa when government pressures forced Christians to forsake their regular buildings and instead hold worship meetings in houses. Even though the assemblies were smaller, which facilitated the development of lay leadership, the government was still able to infiltrate the meetings. People knew this and there was a high degree of distrust in the church, extending even to members of the same family. Children were encouraged to report to the government on their parents' activities.[20]

Propaganda has been in the forefront of the totalitarian state's weapons in every area in which it takes an interest, and that includes activities intended to delegitimate the church. Since people do not easily give up the need for ritual, the regime devises its own rituals to replace and also discredit church rites. The Soviet government established a seminary of atheism for the Communist Youth Party (Komsomol). It instituted anti-religious processions, mocking those of the Russian Orthodox Church, but also seeking to substitute for them. Party meetings to some extent are intended to take the place of church meetings. The theater was another substitute, becoming a kind of temple of the new religion. In 1914 there were about 210 theaters in

Russia; in 1920 the Soviet Union had 6,000, many of them converted churches. These theaters were not provided merely for entertainment and culture; they were full of propaganda for the new thinking. After Lenin's death, when the body was deposited in the mausoleum for perpetual public viewing, the Communist Party organized a "nocturnal adoration" ceremony.[21] The religious symbolism, built on the ruins of the Orthodox tradition, is obvious.

In keeping with their efforts to attain their ends without incurring unnecessary political costs, the authorities normally make efforts to exploit the church's internal weaknesses, especially disagreements and dissension, so as to avoid obvious repression. In 1941 the Soviet Commissar for the Interior wrote to one of the district superintendents, ordering him to prepare reports on the religious organizations within his district. Of the nine points in the directive, two offer good illustrations of this way of obtaining benefits while avoiding costs:

> (5) Point out internal dissension existing within the religious organization or among the clergy, indicating in detail the reasons for the dissension and giving the names of the priests between whom strained relations exist.
> (6) Offer your suggestions as to the best way to make use of these dissensions, so as to enlist certain people as secret agents and thus undermine the Church organisations in your district.[22]

One Polish Baptist recently acknowledged to westerners that his church had benefitted from favors granted by the government whose motivation was not pro-Baptist but anti-Catholic.[23] The long hostility of Polish Catholics toward Protestants provided an opportunity which the government was quick to seize. The Yugoslav government attempted to drive a wedge between the various orders of clergy for the same reason. Party propagandists emphasized class differences, associating the higher clergy with the exploiters and the lower with the exploited.[24]

The *Letter of Instruction* of 1961 which helped split the Baptist and evangelical churches into mutually hostile registered and unregistered groups was intended to do that very thing. Many Christian leaders did not understand this and so played into Khrushchev's hands. It was an attempt to wreck the church. It failed in its larger purpose because Khrushchev hadn't considered what it meant to have two enemies. He ended up making concessions to the registered in order to undermine the unregistered; this was a big help to the former.[25]

A more extreme example is that of the Three-Self Patriotic Movement in China, which is the officially recognized organization used by the government to control the Protestant churches. Writing at a time of severe persecution in Shaanxi province, one believer said: "But what is most painful is that leaders in the Three-Self churches accuse us to the police even when [the police] have not bothered to search for us, so they are then forced to take action."[26]

A standard technique of the secret police is to take advantage of the moral weaknesses of its targets. A paper from the Council on Religious Affairs (CRA) in the Soviet Union advocated finding candidates for bishop who have moral defects so as to keep the hierarchy in its grip.[27] One Orthodox priest in Leningrad reports that when he was a young man the local representative of the party organization invited him to renounce his faith. The official dangled enticing offers before him—the chance for advanced academic study and a good job. When the priest stood fast, the church rallied to his support. He says this is typical of what happened but that he knows of two or three priests who gave in to those temptations.[28]

A 1940 confidential letter from a high official of the Lithuanian Ministry of the Interior to the secret police is very revealing in this respect. It orders the police to bribe priests and other church employees for information about Roman Catholic parties, groups and fraternities. The purpose is to enlist such people as agents to work for the "disintegration" of Catholic organizations and eventually to form a branch of secret agents among monks. Even at this stage of the Soviet experience, after the Russian Orthodox Church had been all but wiped out, the Ministry was urging a more subtle method. "When attempting bribery avoid rash mistakes; consequently get information about the candidates and lead them on gradually. Always remember that many priests are badly off financially." They combined this technique with repression to exploit the weakness of some of the priests. When a priest was arrested on some pretext, he would be offered the possibility of retaining his liberty if he signed an agreement to work for the KGB.[29]

Bribery could also be practiced on a grand scale affecting not just a few priests but the whole church. The newly installed communist regime in Hungary offered a compromise to the Roman Catholic church in allowing it to retain ten important schools in the midst of a general confiscation, and also permitting the monks and nuns to teach in the newly nationalized schools. The catch was that the church would be giving implicit endorsement to the seizure of the bulk of the Catholic schools. In July 1948 the episcopate refused, saying that to accept "would have meant the abandonment of all our principles."[30]

WRECKING THE LEADERSHIP

Since leadership is so important for accomplishing the mission of the church, the regime naturally looks there for ways to destroy its effectiveness. The authorities in Romania systematically moved Christian university graduates far from their homelands. This had the effect of breaking them away from the religious communities from which they had come. When combined with state refusal to allow more than a token number into ministerial training, as well as denial of building permits for new churches to serve the shifting of the population to cities, it made it even more difficult for the churches to provide spiritual sustenance to the leadership of the next generation.[31] More direct means can also be used to get rid of leadership. In 1979 the only Catholic seminary in Mozambique suddenly went out of business when its entire faculty and student body were drafted into the armed forces.[32]

If the leaders are not gotten rid of or dispersed they can be discredited in order to accomplish the same thing. The celebrated case of Cardinal Mindszenty, who became the symbol for resistance of the Roman Catholic Church to the communists of Hungary, illustrates this. "Mindszentyism" was for the regime the symbol of everything evil. What it really meant was resistance. As the pressure on the Cardinal grew and his assistants were arrested he issued this statement:

> Since I have not taken part in any plot I shall never resign. I shall not speak. If after this you hear that I have confessed this or that, or that I have resigned my office (even though this should be authenticated by my signature), you should realise that such a declaration is but the consequence of human frailty.... Likewise I declare null and void any confession which may be attributed to me from this day....

Evidently they broke Mindszenty, and he issued a confession at his trial. The court sentenced him to life imprisonment for the crimes of treason, espionage, plotting and illegal foreign exchange trading. Afterward there was a muting of the anti-Catholic barrage and even some public displays of goodwill toward the Vatican. The purpose of this was to give credence to the fiction that Mindszenty himself was the cause of the problem and not the policy of the regime. This was followed by a one-sided agreement between the government and the episcopate. It included a state subsidy for the church that was to continue for eighteen years. But shortly afterward the arrests of priests and bishops resumed.[33]

The Regelson case in Moscow, mentioned earlier, was similar in its outcome. After Regelson was released there was a report to the effect that he would take up the leadership of the Christian Seminar, and that moreover it would now take on a semi-official status. But there was little or no support from others and the idea petered out. Regelson tried to persuade others to change their views and throw in with him but without success.[34] Since most of the other leaders of the seminar were behind bars, people evidently considered him to be compromised and wouldn't have much to do with him. Of course, the whole case against Regelson, as the other Moscow Seminar leaders, was trumped up from the start. One woman refused to cooperate with the prosecution of Regelson because it was all fabricated. Then the police threatened her by discussing with her what would happen to her nine-year-old daughter were she to be arrested.[35]

This discrediting of the leadership is part of a general motive to isolate the believers from the larger society and thus reduce the damage done by the "infection."[36] The same end is achieved by the constant propaganda that believers are different from other Soviet citizens. People on the receiving end of this propaganda all their lives comes to think of believers as bizarre creatures from the past. One result of the opening of the Soviet citizenry to alternate voices is the surprise in finding out that in most respects Christians are "normal" and that in the ways in which they exhibit unusual traits, such as the willingness to volunteer for social services, they are attractively different.

SUBVERTING THE YOUTH

Along with the leadership, the youth of the country represent a target of prime importance. Hence, the youth movements that are so much a part of totalitarian regimes. The Hitler Youth and the Komsomol have imitators almost everywhere such governments exist. Josef Tson recalls from the indoctrination meetings of his childhood in the Romania of the late 1940s that the atheist ideologues knew well from historical example that overt persecution can be counterproductive. They wanted to profit from the lessons of history and not strengthen religion by persecuting it. Rather they would allow old people to carry on their religious practices without hindrance while eradicating religion from the future generations by indoctrinating the young.[37] In Czechoslovakia the regime disbanded the religious youth organizations.[38] In 1989 the Czech authorities dismissed a teacher named Vera Zak from her job on the grounds that she was a Christian. She appealed this decision, but the court ruled that the school authorities were justified in firing her because of her religious convictions. The reason is that teachers have to swear they will teach in accordance with the spirit of Marxism-Leninism, which Christians cannot do.[39]

The Nazis saw the youth of the church as standing in the way of the general adulation of the Führer and his program, and they launched crude propaganda campaigns to win them over, if not by argument then by intimidation. One of Hitler's spokesmen put it this way:

> The German youth has staked its honour on its ability to stand before the judgment of History as the creator and upholder of the unity of the Third Reich. Catholic Youth, do you want to adhere stubbornly to your special viewpoint, do you want to be branded in the judgment of history as the destructive force which sabotaged the unity of the Reich and the formation of its future?[40]

SUBVERTING THE INTELLECTUALS

If the youth are objects of special concern to the totalitarian regime, so are the intellectuals. These regimes almost all take their justification from the scribblings of the intelligentsia, and they have a natural fear of counter-revolutionary writings. One article published in a Soviet journal in 1976 pointed with apprehension to the modernization of the Roman Catholic Church in the West and expressed the fear that a similarly rejuvenated Russian Orthodox Church could increase its influence among the educated.[41] No doubt similar fears account for the almost total elimination of theological education, which disrupted the intellectual life of the church. In addition much of the church's brainpower died in the labor camps. With four or five candidates for every opening at the theological schools, authorities play a big role in selecting the students. "If you really want this student you must take this one as well." With various pretexts the police arrest the candidates they don't want to attend, sometimes only long enough to prevent their taking exams. They also recruit informers at the theological schools. Some 50 percent are reported to cooperate, which changes the atmosphere in the school.[42]

The authorities in Romania, to cite only one more example, have allowed very few theological students. There are some one thousand Baptist churches in Romania, but less than two hundred pastors. The government likes it this way because when a church does not have a pastor it is more susceptible to the influence of laymen who are controlled by the security force. The tradition is for the pastor to do everything in the church and to control everything. Without a pastor there is a power vacuum that the state can maneuver to fill.[43]

Since the totalitarian regime is as concerned with what is thought as it is with what is done, church literature comes in for special attention. The effect of censorship on the *Journal of the Moscow Patriarchate* has been to deaden it, if not actually to turn it into propaganda. Before his imprisonment, Deacon Vladimir Rusak reported that every issue is sent to the CRA on the twentieth of the month, and they read it for five days. CRA officials

> are the most attentive and the most zealous readers of the church journal. . . . The entire structure of the journal has gradually been defined by the Council, and at best only one-third of the space has been made available to purely church historical events. The remainder is peace-making and ecumenism. The space which is useful to the Church is bought at the price of that which is useful to the government. . . .

Talented writers turn instead to *samizdat.*[44]

The rituals of the church appeal to the imagination similar to the way the doctrines appeal to the intellect, so the totalitarian regime finds it useful to create substitute rituals, although seldom able to come up with more than a pale imitation of the real thing. The Soviet wedding civil ceremonies are a ludicrous example of this. More seriously, the propaganda mills create a substitute religion out of the ideology that undergirds the state. In the attempt to win people's loyalty they even bring up religious concepts that are contrary to the official ideology, if the contradiction can be hidden under emotional rhetoric. Thus in the attempt to fan patriotism in the face of actual or fabricated external threats, the Soviet regime will speak of the *sacred duty* to defend the motherland, language which has no referent in Marxism-Leninism. The Nazis found it easier to do the same thing with the mystical claptrap about the German nation that informed their ideology. An Austrian woman put it this way:

> What the Führer has given me is not only a political ideology, but also a religion. He has given me a faith, which, in its true form, I never before possessed, not even when I was young. This faith is the belief in ourselves, in our strength, in our greatness; the belief in the mysterious power of the Blood, of the soil of our Country, and of the German Nation.[45]

DIRECT METHODS OF SUPPRESSION

These disparate methods of dealing with the church are effective to varying degrees. They are also slow. Often the authorities use more direct methods, even when they are not brutal ones like shooting and imprisonment. Russian Orthodox Metropolitan Nikolai, who died in 1961, told a churchman in Brussels of some of these methods. In the case of an effective priest who is doing a good job, the CRA deregisters him or requires the bishop to transfer him where he can do less harm. The bishop does as he is told and then submits another name for the post. The CRA refuses to agree to that candidate or anyone else the bishop recommends. Consequently, no service is held in the church for six months; since it is a non-functioning church, it is closed. But why wait six months if the job can be done immediately? If that is the desire, the authorities simply see to it that a crowd of a few hundred Komsomol activists shows up one Sunday after services with the required tools, and soon the church is flattened. The valuables are taken away and are never seen again. The police, of course, do not interfere.[46]

The various stratagems may be brutal or soft, but the intent is always to have a church that is tame and compliant, a fit tool for the use of the regime. Outsiders mistakenly focus too often on the means used and thus miss the ends that are sought. Speaking privately after the Tienenman Square massacre in 1989, one house church member cautioned westerners that the whole purpose of the regime's actions is to intimidate and so render the church docile. Westerners may say at a particular time that only twenty or so people are in prison, so things aren't too bad. But they don't realize that when one is in prison it intimidates the rest. The extent of the persecution has nothing to do with how many are in prison. It's the effect of the imprisonment on those who are walking around on the outside. "They don't actually have to put you in prison to stop what you are doing. They can harass you just by putting one in prison."[47]

Harsh treatment may not simply be the result of brutality; it can be a coldly rational way to bring about a compliant attitude. One French priest, Jean de Leffe, tells of this technique in a Chinese prison that he inhabited. The prisoners were made to sit all day in absolute silence in regret for their "sins." Some days they would write out endless letters of confession, or discuss the subject of the radio propaganda programs to which they were forced to listen. Three points were the constant subject of their discussions, always under supervision. 1) They had to confess their crimes against the regime, and they had to do this with evident complete sincerity. An incomplete or half-hearted confession would be met with further demands. 2) They had to convince their jailers not only that they had stated all their sins, but that they were regretful about them. 3) They had to prove that the whole charade was sincere by denouncing all their accomplices, including friends and family members. This placed great psychological and spiritual burdens on the prisoners. Should they state everything, even things the police might not know? If they held something back, what would this mean for their release? Should they admit to false charges in an effort to get out of their fix? Should they reveal facts about others? How many charges against others would they have to invent in order to prove their "sincerity"? They were not only exhorted by their jailers to comply with all these demands, but also by their fellow prisoners who were themselves proving their "sincerity" by this action against their neighbors. One day a fellow prisoner said to de Leffe: "I accused my father and my older brother. Why don't you silence your scruples and turn in the names of the enemies of the people?"[48]

The jailers were creating guilty people with an inner weakness that in turn made them susceptible to doing the bidding of the authorities. There is no end to the manipulation that comes from the spiritual weakness of people sensible of their guilt. This is another way in which the totalitarian regime apes Christian faith while opposing it.

It transforms people. When the regime successfully deals with one of its subjects, he is changed into a weak and pitiful thing that can be manipulated at will.

Of course most Christians are not imprisoned or tortured, and many are hardly conscious that anything is out of the ordinary, so accustomed do they become to the general harassment. A couple of years ago I was sitting with two friends in the Prague living room of a pastor when he interrupted me to say that they were not persecuted in Czechoslovakia, they were only "under pressure." He didn't want me to exaggerate the situation. Yet, we had arrived at his place as he requested: at night, with the taxi dropping us off some distance from his house, and being careful that no one saw us enter. When we sat down to talk, he removed the telephone and set it down outside in the hallway, covered with cushions, and closed the door. Upon our departure, he turned out the light, opened the outside door cautiously, and stepped out to make sure the coast was clear before inviting us out to the sidewalk. But he wanted it understood that there was no persecution in his country. (A complicating factor in this case is that he was a Protestant in a country in which the regime saved its most severe treatment for Roman Catholics.)

In Romania during the long night of the Ceausescu regime, pastors' telephones were tapped, *securitate* officers were present in each service taping sermons, baptisms were restricted, church members who refused to become informers were harassed at work. Pastors were forbidden to preach from specified texts. For example, the book of Revelation was forbidden because the government wanted no talk about the return of Christ to rule the world.[49] They realized, in ways that many Christians don't, that the gospel has political implications.

A Baptist in Leningrad reports that when he moved into his apartment, for years afterwards his family was spied upon by the neighbor across the hall. When his doorbell rang, the neighbor's door opened so he could take a good look at the visitor.[50]

Even when the totalitarian regime moderates its harshness, one never knows how deep down the change is or how permanent it will prove to be. The periodic thaws and refreezes in Soviet religious policy are largely unknown to westerners with short memories who are ready to proclaim, if not the millennium, then something close to it whenever the bear stops roaring and issues forth sweet talk. But the reality may be very different from the appearance. Five years into *glasnost* the KGB was evidently still killing religious figures while the

National Council of Churches in the United States was warbling its enchantment with the ruler. Sergei Sevchenko was killed by the KGB on October 23, 1989, by means of a staged automobile accident, a favorite method of theirs. A car leaped the curb, rolled onto the sidewalk and crushed him. He was associated with Alexander Ogorodnikov and the Christian Democratic Union. This happened less than a year after Ogorodnikov's brother Rafail, an Orthodox priest, was killed in a car accident, also widely thought to be a KGB action. Shortly before Sevchenko's death KGB goons struck at the editorial office of Ogorodnikov's Bulletin of Christian Opinion; one of their people was beaten up and some equipment taken. Two weeks after Sevchenko's death the editorial offices again received visitors. This time Fr. Victor Grigoriev was beaten, and the place was cleaned out of its equipment and files. The priest was left bound and gagged, suffering a concussion.

Such incidents are of course out of the ordinary in recent years, although at one time the regime's victims had to be counted not as single incidents, but by the thousands. Even at that we can perhaps learn more from the systematic subjection of the church to the wishes of the totalitarian state than we can from bursts of random violence. To that we shall now turn.

TOTALITARIAN CONTROL OF THE CHURCH STRUCTURE

The totalitarian regime often concludes that the challenges presented by the presence of Christianity can be better handled by other means than violence. Taking "active measures" —to use the typical euphemistic language—carries with it the disadvantages associated with creating martyrdom and resistance at home and diplomatic defeats abroad. Usually the regime prefers to attain its ends by softer means, by controlling the churches and minimizing the damage that might come from Christian challenges to its legitimacy. Or even better, by turning the churches into tools usable for the consolidation and expansion of state power.

ATTACKING THROUGH INDIRECTION

Although there are many common features between persecutions in the various totalitarian countries the manifestations are somewhat different in all of them. Albert Galter studied the Roman Catholic Church during the early years of the European communist regimes and arrived at some conclusions on how they operate in different circumstances. These are the main determinants he found:

1) How many Catholics there are, their degree of organization, and the vitality of Christian life among them. Thus there was a very severe persecution in China, Bulgaria and Romania compared with

Poland or Yugoslavia. Where it seems expedient, the communists can even appear to be defenders of religious liberty. This is especially true when they have not yet come to power and are faced with the need for the Catholic vote before an election. 2) The rite—they are tougher on eastern rite or Uniate than Latin Catholics. 3) Existence of strong denominations (Eastern Orthodoxy, for example) that can be used as counterweight to the Catholics, thus permitting a more repressive policy. 4) Strength of the communist position within the country. Thus with the economic crisis in Hungary during 1953-55 anti-religious pressure was eased and the government even appealed to Catholics to support the national front as a sign of their patriotism. 5) Contact with countries abroad. They were tough in China and the U.S.S.R. which were relatively isolated, but felt they had to be more cautious in East Germany because there was so much more contact, especially before the Berlin Wall was in place. 6) The requirements of psychological warfare. The authorities place great restrictions on the church, or even treat it with severe brutality; if they meet with resistance they ease up to some degree, and the church may be satisfied at the easing of pressure even though the situation is very bad. The church's will to resist has been sapped by the concession. The authorities also may tighten the vise in one place when the outside world is focusing on the loosening elsewhere.[1]

The fundamental dilemma of the communist world, which accounts for the paradoxes and contradictions (but also the befuddlement and weakness of both Christians in the West and their governments) is on the one hand the desire to destroy religion and the transcendence that relativizes the totalitarian dream, and on the other hand to demonstrate to onlookers that these countries are democratic and free. How is it possible to do both at the same time? Deception is central.

Josef Tson reports on his youth in Romania: "We heard the communist leaders say again and again, that they fight religion but 'not by administrative actions,' that is, not by closing the churches or by imprisoning Christians." The plan in the case of the Baptists was to leave the church structures in place but see to it that they do the bidding of the state. The authorities did not put the new rules on paper, but communicated them orally. Nevertheless infractions brought punishment, which the Baptist Union executed under government direction. The advantage of this indirect action was that the state was not seen as the cause of the sanctions, which appeared to outsiders to be the work of the church itself. When a pastor lost his position it was his peers that did it, or so it was made to seem. The following numbers give some idea of the effectiveness of this tactic. In 1959 the Romanian Baptists had 540 active Baptist pastors. Five years later four hundred of them had been dismissed, and as far as the outside world was concerned it was the Baptist Union which did it. In 1973, a group of younger pastors exposed the whole sham, writing papers that were published in the West. The next year the government was forced to abolish the unwritten rules, so severe had the damage to the government's reputation become.[2]

Another approach is to attack not the church, but the church *member* in order to destroy his motivation for supporting the church. They do this principally through job discrimination. Good jobs are closed to Christians, and no matter what job they get they receive harassment by managers and by police. People are dismissed from their jobs, allegedly for incompetence. Christians attending universities may not study such sensitive subjects as history, law, philosophy or sociology. Pastors are subject to harassment and pressure, threats, blackmail and smear campaigns.[3]

MERGERS AND ACQUISITIONS

Even though Stalin almost erased the church from existence in the Soviet Union, he recognized belatedly that political control could be more effective if it were allowed to exist in a strictly controlled way. Why try to wipe it out and run the risk of driving it underground where he could not keep an eye on it?[4] One Soviet innovation in this area was the creation of a fake church to supplant the real one. They called it the Living Church when it was founded in the 1920s. It petered out in the 1940s, as the state found it could achieve its ends through controlling the patriarchal church.[5] Soviet leaders tried the same thing with Roman Catholicism in 1944 when the German forces were expelled from Lithuania. They created a Lithuanian National church in order to entice young Catholics to join it. They agitated clergy groups to act against the hierarchy while intensifying a campaign of lies against the Pope, using falsified documents.[6]

The Romanian regime forcibly combined the Uniate Catholic church with the Romanian Orthodox Church in 1948.[7] It was helped in this by shameful collaboration on the part of the Orthodox leadership. This was pretty much the same situation as the forced merger of the Ukrainian Orthodox Church into the Russian. And similarly the Czech communists disbanded the Uniate diocese of Presov in May 1950 despite universal dissent among the population. This broke up a church in existence since 1649.[8]

Idi Amin's church policy in Uganda was based on similar considerations. He banned all churches except the Roman Catholic, Anglican and Orthodox. It was all a matter of facilitating state domination, since it was easier to control three archbishops than a multiplicity of groups.[9]

The Romanian Baptists, alluded to earlier, deserve some closer attention in connection with the method of control because they accepted a system of governance wholly at odds with their tradition and their convictions. The regime in 1954 forced on the Baptist Union a scheme which would have drastically reduced the number of worship services. The specific measure was not the significant issue for our purpose here, but rather the notion that the Union could control the churches and in so doing become a conduit for government policy. In keeping with the traditional Baptist polity the Union was not a governing body but had been formed rather late, in 1920, purely as a consultative group for mutual assistance. The individual congregations were self-governing until this move by the regime to turn them into something else. Recognizing the radical nature of the government demand, the Union balked. The Ministry of Cults responded to this defiance by withdrawing recognition from the Union's leaders and requiring the denomination to elect new ones. Under great pressure the Union did this in 1955, and selected the leaders acceptable to the Ministry. Josef Tson concludes that this action to vote in opposition to their own convictions was equivalent to lying and had serious consequences for the future. "Those who voted, yielded and were inwardly crushed. They started down the slopes of compromise which one after another followed the congress."[10] The lesson here is that a centralized church is easier for the regime to control, but if the centralized structure does not exist—even if it is contrary to the doctrine and organization of the church, as in this case—the regime may simply ride roughshod over the traditions of the church and the convictions of its people and force it to centralize as a prelude to dominating its processes.

The Soviet regime analogously overturned the governing structure of the Orthodox parishes in 1961 by forcing the Church to place the governing power in the hands of a lay committee. The same act removed the priest's authority over the financial affairs of the church; thus he was in charge of the worship and all that was connected with it but had no commensurate fiscal authority. In practice it put the priest in the hands of laymen who might not even make any claim to Christian faith, but had the advantage, to the regime, of taking orders from the local representative of the Council on Religious Affairs.[11] Thus if a conscientious bishop or priest somehow got through the screening process and began having a spiritual ministry he might be neutralized at the parish level by this hand-picked demolition squad.

Even when the state has put its apparatus in control, it is sometimes possible for the church to wrest some degree of independence from the situation, often by exploiting the drive for international respectability that many such regimes seek. In the spring of 1988 the pastor of the largest Baptist church in Romania (and in Europe), Nicolaie Gheorghita, found himself in a clash with the Ceausescu government over the presidency of the Baptist Union. He was the clear choice of his fellow pastors, but the government was pushing for the election of Vasile Talpos. A solution was effected in which both candidates would be given other posts while a compromise candidate would become president.[12]

Where the church cannot be controlled, the regime may try to make it irrelevant. Analysis of the joint declaration between the Roman Catholic Church in Poland and the government shows it to be an obvious attempt to privatize the church, divorcing it from the life of the nation. For example, Article 2 put the church on record as being completely behind the Communist Party program for national reconstruction and made it impossible to dissent from state policy. Article 6 took away from the bishops the right to oppose the collectivization of agriculture. Article 13 allowed the church to continue its charitable work, but granted to the state the right to restrict this activity. As disadvantageous as this joint declaration was to the church, the government began violating it almost immediately, restricting the church's influence even further.[13]

CHANGE IS THE NORM

Almost any generalization that might be made about the church under the totalitarian regimes should be met with this question: When? In no case did the situation remain static, but underwent bewildering shifts as both government and church leaders succeeded their predecessors, and as the requirements of foreign or internal policy dictated the adoption of tactical changes. One of the reasons westerners, including western Christians, have been fooled by the activities of the communist regimes is that they place the wrong interpretation on periods of relaxation which have occurred from time to time. These periods occur partly for tactical reasons, in response to this or that requirement, but also because of the Leninist ideology. The assumption has been that once the church organization is brought under the domination of the state and can do no harm, the internal contradictions will assert themselves and the necessary disintegration will eventually commence.[14] The relaxation is taken by the unwary to signal a fundamental change of policy. "Perhaps they won't be so bad once they get over their insecurities. See, they're already changing."

Some of the shifts are justified by recourse to theorists. The Chinese leadership, for example, has been impressed by Mao's theory of contradictions. There are primary and secondary contradictions, and in order to devote proper attention to the former, it may be necessary to tolerate the latter. That is why they could cooperate with the U.S. when the U.S.S.R. seemed a greater threat. Chinese politicians see religion as secondary and relatively non-antagonistic in comparison with more pressing concerns. So they're willing to take a softer line while striving to change the secondary contradiction by persuasive means. This is part of the United Front strategy but it has its limits, and to those who persist in refusing to be persuaded the Party is ready to drop its lenient means and take to criticism, threats, and force.[15]

The difficulties of working out a more or less permanent settlement to the church-state problem in Poland is suggestive of what happens almost everywhere. Seldom do we find these artificially contrived "solutions" persisting past the circumstances which gave rise to them. Jonathan Chao has identified different phases through which the relationship has gone. During the period 1954-58 the state attempted to bring the Protestant churches under control by enrolling them in the Three-Self Patriotic Movement. Pastors who refused to join were imprisoned. The leaderless churches were in trouble, and their numbers were reduced drastically. Wang Ming-tao in Beijing and Lam Hin-ko in Canton were among the best known of these pastors.

The years 1956-66 saw a virtual union of church and state. Intensive political study became mandatory for pastors. Many pastors were forced to be away from their churches, which then withered away. In Shanghai the number of churches declined to eight from more than two hundred; Beijing went from sixty-six to four. The Great Proletarian Cultural Revolution lasted from 1966 to 1976. During this period the state tried to destroy the church. This was a drastic shift from the United Front policy by which the regime attempted to put a fig leaf over its control of the church. During the cultural revolution Christians met secretly in their homes, especially in the countryside. In 1979, several years after Mao's death and the arrest of Gang of Four, the church began to reappear from apparent death. The regime reestablished the United Front Work Department in March 1979, and the following month the Religious Affairs Bureau; this meant the reappearance of the control mechanism, now necessary again since the church had refused to die according to plan. Now the Chinese Communist Party began talking again of freedom of belief, as they had before the cultural revolution.

In October 1980, the Three-Self Patriotic Movement came back to life as a mass political organization to assist the government in its religious policy. The Christian Council of China was formed to take care of purely ecclesiastical functions. But the staffs of both organizations are essentially the same, and they usually meet jointly. The CCC is the organ that sends officials abroad to meet with foreign churches and other groups. Persecution again intensified after 1982. The house churches that would not join the TSPM suffered greatly. With the liberalization of the economy in 1984 the regime backed off on the pressure against the house churches. Many in jail were released or had their sentences reduced.[16] Several years later the pressure again began to mount, becoming much worse after the killings in Tienenman Square in 1989.

The Chinese experience can be examined further to see how the mechanism of state control is used. As suggested in the previous paragraph, the United Front is used to gain goodwill for the communist regime. The Front encourages the Three-Self movement to form relationships with foreign bodies, including foreign churches, even though those churches cannot establish relationships directly with Chinese churches. In domestic policy the United Front organizations are expected to win the support of the Chinese people for government policy. These policies come from the United Front Work Department of the Chinese Communist Party Central Committee. The policies of the government toward religious groups are implemented by the Religious Affairs Bureau and also the national leaders of the patriotic religious organizations. The Religious Affairs Bureau national office has affiliates that administer its policies through provincial, country and municipal level bureaus. These control not only the Three-Self Patriotic Movement Committee of Protestant Churches, but also analogous Buddhist, Moslem, Taoist and Catholic groups. (The China Patriotic Catholic Association was severed from the Roman Catholic Church and has not managed to win much support from Catholics.)

These patriotic associations report to the Religious Affairs Bureau, which is often part of a local United Front office in the local party organization. The RAB works closely with the Public Security Bureau—which is to say the secret police. Three-Self officials often act as informants who keep the police aware of what is going on, especially when they learn of religious activity that is taking place outside of TSPM control.[17]

ESTABLISHING CONTROL

Thus we see that the Chinese have set up an ecclesiastical type of structure headed by a "bishop"—although "Three-Self Patriotic Movement" does not *sound* much like the name of a church —to relate to easily duped foreign churches, while tying that structure tightly to both the ruling party and the secret police. The purpose of the whole ungainly edifice is to turn the churches into expressions of the Party's will while preserving for them some semblance of legitimacy both within and outside of China. (This, of course, does not impugn the motives or sincerity of large numbers of Christians who belong to the TSPM churches.)

Another variation on the same pattern may be seen in the way the Bulgarian regime kept control of the Pentecostals. The Protestant population of Bulgaria is minuscule, the Christian heritage of the country being mainly Orthodox. Of the Protestants the largest denomination is the Pentecostal. The chairman and vice chairman of the Pentecostals in 1985 were Ivan Zarev and Kinko Zhelev. There was bad blood between the two, however, and moreover, neither one had a spotless reputation in the church. As a result of their quarrel Zhelev approached the Bulgarian secret police and the Committee for Religious Affairs and gained their support for his elevation in Zarev's place.

Several months later the council of pastors, about forty in number, met in Sofia, and to the surprise of the assembly Zhelev announced that Zarev (who was seventy-five years of age) was going to retire and that the Committee for Religious Affairs was proposing a new list for the leadership of the Pentecostals. The list was headed by himself for chairman, and several others were ready to assume other offices. It was understood that the pastors had no choice in the matter. The few that voted against the new leadership all lost their positions in the next few years. The pastors who were most respected by the church members, those who refused to vote for Zhelev, could no longer provide leadership to the church. The most effective of the pastors, the ones with growing churches, were dismissed in the years following the coup.

There were gross financial irregularities during those years as well, and Zhelev destroyed many records, even though this was contrary to the laws of Bulgaria. In 1989 some of the pastors tried to do something about this unhealthy situation. They circulated a "yellow letter"—named from the paper on which it was written—which revealed many details of the Zhelev years of leadership. This led to a meeting of twelve pastors in northern Bulgaria to which Zhelev was invited. Zhelev threatened the participants with disciplinary action and did not attend the meeting. Out of the meeting came a request for a conference of all the pastors—a "pink letter." This time there was a strong government reaction, with the secret police questioning one pastor accused of being the ringleader and Zhelev and the central leadership of the pastors issuing threats of severe disciplinary action.

This reaction only served to increase the unrest in the churches. The church in Plovdiv, for example, began opposing the actions of their pastor, one of the men who had been quick to do the bidding of the Zhelev and the government. The pastor in turn brought police representation to keep an eye on people during church meetings. These tensions led to an "initiative committee," consisting of forty-seven church members in southern Bulgaria, intended to bring about a change in church leadership. The police called in some of the pastors for questioning and Zhelev at first said he would not come, then changed his mind. Zhelev reported at this meeting, held in Jambol, that things were going well in the denomination and that the leadership was taking care of such problems as existed. Another of the pastors gave a very different and much more realistic report, systematically pointing out the problems of the church. He frankly explained Zhelev's service to the government rather than to the church and demanded that he resign, along with the rest of the denominational leadership. The assembly greeted this report with enthusiasm, then voted Zhelev and the rest of the leadership out of office, restoring to the ministry pastors who had been dismissed by him and his predecessor. By the end of January 1990, after the revolution that had toppled the old regime, the new government had still not recognized the new leadership of the Bulgarian Pentecostals.[18]

In Hungary the Free Church Council was the organ the regime used for controlling the smaller churches with which it did not have formal documents which guaranteed their subservience. By the spring of 1989 the use of this Council to carry out the will of the state had become intolerable in the gradually liberalizing atmosphere in the country. This was admitted openly by the president of the Council at that time. He also promised a "turning point" in the history of the Council. This came at a time when the Adventist church decided to pull out of the Council with other defections expected to follow. One of the main forces in this disintegration was a newly formed opposition group called the Evangelical Christian Group.[19] Several months before this event I talked to a pastor in Budapest who was one of the leaders of this Group and learned about the long history of the state domination of the Council to control the churches. Of course, for most of that time church leaders could not even discuss pulling out of the Council except at the risk of long prison terms.

In the German Democratic Republic the Soviets treated the confessing church gently, acknowledging the part it played in opposing Naziism. They also wanted to avoid unnecessary hostility to the new order among the German people. But the church in turn accepted a completely non-political role and became marginalized, similar to the position of Polish Catholicism. Even though the constitution of 1949 allowed the church to take public positions on public policy, it kept a low profile in this area.[20]

In Czechoslovakia the Roman Catholic Church is dominant and occupied the center of government attention, suffering much more pressure than did the Protestants. In addition to controlling the hierarchy so tightly that it kept most of the bishoprics vacant for years, the regime set up an organization of tame priests called Pacem in Terris. About 10 percent of the country's priests became members, but received disproportionate favors from the government.[21]

More important than the institutional arrangements for control is the extent to which the individual leaders of the church become active in carrying out the will of the regime. A secret report issued by the Council on Religious Affairs in 1974 divided the bishops into three categories. The first, composed of seventeen bishops, show little or no interest in extending the religious influence of the church. The second, twenty-three bishops, appear to be loyal to the state, but also try to heighten the role of the church in personal and public life and select zealous people for the priesthood. The third is the dangerous party. Consisting of seventeen bishops, they try to evade the restrictions of the law, and even act disrespectfully toward the officials of the Council on Religious Affairs.[22]

There is a letter of the Christian Committee for the Defense of Believers' Rights in the U.S.S.R. that describes as "widely known among the clergy and People of the Russian Church that Metropolitan Nikodim was an active collaborator of the KGB."[23] A Russian Orthodox priest in Leningrad with whom I discussed this question told me that such statements were typical of "western opinion" (although the statement of the Christian Committee is proof enough that people in the Soviet Union also believe it). This priest had worked as an assistant to Nikodim, and he attested that the Metropolitan only appeared to go along with the state while actually serving the church.[24] Even if this is correct, it's not difficult to see the tremendous damage done to the church by the regime when innocent people, especially leaders, within it are suspected of being spies.

The Vietnamese Communist Party policy since 1976 has tried to bring religious and cultural life under state and party control by establishing "mass" organizations, the most important of which is the Viet Nam Fatherland Front. This is evidently modeled after the Chinese pattern. The 1980 constitution charges this organization with the task of promoting national unity and educating and motivating the people to build socialism and to defend the country. Various religious organizations and others have resisted this effort to incorporate them into "representational" organizations. People refusing to be incorporated have been charged with counter-revolutionary activities, many of them being imprisoned or confined to "re-education" camps, placed under house arrest or restricted to their own villages.[25]

After the defeat of the Khmer Rouge terror in 1979, during which reign all religious activity in Cambodia was banned and multitudes of Christians and other Cambodians murdered, the government installed by the Vietnamese continued a milder form of persecution, although still with harsh restrictions. But with the armed resistance movement gaining strength they reversed their stand in January 1989. Prime Minister Hun Sen acknowledged regretfully the mistakes his regime had made over the years, mistakes that had caused people to believe that the government was hostile to religion. At an extraordinary session of the National Assembly on April 30, 1989, the communist leadership made Buddhism the religion of the state. The revivified Buddhist hierarchy was now placed under control of the semi-official United Front for National Construction and Defense. This Front is publishing much Buddhist material and stressing the new policy of favoring religion. But there is little chance this will allow Buddhism to function in its former role as a leading force in society. The regime is keeping it all under control.[26] It was only in early 1990 that Christianity was legalized in Cambodia. Now the formerly illegal churches are permitted to meet.[27]

As elsewhere the one-party Marxist regime in Zimbabwe intends to use the church to further its own program, although it is more frank about this than in some parts of the world. Using the cover of Party Chief Robert Mugabe's so-called "Christian-Marxism," the ZANU party officially declares its intention to have the churches in the forefront of bringing in the new order. "The churches are well placed to perform this revolutionary task because they deal with the people at the grassroots levels."[28] Repeating the pattern of the Russian Orthodox Church in the Soviet Union, a number of Zimbabwe's churchmen are justifying the gospel of subservience and the necessity for an increasingly repressive regime. Methodist clergyman Canaan Banana is a frequent speaker at events intended to highlight the compatibility of Christianity and Mugabe's brand of socialism along with an explicit disavowal of any kind of cooperation between the faith and capitalism.

THE RESULT OF CONTROL: A COMPROMISED CHURCH

Thus far we have been considering the strategy and tactics of the totalitarian regime's control of the churches. We now turn to the effects of the methodology on the church. How successful is the regime's efforts to go for control rather than extermination?

Anatoli Levitin, a prolific *samizdat* writer and labor camp alumnus, argued in 1975 that the entire episcopate of the Russian Orthodox Church was uncanonical, which is to say illegal. His reason is that canonicity requires that the bishop be chosen by the flock and consecrated by a council of bishops. If the civil authority intrudes, the consecration is invalid.[29] A legal argument of this type may be too abstruse to appeal to the masses, and therefore of little practical effect. And state interference with the Russian Orthodox hierarchy long predated the coming of Bolshevism. But the underlying reality is of great importance. The general realization that the hierarchy to a large extent speaks for the state rather than the church cannot but have a dampening effect on the authority of the church's teaching with those who otherwise would be willing to listen. Thus the official status of the church, deriving from its relationship with the state, has resulted in a grave loss of its real authority, the kind that would make it influential with the people. Dissident priest Gleb Yakunin issued a report in 1979 which described the Moscow Patriarchate as so spiritually weak because of state control that it was incapable of giving any assistance to the spiritual revival that was taking place in the Soviet Union.[30]

As the hierarchy, so with the lower clergy, which suffered violent changes in their status—from being outlaws after the revolution to people of great privilege after 1945 to having power taken away once again. When they prospered they were irresponsible. They were in such a bad state that the patriarch was quoted by an observer as saying that only the laity could save the church.[31] But with the parish priest's reduction in authority to the benefit of the lay committee, often deliberately stacked with non-believers, if the laity were going to do any good it might have to be completely outside of the established structure. That may account for the locus of the Seminar movement in Moscow and Leningrad in the 1970s; it was a lay movement of Orthodox believers, but not connected with particular parishes.

Most of the totalitarian countries saw the churches similarly becoming badly checkered in effectiveness, although in no case that we have seen in the twentieth century has the church been under severe pressure for so long a period as in the Soviet Union. In China, as we saw earlier, many of the Three-Self pastors allowed themselves to become tools of the state. Early in the Nazi period much of the church became composed of "German Christians," which is to say more *German* (in the Nazi meaning of the term) than Christian. Many of the clergy adopted a theology that might be called Führerolatry, departing far from any traditional understanding of the gospel. In fact they caused such a great uproar within the church that Hitler found it expedient to disavow them on the grounds that they had become a source of disunity in the Third Reich.[32]

DIFFICULTIES FOR THE REGIME IN SUBVERTING CHRISTIANITY

Given the array of weapons in the hands of the modern totalitarian state and the ruthlessness it normally has in using them, it might be

thought that destroying the effectiveness of the church is a rather simple operation. But these regimes have had a more difficult time than
they expected; Soviet authorities are now acknowledging this with cha-
grin, and sometimes even with expressions of remorse.

The Soviets recognized in the fifties that harsh repression was
counterproductive. In 1954, not long after Stalin died, the Central
Committee of the Communist Party of the Soviet Union issued a
famous resolution signed by Khrushchev which provided a theory for
relaxation.

> Propaganda which is scientifically atheistic, used in a profound and
> patient manner and employed judiciously amongst the faithful, will
> eventually succeed in liberating them from their religious errors. On
> the other hand every administrative measure or illegal attack
> against the faithful and the clergy will turn only to our disadvan-
> tage and will definitely strengthen their religious prejudices. . . .[33]

The meaning here evidently is that the years of utter brutality had failed
to accomplish what the communist leaders expected. They were now
going to try a different method. So enlightened. Yet, five years later
Khrushchev began his brutal anti-religious campaign that by 1964 had
closed down half the Orthodox churches in the Soviet Union.

Romania analogously changed the method of harassment in the
last years of the Ceausescu regime. During that period the persecution
intensified, but it was deliberately done in such a way as to avoid
putting believers on trial and making martyrs and heroes. Rather,
quiet means of pressure were placed upon them in order to bring them
to heel. The authorities harassed the families of activists. Doru Popa's
wife was dismissed from her job in a hospital and forced to work in
a village far from their home. Whenever he was picked up for questioning he never knew if he would reach home alive.[34] In Romania as
elsewhere, however, the soft method proved too much a trial for the
patience of the communist rulers, and with the church demolitions
increasing the bad publicity in the West, the regime could no longer
maintain its favored trading status with the United States.

Some idea of the contrary demands of policy may be seen in the
advice the Chinese regime gave to the newly installed Castro government in 1959. The Chinese urged destroying the church in Cuba
obliquely, for to do it directly would be to increase the control of the

church over the masses by creating sympathy. They warned the Cubans to be especially concerned not to produce martyrs.

> The line of action to be followed against the Church consists in instructing, educating, persuading, convincing, and gradually awakening and fully developing the political consciousness of the Catholics through obtaining their participation in study groups and political activities.[35]

Still, Armando Valladares, who was wasting away in a filthy Cuban prison camp not long afterward, heard the cries of prisoners shouting "Long live Christ the King," interrupted by the crash of the firing squad rifles that ended their lives. The communist jailers, soon tiring of this, began stuffing their mouths with rags before killing them. The "soft" Chinese advice to the Cubans should be read in conjunction with the dedication to Valladares's book: "To the memory of my companions tortured and murdered in Fidel Castro's jails, and to the thousands of prisoners still suffering in them."[36] Contradictions like this point to the highly pragmatic nature of totalitarian policy: they do what they think they have to do in a given situation. If it doesn't seem to be working they try something else, often managing to justify every shift in accordance with their ideology. The Chinese themselves, of course, frequently ignored their own advice to the Cubans, killing millions of their own victims over the years.

Apart from all the other difficulties the Party has in controlling the church, it cannot even rely completely on the information it gets from those it assigns the task. In the Soviet Union, for example, the Council for Religious Affairs may or may not give accurate information to the Party. It performs a balancing act in that it has to control the churches while proving that its existence is still necessary so that the churches will be controlled. So its reports cannot be taken at face value.[37]

There is another internal contradiction that plagued the Soviet program. When the U.S.S.R. geared up its propaganda machine to isolate believers by picturing them as peculiar and different from ordinary people, the message hardened them in their separation.[38] There is an irony here in that a softer approach might have integrated them into the life of the nation and thus gradually dulled their distinctiveness, making them more amenable to other forms of manipulation.

Evidently the impatience of the Soviet authorities made this option seem unattractive.

LAWLESSNESS

One trait which is uniform in all totalitarian societies is that they are lawless. If the regime is to do whatever it wants with its citizens it cannot allow a law transcending political expediencies to which the citizen can appeal. The law may be on the books, of course, but in practice it must be of no effect. The law is intended in these societies only to serve the authorities in their desire to control everything that takes place in them. That lawlessness accounts for the fact that the 1929 Soviet law regulating religion has been very difficult to obtain, so that believers have known neither their legal responsibilities nor their rights. Mathematician Igor Shafarevich was able to get the law and also access to a secret volume entitled *Legislation on Religious Cults* which was intended for use only by officials. This provided practical information that believers could use for their protection.[39] In a society in which the law is intended to protect the citizens, it is inconceivable that they should not be able to find out what it says.

Just as individual rights are abrogated in the totalitarian regime, so are corporate rights. Thus the church has no legal standing. In a remarkable interview published near the end of his tenure as the head of the Soviet Council on Religious Affairs, Konstantin Kharchev spoke of the lack of legal status of the church. "Nothing prevents local authorities from building a road across the church fence or knocking down the church's dome, since the church, deprived of the rights of a legal body, cannot stand up for its rights by taking them to court." His interviewer, the writer Alexander Nezhny, compared the church with the individual who lives in a city without having a residence permit; he knows that a policeman can show up at any time and expel him.[40] This, of course, points up for us what we must not forget: the state which takes away religious rights has plenty of other restrictions operating at the same time.

Kharchev made one point of overriding importance in that interview. He drew the distinction between a law-based organ and an administrative-based organ, and said that he hoped the future direction of the Soviet Union would be from the latter to the former.[41] To illustrate this Kharchev spoke about "rule by telephone." He reported that in 1988 the CRA headquarters in Moscow had overturned local decisions eighty-three times and allowed the opening of churches. When the local authorities asked on what basis he overruled them, he replied "on the basis of the law." But many people remember the rule of the telephone. Someone makes a telephone call and is told *no*, without reference to the law.[42] (But Kharchev still didn't get the point. He stated as a positive sign that although the repressive legislation that came from Stalin in 1929 was still in force it was disregarded. He failed to see that this was the opposite of the rule by law he was calling for; it still depended on arbitrary administrative decisions about whether and how to enforce the law, which is the opposite of a rule by law.)

The lawlessness of these regimes is such that even when the church complies with the most unreasonable legal procedures there is no protection against arbitrary state actions. In the Romanian town of Comanesti the Baptist church had verbal but not written agreement to build a church building. But they slightly exceeded the stated dimensions. They paid a fine for this which they thought would solve the problem. Nevertheless, the bulldozers came and flattened the new church. Four people were arrested and beaten, and the Department of Cults demanded that the Baptist Union take away the pastor's license.[43]

In spite—or because—of the pervasive lawlessness the totalitarian regime usually goes out of its way to try to demonstrate the legality of its actions. When Stalin was executing his millions in the purges of the 1930s or when Christians and dissidents in later periods were sent to labor camps, it was normally after a trial, perhaps even a show trial. The Romanian regime in the early 1970s asked Josef Tson's wife to go to Bucharest and fill in papers for him requesting permission to study in England. But he was already *in* England where he had made a belated request for permission after beginning his studies. They made her backdate the papers and sign his name for him. Tson says the reason they went to such lengths in pretending that he was in England legally is that they wanted to save face, to show if necessary that he was not getting away with defying the government and that the law was being upheld.[44]

Finally, we should note the main reason why, despite all the twists and turns in state policy, all the deceptive adoptions of a "soft" policy, the totalitarian state is inevitably hostile to Christian faith. There is no higher authority than the state in its conception of government. If the state is the final judge of everything, by definition it is idolatrous; it has put itself in the place that only God rightfully occupies. Any Christian church worthy of the name will find that intolerable. Thus the totalitarian state cannot abide a church it cannot make subservient to itself. The followers of Christ are the ones who not only can oppose it but also connect that opposition to a transcendent source that will not be bought off or placated.

THE AMERICAN CHURCH ON THE DEFENSIVE

NEBRASKA V. FAITH BAPTIST CHURCH

When Everett Sileven became pastor of Faith Baptist Church in Louisville, Nebraska, he was convinced that the church would have to provide an alternative to the public schools. The problem he perceived was not just the well-known deficiencies in public education, but also the fact that the system was undermining the Christian convictions the church was seeking to instill in its children. The aggressive secularism championed by curricula and texts carried with them values and philosophies fully as much as they did standard academic subjects like mathematics, grammar and science. The church's efforts to teach children a Biblical understanding of reality would be undermined by the schools teaching them the opposite.

For Faith Baptist Church this was not just a prudential matter. Rather it came from the conviction that God had given the responsibility for educating children to their parents. Since the state had proven itself incapable of doing the job properly, the parents must provide the education directly. When Christian parents work together in producing what is needed for educating their children, it's natural that the church should be involved. Thus the church resolved to begin a day school. Even before the church school opened, two representatives of the Nebraska department of education, tipped off by the local superintendent of schools, paid Sileven a visit and informed him that the school would not be permitted to operate unless it received a license from the state. Sileven replied that the school was a ministry of the church and that the state did not have the authority to regulate the ministry. The church had a right to carry on without harassment from a government agency. When the visitors left, it was with the comment that they would meet again in court. The church discussed the matter again and concluded that it could not agree with the principle that its ministry should be subject to evaluation and licensure by the state.

They heard no more about the state's interest in their school until about a month after classes began. Sileven returned home one evening about nine o'clock, just in time to hear the phone ring. The caller said, "I am Sheriff Fred Tesch. I have a warrant for your arrest, but if you promise to be at the hearing on Monday morning at 9 A.M. I will not come and arrest you." That was the beginning of a long nightmare, in which the pastor and a number of others from Faith Baptist Church spent time in jail, with other parents escaping that fate only by fleeing the state. For several years their lives were dominated by the specter of fines and imprisonment—not for engaging in criminal activity but for conducting the ministry of the church in accordance with their convictions.

In September 1980, acting under court orders, the sheriff entered the church during the evening service, ordered the whole congregation out of the building, and padlocked the doors. (The judge also ordered the church to pay for the padlocks and chains.) Classes resumed the next day outside the building. In succeeding days they met in other buildings or in buses and even conducted instruction in locations across the state line.

After a complicated series of legal moves and countermoves, Sileven began serving a four-month jail term early in 1982 on a charge of contempt of court. He was released after eighteen days when he resigned from his position in the school—mistakenly taking bad advice, as he later came to believe. He renounced this decision and informed the court that he was back on the school staff. Sheriff Tesch then arrested him as he addressed the students at chapel, and he went back to jail.

At six o'clock one morning while Sileven was serving his second stretch in jail, Sheriff Tesch arrived at the church accompanied by eighteen armed State police and some deputies. There were about ninety people in the church then, mostly visiting pastors from out of town who had come to support the church in its troubles. The lawmen physically carried all the occupants out of the building and padlocked the doors again. The visitors quickly began meeting in another church, formed committees, and started a campaign on behalf of Faith Baptist. Within a couple of days there were something like a thousand pastors in the town as part of the protest movement. More complicated events ensued, and Pastor Sileven went back to jail once more and finished his original four-month term. When a new judge entered the case he jailed seven fathers of the school children and issued warrants for eight mothers as well, including Sileven's daughter who was a teacher in the school and nursing an infant. He also issued a fresh warrant for Sileven, who was traveling out of state at the time.

This harsh treatment by the judge seemed to the church to be a calamity but it was what broke the case in the end. It led to a great deal of publicity, and consequently heavy political pressure came to bear on the authorities. The White House received 200,000 phone calls in two days. But this only confirmed what the church knew from the start: the whole thing had been much more a matter of politics than of law, and the governor had hoped to make gains out of his opposition to the church. The governor finally negotiated his way out of the impasse by striking a deal with the Nebraska Education Association, which had funded much of the public relations campaign against the church. With the backing of the NEA, he allowed a bill freeing church educational ministries from state control in exchange for the passage of a large tax increase to be used for the benefit of public education. As part of the deal all charges were dropped except for those against Sileven and his daughter. They returned to Nebraska, and she was freed from further harassment. Sileven went to jail for another forty-five days. Later the Nebraska Supreme Court overturned his conviction.[1]

THE CONSTITUTIONAL HERITAGE

The situation existing before the current spate of church-state battles was that of a de facto state establishment of Protestant Christianity as the official religion. In the early nineteenth century a number of states enacted statutory or even constitutional provisions to provide for this.[2] The courts had always upheld these actions as being in keeping with the federal Constitution. In 1811, for example, the New York courts approved a case in which a man was charged with blasphemy against Jesus Christ. The justices explained this decision by saying that "we are a Christian people and the morality of the country is deeply engrafted upon Christianity." Even as recently as 1952 the U.S. Supreme Court in *Zorach v. Clauson* said that "we are a religious people whose institutions presuppose a Supreme Being." That, of course, is already seriously watered down from earlier formulations, even twentieth-century formulations. In 1931, to illustrate, the Court had said in *United States v. MacIntosh* that "we are a Christian people."[3] Now even the 1952 statement would be inconceivable. A variety of beliefs coexist, the present argument says, none of which can be assumed to be normative for the American people.

In recent years the religious liberty issue that has caused so much controversy is found in varying interpretations of the First Amendment to the federal Constitution. The relevant passage—a total of just sixteen words—consists of two short clauses, and its interpretation depends largely on how much attention is paid to the first at the expense of the second. "*Congress shall make no law respecting an establishment of religion* or prohibiting the free exercise thereof." *Everson v. Board of Education* in 1947 applied the establishment prohibitions to the states. This was on the basis of a 1940 case, *Cantwell v. Connecticut*, which held that the Fourteenth Amendment had declared that whatever restriction was placed on Congress in the First Amendment due process clause ("nor shall any State deprive any persons of life, liberty or property, without due process of law") was thereby placed also on other levels of government. All government actions at any level, then, are bound by the same restrictions as federal actions. *Everson* also drew heavily on a statement of Thomas Jefferson in a letter, and called for a "wall of separation" between church and state, without the "slightest breach."

This set the stage for what is called the "separationist" position on questions of church and state, one which created complete separation between religious activity on the one hand and civil authority on the other. In order to explain how this should work in practice, the Court spelled out a three-part test in the *Wolman* case (1977): "In order to pass muster, the statute must have a secular legislative purpose, must have a principal or primary effect that neither advances nor inhibits religion, and must not foster excessive governmental entanglement with religion." In effect the "primary" provision of the second part of the test has not stood up, and the Court has disallowed laws with even *possible* religious effects.[4]

The second of the two First Amendment clauses relating to religion is the free exercise clause. "Congress shall make no law respecting an establishment of religion *or prohibiting the free exercise thereof.*" What is protected here is belief, not action. This was established in the nineteenth century with Mormon cases disallowing claims that religious belief required polygamy. Court decisions have modified this somewhat, but the principle remains that some activities that are claimed to derive from religious convictions can be restricted. The obvious problem is that if only belief is protected then free exercise is a travesty; we saw in an earlier chapter that the common totalitarian "guarantee" of freedom of religion gives people the right to believe whatever they wish while restricting their ability to act on those beliefs, and therefore is no guarantee at all.

Justice Robert Jackson in 1943, writing for the Supreme Court in affirming the right of Jehovah's Witnesses not to salute the flag, promulgated the widely quoted "fixed star" formulation. "If there is any fixed star in our constitutional constellation, it is that no official, high or petty, can prescribe what should be orthodox in politics, nationalism, religion or other matters of opinion or force citizens to confess by word or act their faith therein." The three questions the Court specified that are to be asked in these cases are: 1) Has the government placed a burden on the free exercise of religion? 2) Is there is sufficiently compelling state interest to justify that burden? And 3) Has the state accomplished a legitimate purpose in the least intrusive way possible, so that there is no greater infringement on free exercise than is necessary to achieve the legitimate purpose of the state?

In all such cases the courts cannot determine the truth of a claim but they will test its sincerity. For example, they tossed out the sabbatarian claim of one man on the grounds that he was known to conduct business on Saturday. So the courts will not be ruled by a mere unsubstantiated claim of religious belief.[5]

THE CLASH BETWEEN THE CLAUSES

There have been more church-state cases tried in the last twenty years than in all of prior American history.[6] Our increasing difficulties come from uncertainties in adjudicating apparent contradictions between the two clauses. Chief Justice Warren Burger: ". . . the court has struggled to find a neutral course between the two religious clauses, both of which are cast in absolute terms, and either of which if expanded to a logical extreme, would tend to clash with the other." In school cases the Court has given the establishment clause precedence, and this has brought caustic dissents from Justice (later Chief Justice) William Rehnquist and Chief Justice Burger. Rehnquist critically noted that the Court has come down "on the side of those who believe our society as a whole should be a purely secular one." These defenses of the place of religion in public life are normally associated with conservatives, but liberal legal scholar Lawrence Tribe has said that free exercise "should be dominant in any conflict with the anti-establishment principle" even at the expense of some slight appearance of establishment.[7]

It is often supposed that the concept of "neutrality" will serve to do justice to both clauses of the religion portion of the First Amendment, but that is an illusion. Justice Arthur Goldberg identified the crux of the problem. Such neutrality, he said, could lead to "a brooding and pervasive devotion to the secular and a passive, or even active, hostility to the religious." This would be counter to the constitutional guarantees.[8] And Justice William O. Douglas, whose own beliefs were far from any personal sympathy with organized religion, similarly downplayed the absoluteness of the separation of religion and society. He even said that our institutions "presuppose a Supreme Being."[9]

The current situation in church-state conflicts is dramatically different than it was only a few years ago, not only in the vast increase of the number of cases but also in the nature of the cases. Beginning in the 1970s Protestants began to be affected by court cases, in addition to such groups as the Roman Catholics, Anabaptists, Mormons and others who could be judged out of the mainstream. Legal scholar Carl Esbeck explains how that happened:

> The line of confrontation has shifted and the antagonists have regrouped along a broader front. It is no longer sect versus state. Now all religious groups including traditional denominations are finding a state increasingly uninformed, indeed, insensitive, to the unique nature and role of church and parachurch ministries.

Esbeck says this situation has been brought about by the separation and increasing hostility of two groups which formerly were allied for the purpose of insuring the continued constitutional separation of church and state. The first he calls "secularists." They are the descendants of the eighteenth-century rationalists, some of whom were prominent at the founding of the republic, and who today are joined by some members of religious and ethnic minorities who fear discrimination should Christians gain control of state policy. The second group Esbeck calls the "institutional-separationists." They view the separation of church and state as a benevolent and friendly relationship, without the hostility that has become so evident in recent years. The breakup of this old alliance came when the secularists could no longer hide their complete disdain for religion and their conviction that it is either irrelevant or harmful to the cohesion of the social order. These two groups could paper over the cracks as long as the trend of legislation and court cases concerned the imposition of religious tests on public policy. But now that the main issue has shifted to the question of the state's domination over the church, there is sharp disagreement between them.

Esbeck further argues that the differences are more basic than is commonly supposed; it is a question of basic worldview. ". . . the secularist is anthropocentric and enthrones individual conscience, while the institutional-separationist is theocentric and derives individual rights from the relationship of humans to God the creator."[10] The upshot of this conflict in basic views of reality is what an experienced religious liberties lawyer, William Ball, calls a "lava of governmental regulation" that is inundating us.[11]

SCHOOLS ARE THE FLASHPOINT

Perhaps in no other area has the controversy on church-state relations been so divisive as in public education. It's not hard to see why this should be so. Citizens evidently agree to a substantial degree with the Biblical teaching, first that parents are responsible for their children's education; and second, that education necessarily carries with it substantial worldview teaching, and therefore partakes of the religious. This is related to Carl Esbeck's point in the preceding paragraph.

We have already seen in the case of First Baptist Church in Louisville, Nebraska, the way state authorities can erase the free exercise guarantee of the First Amendment. Now let us consider that of Levi Whisner. The pastor of a church in Darke County, Ohio, Whisner and the congregation determined to begin a school in 1973. They wanted an alternative to the public schools, which they believed exposed the children to an anti-Christian philosophy. A year after the school opened, the state of Ohio pressed criminal charges against

Tabernacle Christian School, its twenty-three students, and the church's members. The crime was sending children to a private school without accreditation.

The next year the pastor and the parents were convicted and faced imprisonment or fines if they did not meet state standards. Whisner argued that if the school did what the state demanded, it would not have the time to devote to the studies for which the parents established the school in the first place. The state curriculum requirements, he went on, gave the state "a blank check to control the operations of the school." After the church appealed through two levels, the Ohio Supreme Court reversed the conviction, explaining that the state educational standards were "so pervasive and all-encompassing that total compliance with each and every standard by a non-public school would effectively eradicate the distinction between public and nonpublic education."[12]

None of the rights secured either by constitutional provisions or by favorable court decisions regarding them can be taken as permanent, as if they can be maintained without further concern and defense. As a matter of both realistic expectations and normal prudence we should regard all alleged "fixed stars" of jurisprudence as temptations to let down our guard. As this is written, a fresh case shows the continuing saga of anti-religious activities on the part of state authorities. A Long Island school district refused to allow a church to rent an auditorium for the showing of a James Dobson film on the family, even though the district rented to other organizations. The district cited a New York State law prohibiting the use of schools by religious organizations. Lawyers for the church argued that the district's position amounted to discriminating against people on the basis of the religious content of their speech. They cited a U.S. Supreme Court ruling in 1981, *Widmar v. Vincent*, in which the University of Missouri was forced to allow a religious club to hold meetings in a facility open to other student groups.[13]

FAMILY ISSUES

On August 18, 1989, state and local officials raided the home of Steve and JoAnn DeCosta of Rumney, New Hampshire, and forcibly removed their children. They did not disclose where they took the children. The officials claimed to be acting under the New Hampshire Child Protection Act which prohibits any corporal punishment, even the mildest. The DeCostas believe because of Biblical teaching that they have a responsibility to shape the children's moral character and that they should use corporal punishment as part of their method. The authorities told them that if they even spoke to anyone about the abduction they would be fined $1,000. New Hampshire regulations require a hearing within twenty-four hours in this type of case, but the state refused a hearing until the children had been gone for four days. At the hearing a doctor appointed by the court testified that he found no evidence of child abuse, although there were red marks from a spanking on the buttocks. The family pediatrician agreed, stating that he had never seen any evidence of child abuse in the family. Nevertheless, the judge kept the children in foster homes and ordered the parents to undergo psychological testing.

The DeCostas are members of the Calvary Independent Baptist Church, whose teaching includes corporal punishment and which runs its own school, attended by the DeCosta children. The judge permitted witnesses to denounce the church and its teachings at the hearing, including hearsay evidence about abuses at the school. The church asserts that it has not permitted children to be struck at the school for at least ten years. According to a local newspaper (which broke the law in reporting the case), zealous officials violated numerous legal safeguards in this action. They dropped criminal charges against the DeCostas within weeks, but there were long delays in returning the children. The youngest went back to the family in January, two more in February. The oldest remained in foster care at the time the report was published the following May. The publicity has resulted in restructuring the state bureaucracy. It remains uncertain whether the restructuring will make any substantial difference or whether it's intended only to tide the bureaucrats over a rough spot in their public relations program.[14]

As in many of these cases, the basic issue is broader than religious liberty; the question is how broadly the powers of the state can legitimately be extended without violating other provisions of the Constitution intended to insure our liberty. No doubt there are many opinions about the proper way to bring up children, and these might profitably be argued. But it's difficult to imagine that there will be no violations of the rights of the citizens when the views of one group are legislated to apply to all.

REGULATING WHAT WE DO AND WHAT WE THINK

The lines between the exercise of legitimate authorities are not always easy to draw. It's clear that the state has no legitimate authority under any form of government to compel its citizens to believe or disbelieve any particular doctrine. But it does have the right to compel citizens to do or refrain from doing particular acts. To some people that is sufficient clarification: "The state may not say what we can believe but can control what we do." But that distinction will not serve us at all. Christian faith has a "do" component as well as a "believe" component. It is activist. It believes that God is sovereign over the earth, that His people are obligated to act in particular ways, and that all other authorities are relativized and therefore limited by His sovereignty. In fact we could use as an organizing structure of human history the story of the challenging of God's authority by lesser authorities. If that is the case, then we should expect the state to be engaging in a continual tug-of-war with those whose ultimate loyalty is to Jesus Christ. Public officials prefer that they be the recipients of such loyalty, whether or not they say it. Thus we should expect that even with the best and most just political structure in the world we would encounter challenges to religious freedom.

Licensing laws illustrate how the expanding role of government leads to control of religious groups. An organization called Family Ministries brought twenty orphans out of Cambodia just before the Khmer Rouge took over the country in 1975 and placed them for adoption. In keeping with its charter, the ministry considered only members of evangelical churches as adoptive parents. One of the attending physicians who wanted to adopt a child challenged this policy. The court found for the physician and granted the injunction he requested. The appellate court affirmed the decision, declaring that the fact that the state licensed the agency's activities made the agency subject to the restrictions of the establishment clause. Since the state had to be neutral in religion, the private agency it licensed also had to be neutral. The Court of Appeals gave no indication in its decision that it had considered the free exercise rights of Family Ministries and those who funded and administered it. The Los Angeles County Department of Adoptions evidently believed the case might be too shaky to survive continued appeal, since it agreed to allow the organization to proceed with its adoptions in return for the promise not to appeal further. But the cost of litigation forced the liquidation of the ministry. This case shows how the right to license can become the right to destroy.

> The implications are far-reaching. Family Ministries exists for the very purpose of discriminating in favor of its particular religious persuasion, as do other adoptive agencies sponsored by other faiths. . . . The holding of *Scott v. Family Ministries* hopelessly frustrates the religious activities and underlying motivations of social service ministries. Not only is a ministry not allowed to choose the community it seeks to serve, but its evangelization and spiritual counseling would be prohibited altogether. In light of this decision, one can understand the clergy's hesitancy to license their social service ministries.[15]

This explanation by Buzzard and Ericsson suggests that once the state exercises the right to license social service activities of almost any kind, there is bound to be a conflict with the church that engages in such activities. For the long history of church service in hospitals, schools, and charitable activities of an endless variety is firmly established by Biblical and traditional heritage. These services are part of the function of the church and cannot be isolated without severing the church from much of its ministry. Therefore, when the state regulates their provision, it is interfering in the religious mission of the church as surely as if it were adjudicating disagreements about doctrine. If the church does not challenge this supposed right of the state, there is little chance that we can avoid further threats to the church's freedom to conduct its ministry without interference, and the continued whittling away of the protections of the free exercise clause.

In a very recent case that illustrates the point the U.S. Department of Labor sent an ultimatum to the Salvation Army that threatens to shut down the Army's charitable efforts. The Department is interpreting the Army's relationship with its beneficiaries as employer to employee and demanding that employment regulations be followed, including minimum wage laws, on the grounds that such people perform chores on the premises. The Army's response is that it provides housing and food to over seventy thousand people every year without any government support.

> A requirement that the minimum wage be paid to the beneficiaries of the centers will find them back on the streets since the Salvation Army will no longer be able to afford to support them

or to provide them with the religious and charitable rehabilitation program conducted at the centers.[16]

The supremacy of state action in almost all areas of life is usually given the name *statism*. This is essentially a religious idea. It implies, or may even state explicitly, that the sovereignty of the state is absolute, meaning there is no higher authority. In Christian perspective that is idolatry, since it erects a "god" above the Creator. The proponents of what they call state "neutrality" almost always use this expression to mean the cessation of governmental support for all religious ideas except one—theirs.

This contradiction is often evident in the religion cases handled by the American Civil Liberties Union when they deal with the issue of value-free, or neutral, education in the public schools. The longtime president of the ACLU's Minnesota affiliate, Matthew Stark, says that the public schools should attract children away from the religious schools because it's better for all children to study together. And they have to study in an atmosphere of religious neutrality. He gives an example of a fifteen-year-old girl telling a school counselor that the girl is pregnant and the counselor answering in "valueless terms." Some people are opposed to abortion, some are for it, the counselor is to say. Do what you want and be prepared to live with the consequences.[17] Stark doesn't consider the possibility that the girl is pregnant in the first place because of the valueless terms in which schooling is conducted—at his organization's insistence.

But more basically, where does Stark get the notions of freedom, constitutionality, and so on, all these *values* that drive his organization's influence on public policy? If values must not be imposed on anyone by anyone, whence comes the legitimacy of the values-pushing that he is doing? The obvious answer to this puzzle is that law is never without values, and those who advocate value-free education are, whether they realize it or not, advancing their values at the expense of competing values. They have a right to do this, but not with the imputed legitimacy of a spurious neutrality. They must not be permitted to get away with saying that their values are neutral and therefore privileged while ours are religious and therefore inadmissible. The Constitution was never intended to permit the state to wreck the public influence of those whose motivations are overtly religious.

There was considerable grumbling in the aftermath of the recent Supreme Court ruling (*Mergens v. Westside Community Schools*) upholding federal law granting religious groups the same rights as other groups in the use of school property after school hours. An official of Americans United for Separation of Church and State saw in this the schools turning into "some kind of revival campground." Dean Kelley of the National Council of Churches, however, put the matter in the proper perspective:

> There's a great deal of evangelism that goes on in public schools now. You have evangelism for drug use, you have evangelism for sexual promiscuity, you have evangelism for all kinds of behavior that society doesn't particularly like. I think [the ruling] gives just a little bit of equal time for influences that might serve as a corrective to some of these activities.[18]

Most challenges to the free exercise of religion, as we have seen, concern external actions taken in response to perceived religious duties—those relating to family life, education, charitable enterprises, and so on. Expansionist versions of state power, however, are now going beyond the external and are bringing challenges to psychological and spiritual life itself. They now seem ready to say not only, "We're going to regulate what you do," but also, "We're going to regulate what you experience and believe." In 1981 a number of states passed "deprogramming" or "anti-conversion" statutes. This type of legislation is ripe for abuse.

In reversing a lower court decision, Justice William O. Douglas earlier had written that the First Amendment prohibits the courts from examining whether a religious doctrine is true or false. "Men may believe what they cannot prove," he wrote. "They may not be put to the proof of their religious doctrines." A New York bill, vetoed by Gov. Carey, authorized state courts to appoint temporary conservators for people who experienced "psychological deterioration." Proof of this condition would be shown by any of several symptoms, including abrupt changes in values and lifestyle, odd emotional responses, childlike behavior, psychotic symptoms. Some proposals have added weight loss and changed friendships as sufficient evidence for state action to restrict individual liberty. As Buzzard and Ericsson put it: ". . . these characteristics are wholly subjective, overly vague, and in many cases undefinable. Much of the legislation could easily apply to a conversion to Christianity."[19]

THE PHILOSOPHY OF HUMANISM

Humanism has a nice ring to it, allied as it is with such positive-sounding words as *humane* and *humanitarian*. This connotation serves mainly to hide the roots of what has to be called a religion. When the serpent said to Eve, "You shall be as gods knowing good and evil" (Genesis 3:5) that was the call to autonomy, placing into human hands the ethical standards that rightly come only from God. Unifying the various forms of humanism is their rejection of the Christian view of humanity.

Auguste Comte, the nineteenth-century French philosopher who is regarded as the founder of the discipline of sociology, was one of the most influential of the theorists who deified the human race. His Religion of Humanity, as he called it, advocated the worship of the Great Being, defined as humanity past, present, and future. This religion had a catechism, sacraments, a sacred calendar, a priesthood, prayers, and something imitative of the Trinity. It also had a social system of which Comte was the chief planner. The Religion of Humanity, as a visible institution, for a time had great vitality. Comteans formed societies for the worship of great people, and their churches spread even to South America.[20]

Interpreting modern humanism from this perspective allows us to get past its cover of toleration for diversity—"pluralism" is the favorite term now current—and understand why it is so intolerant of those who disagree with it. Widely supposed to provide freedom for diversity,

> instead it seems to demand a conformity to a humanistic philosophy. It is a pluralism that encourages the expression of all kinds of views—but only if they coincide with the prevailing consensus. This philosophy is perhaps primarily manifested in public education and media circles. . . . This humanism is as evangelistic and expansive as any religion the world has ever seen. Advocates promote its ideas subtly, but vigorously. It is a philosophy so total that it amounts to a religion, a system of values and commitments that shapes life.[21]

Since human autonomy and the freedom to decide right and wrong for ourselves—that is the meaning of "You shall be as gods knowing good and evil"—is the essence of humanism, this is bound to have a profound effect on legal and legislative matters. One justification that Soviet apologists have used to bolster this is the conception that all rights are granted solely through the provision of statutes.[22] No statute, no right. Similarly if a statute does grant a right but then is repealed, the right no longer exists. All rights therefore are subject to politics. This conception is known among legal theorists as *positivist law*. It was widely discredited after the Nazi period, since it dominated in German legal circles in the decades prior to Hitler's accession to power, and it gravely weakened any opposition to his regime. But it has gained much ground since then and is now generally defended in American law schools.[23]

The conception of law in the West has changed to such an extent that the safeguards built into the legal structure have been gravely weakened. It used to be thought that transcendent principles not subject to human manipulation formed the basis for the law's legitimacy. This notion had two primary effects: first, it restrained human actions that violated those principles; and second, it provided the law an aura of legitimacy that gave it dignity and the power to influence people's thinking and actions more than the mere threat of punishment could do. Legal scholar Harold Berman explains what happens when these principles are no longer believed:

> Today those beliefs or postulates—such as the structural integrity of law, its ongoingness, its religious roots, its transcendent qualities—are rapidly disappearing, not only from the minds of philosophers, not only from the minds of lawmakers, judges, lawyers, law teachers, and other members of the legal profession, but from the consciousness of the vast majority of citizens, the people as a whole; and more than that, they are disappearing from the law itself. The law is becoming more fragmented, more subjective, geared more to expediency and less to morality, concerned more with immediate consequence and less with consistency or continuity. Thus the historical soil of the Western legal tradition is being washed away in the twentieth century, and the tradition itself is threatened with collapse.[24]

From all this we can draw at least two conclusions. First, those who think the establishment clause of the First Amendment should be extended to require the exclusion of religious principles from political life are advocating the impossible. For to exclude, say, Christian doctrine, from consideration in public policy is merely to invite rival doctrines to take its place. If we say that the statutes must not be considered as having any transcendent reference, to God's law for example, that is equivalent to saying that they must be considered as wholly immanent—based purely on human desires. But that principle is no more scientific and no less religious than a Biblical statement of reality, although that is seldom recognized by strict separationists. One person *believes* God's law should inform human ethical behavior, and the other *believes* that God's law does not exist or if it does is irrelevant. Putting it that way reveals both points of view as faith propositions, and there is no reason to give one a privileged position with respect to constitutional acceptance as opposed to the other, however much we are inclined to argue on other grounds.

Second, we can infer from Berman's analysis that the extent to which the new conception prevails in statutes and court decisions is the extent to which Christians can expect to find themselves not only in disagreement with this or that point of law—which is the inevitable fate of all citizens of all countries—but with the whole political and legal structure, which they will rightly perceive as being increasingly in conflict with the law of God and therefore illegitimate.

HOSTILITIES ON THE SECULAR-RELIGIOUS FRONTIER

ACLU positions on church and state have almost become a fracture point between American liberals and conservatives. Seldom do the former exercise their critical judgment of those positions. Yet it was a man of the left who in 1958 said this of positions taken by the ACLU: "They are the result of one theory of the role of the state in a pluralistic society—a theory not subscribed to by a large body of eminent constitutional law experts in this country and not at all considered to be 'non-partisan' by many religious groups."[25] Since then the ACLU positions have been subscribed to by increasing numbers of the legal profession, largely as a result of the work of the Union and similar groups, and the effectiveness of their efforts is shown by the large numbers of people who do not recognize that this view is only one possible theory, and not at all "non-partisan."

One of the points of confusion on First Amendment matters is that people use different definitions of "religion," so that there is uncertainty about what it is that is supposed to be protected by the Constitution. As society is increasingly centralized (and therefore politicized), it's natural that some activities that used to be thought of as within the church's (or the family's) province come to be thought of as being within the state's. Education, child care, support for the poor, disabled and handicapped, health care, and innumerable matters relating to economic life are common examples of this process. This means that religious life is thought to cover a greatly restricted scope compared to even a couple of generations ago, and therefore increasingly is regarded as having its proper sphere of influence only within the four walls of the church building.

As we saw in the previous chapter, this conception has dominated church-state practice in the totalitarian countries and has facilitated the oppression of the churches. Soviet spokesmen have pointed to the freedom of the church to do its business unhindered in the church buildings (which is untrue in any case) while placing numerous restrictions elsewhere. Document No. 19 of the Central Committee of the Chinese Communist Party defines religious freedom as the freedom to believe or not believe in your heart.[26] This is bad constitutional policy in the American context, and it is bad theology in any Christian church, since it makes Christian faith purely an inward phenomenon and misses entirely the cultural transformation that ought to accompany it. Comparing the increase of statist thinking the U.S. with totalitarianism is not fanciful. Even a generation ago a prominent social scientist, now a United States senator, said that American society was moving toward the totalitarian model and that he had no objection to this.[27]

Theologian Richard John Neuhaus has called the resultant stripping of religious sensibility from public discourse the Naked Public Square—naked, that is, of any transcendent meaning that can be given to the bare facts of social and political life:

> The naked public square is the result of political doctrine and practice that would exclude religion and religiously grounded values from the conduct of public business. The doctrine is that America is a secular society. It finds dogmatic expression in the ideology of secularism. . . . [T]he doctrine is demonstrably false and the dogma exceedingly dangerous.[28]

The doctrine is false because of the sociological truth that America's most fundamental values are religious in nature, and without religious sanction its policies and programs cannot attain to the kind of consensus that would bring about a sense of legitimacy.[29]

For our purposes the main point of this part of the analysis may be expressed in this idea from Neuhaus: *The naked public square cannot remain naked.* "It is a vacuum begging to be filled."[30] And the vacuum is filled by ideologies that do not dare admit they are religions. This is a similar point Carl Esbeck made, cited earlier, about the split between the secularists and the institutional-separationists. These are not only two different legal theories, but also two opposing world-views. For our purposes here *worldview* is equivalent to *religion* because it means, among other things, an interpretation of the meaning of life. That is why it is completely in order for Neuhaus to say that taking Christianity out of the schools doesn't mean making the schools secular; rather it means filling them full of no-name religion.

Theologian Carl Henry has highlighted the hostility of the no-name religions toward Christian faith. In particular the transformation of humanism to an increasingly militant naturalism carried with it the deliberate neo-pagan repudiation of the Christian heritage.[31] Even in academic life, which has always prized the freedom to speak freely, those coming from an explicitly Christian framework *even if they say nothing about it in the classroom* sometimes lose their jobs, to the manifest unconcern of academic organizations and legal protection agencies.[32]

A recent Supreme Court decision shows that conservative jurists are no panacea when it comes to the preservation of liberties. *Oregon v. Smith* is the case of two drug rehabilitation counselors who lost their jobs for using an illegal drug as a part of their religious ceremonies. Alfred Smith and Galen Black used the dismissal as a basis for applying for unemployment compensation. The Oregon Employment Division turned them down on the grounds that they had been discharged for misconduct. The Oregon Court of Appeals reversed the decision, holding that this denial by a state agency violated the free exercise clause of the First Amendment, and ordered that benefits be paid. Justice Antonin Scalia wrote the majority decision in which the Supreme Court upheld the original denial of compensation. The operative point of his decision was: "If prohibiting the exercise of religion is . . . merely the incidental effect of a generally applicable and otherwise valid provision, the First Amendment has not been offended." In explicating the decision he said that the Court has never allowed religious beliefs to excuse anyone from complying with a law that is otherwise valid in an area that the state is free to legislate. It is only when the religious restriction is combined with some other constitutional provision, such as the freedom of speech or of the press, that the religiously motivated action is protected.

We should emphasize here that the issue is not whether drug use is either condoned or condemned. Justice O'Connor agreed with the majority judgment in the case, but strongly dissented from the reasoning behind it. "In my view, today's holding dramatically departs from well-settled First Amendment jurisprudence, appears unnecessary to resolve the question presented and is incompatible with our nation's fundamental commitment to individual religious liberty." The crux of the matter for her is that the Constitution does not distinguish between religious belief and religious behavior, so that the free exercise clause must be presumed to cover both. This decision, she went on, permits the government to prohibit religious conduct as long as the prohibition is general. And she rejected Scalia's contention that there was no need to find a "compelling state interest" in the application of religious liberty cases. That contention means that religious liberty can be denied without any need to show extraordinary requirements. She went so far as to say that Scalia's interpretation serves "to denigrate the very purpose of the Bill of Rights." She dealt with the heart of the issue for those who are non-mainstream in any way: "There is nothing talismanic about neutral laws of general applicability or general criminal prohibitions, for laws neutral toward religion can coerce a person to violate his religious conscience or intrude upon his religious duties just as effectively as laws aimed at religion."

Then she gets to the point that conservatives, such as the supporters of Scalia who oppose the imperial court acting like legislators, often miss: the Constitution is designed as a check on the actions of legislators as well as those of the other branches of government. Scalia wants such issues to be decided legislatively rather than judicially, and that is why he upheld the Oregon law. But O'Connor pointed out that the First Amendment "was enacted precisely to protect the rights of those whose religious practices are not shared by the majority and may be viewed with hostility." O'Connor was writing for a minority of four to five, so there may be grounds for thinking that the course of future decisions will be more favorable. Nevertheless, this decision alone could be extremely damaging for Christians in a society whose elites are increasingly willing to hold the principles and practices of Christian faith as somehow anti-American.

At issue is much more than the use of the drug, a number of critics stated. Jordan Lorence, lawyer for Concerned Women for America, said: "I thought the Indians should not have the right to use peyote, but what the Supreme Court did was to rule much more broadly than they needed to in this case. They swatted a fly with a nuclear bomb."

He was especially concerned because it was the conservatives who got together and made this ruling possible: Scalia wrote the decision, and Rehnquist and Kennedy joined him. John Whitehead, president of the Rutherford Institute, concluded that the opinion will allow the state to violate religious liberty while claiming that the statute is religiously neutral and get away with it.[33]

One prime lesson in all this is that legal provisions by themselves guarantee nothing. Some of the most repressive regimes on earth have similar paper protection. If such promises could of themselves avail anything, there would have been no religious liberty abrogations in American history. American society, like all the others, faces the temptations of power unjustly used. Personal sin and corporate failures combine to cause injustices, and when civic responsibility declines people lack the will to set things right. That is why the future of the liberties of the country depends not so much on elections and court decisions—which are symptoms more than they are causes—but on the determination of the people to see justice done. And that question in turn is likely to depend in part on how well the church carries out its responsibilities.

The process of deciding what it is that covers the naked public square is one in which religions vie against each other. That is another way of saying it is an evangelistic process, although it is seldom recognized as such. It goes on all the time in the schools where only some religions are barred. Bryce Christensen is one teacher who recognizes what is happening in those "secular" classrooms:

> It is not difficult to see . . . that for a teacher to require public school students to read Bunyan's militantly Protestant *Grace Abounding*, Flannery O'Connor's intensely Christian fiction, or John Dryden's poetic apologia for his conversion to Catholicism, *The Hind and the Panther*, is to make a tax-supported religious statement. But deliberately and systematically to exclude such accomplished literature from the classroom in favor of literary attacks upon scriptural beliefs by such writers as Theodore Dreiser, John Steinbeck, or A. E. Housman is just as surely to adopt a tax-subsidized religious position, though one antithetical to most of those paying the tax.[34]

Christensen's work is part of a study by New York University psychology professor Paul Vitz on the religious content of public school textbooks. Vitz's conclusion is symptomatic of the whole issue:

"Religion, traditional family values, and conservative political and economic positions have been reliably excluded from children's textbooks." *Religion* in Vitz's usage means the religious traditions of the nation. He doesn't mean that the secular religions are excluded. The opposite is true, and the exclusion of Christian faith from the public policy arena necessarily means the forcible intrusion of other religions which are then backed by the power of the state.

Thus the problem of religious liberty in this context cannot be solved by dealing only with religious liberty. We have to deal with the proper role of the state. We can do that historically by recapturing the constitutional limitations of the power of central authorities; or we can do it Biblically by noting the limitations to human authority enjoined on us by divine revelation; or we can do it by pointing to the practical effects of the usurpation of power by officials. We should use all three methods. But if we do not solve the problem we shall be in the position envisioned by C. S. Lewis, who wrote that with an expansionist state there is no point in telling officials to mind their own business and leave us alone. "Our whole lives *are* their business."[35]

EIGHT

A THEOLOGICAL UNDERSTANDING OF THE PERSECUTION OF THE CHURCH

A CENTURY OF HUMAN RIGHTS?

The history of Israel and the history of the early church both tell the same lesson, in example and precept, concerning the nature of persecution. That lesson is that wherever people seek to follow the God of Abraham, Isaac and Jacob and the Father of our Lord Jesus Christ they can expect to suffer persecution. The classic New Testament formulation is expressed this way: "Indeed all who desire to live a godly life in Christ Jesus will be persecuted . . ."(2 Timothy 3:12). This suggests that our whole approach to this should not be one that seeks to eliminate the persecution—which will never happen—through some rearrangement of social and political institutions. Rather we should deal with persecution as a normal part of life to be dealt with realistically. We don't expect to rid ourselves of persecution once and for all; we seek to meet it in a way that will mitigate its effects, while remaining faithful to the Lord on whose behalf we are made to suffer. Persecution is not a passing problem to be "solved" but a perpetual condition to deal with, a normal part of our expectations of life.

In the apostolic warning to the first-century church about the prospects for persecution, we have an excellent summary of the example of the prophets which the Christians were to emulate:

> Some were tortured, refusing to accept release, that they might rise again to a better life. Others suffered mocking and scourging, and even chains and imprisonment. They were stoned, they were sawn in two, they were killed with the sword; they went about in skins of sheep and goats, destitute, afflicted, ill-treated—of whom the world was not worthy—wandering over deserts and mountains, and in dens and caves of the earth. (Hebrews 11:35ff.)

This warning was in keeping with the expectations of Jesus: "They will deliver you up to tribulation, and put you to death; and you will be hated by all nations for my name's sake" (Matthew 24:9). Persecution, then, was to be one of the norms of Christian life.

But normalcy is not the same as legitimacy. Although continuing persecution throughout history is to be expected, it is nevertheless unjust and illegitimate. This is caused by a discontinuity between history and law, and is one of the ironies introduced into human events by sin. Being based on a theological fact, this discontinuity is misunderstood by the various ideologies that dominate the culture of the educated classes.

A STRUGGLE BETWEEN GOOD AND EVIL

Just as there is no bloodier century in history than the twentieth, there is also no century in which more Christians have suffered from their persecutors. This cannot be accounted for simply by references to Communism, the cold war, the struggle between totalitarianism and democracy, or the various ideologies. It is at its heart a spiritual struggle and always has been. When Paul wrote to the Galatians to persuade them to depart from the false gospel of salvation by works, he contrasted it with the true gospel of grace and concluded that the hostility between the two had always existed. He drew on Abraham's experience some sixteen centuries earlier. "But as at that time he who was born according to the flesh [Esau] persecuted him who was born according to the Spirit [Isaac], so it is now" (Galatians 4:29). The argument seems to be that no matter what the age, those who seek salvation by some form of self-righteousness would war against those who relied on God's grace.

Thus there is a connection between believing what is false and doing what is evil. Philip Steyne, professor of missions at Columbia Biblical Seminary, stresses that persecution comes as a result of Satanic attack and is intended to strike at God. Saul's encounter with the risen Christ on the Damascus Road came with this question to him: "Why are you persecuting me?" (Acts 9:4). Steyne believes that when persecution is not recognized as the "assault of the enemy," people become passive and adopt a nominal position, in which there is little difference between Christian and non-Christian. "Sin and worldliness are the norm, and some of those who have converted to Christianity have turned to Christo-Paganism." Steyne says this is because they don't understand that this is a "power showdown." Christians in the poor countries have done better in this respect than those in the West because they understand the reality of the spiritual forces better than do secularized western Christians.[1]

This interpretation seems to follow from the fall itself. God's word to the serpent was that there would be constant enmity between humanity and the forces of evil, and that the coming Messiah would enter into the struggle and win the final victory (Genesis 3:15). The psalmist writes of the rulers conspiring "against the LORD and his anointed" (Psalm 2:1ff.). The very notion of righteous deeds and righteous people is offensive to those who persecute the faithful. One of the apostles wrote of the murder of Abel and asked why Cain had done it. And his answer was, "Because his own deeds were evil and his brother's righteous" (1 John 3:12). Jesus Himself associated the hatred for the church with the hatred people bore toward Him. "If the world hates you, know that it has hated me before it hated you. . . . But all this they will do to you on my account . . ." (John 15:18, 21).

THE ROLE OF THE CHURCH IN BRINGING ON PERSECUTION

The preceding section could be taken to imply that the church is simply the passive recipient of the persecutor's zeal—as if occupying purely a victim's role, it bears no responsibility for its plight. But that is not likely. Alexander Solzhenitsyn considered this question in trying to understand the causes of the manifold disasters that had taken place in the Soviet Union. "The truth requires me to state that the condition of the Russian Church at the beginning of the twentieth century is one of the principal causes for the inevitability of the Revolutionary events."[2] And since the Russian Orthodox Church felt the hand of Bolshevik persecution more than any other segment of society, we can look on that whole experience as a vindication of the New Testament teaching that judgment begins with the family of God (1 Peter 4:17). This was a continuation of the pattern under the Old Covenant. The Lord said to Ezekiel that the Israelites would never become "like the nations," no matter how much they might desire it. The reason is that they are joined to God by the covenant and He would not permit that kind of apostasy to occur without consequences. They would fall under judgment first (Ezekiel 20:32ff.). Ezekiel was told to preach judgment against the southern kingdom, the part of ancient Israel that had remained faithful to the Lord in the Temple worship while the northern kingdom had erected idols to substitute for it (v. 46). Ezekiel replied, in effect, that the Judeans wouldn't listen to him; they referred to him as a "maker of allegories."

Thus persecution is properly regarded in part as a judgment of the Lord against his people for their apostasy. If they will not repent, they can expect judgment, and persecution is one of the means at God's disposal. But mercy and restoration are on the other side of judgment, and the prophets taught that the purpose of judgment was to bring the newly repentant nation back to fellowship with the Lord (vv. 40ff.).

Josef Tson, the Romanian pastor expelled by the Ceausescu regime, thinks a similar lesson is contained in the parable of the prodigal son. The father allows the son to wreck his own life because he wants his heart, which unfortunately is bent on dissipation. There is no way to regain the son's loyalty until he begins to experience the results of dissipation and finds that there is no satisfaction in it. Then his heart turns toward home. Persecution, then, is the means whereby God disciplines a church whose heart has turned elsewhere and makes it see where its true home is. It's a form of discipline. Tson believes that is the reason for the readiness of the communist (and formerly communist) world for the gospel, equaled nowhere else.[3]

WHAT ARE THE MOTIVES OF THE PERSECUTORS?

The motivation of the persecutors—as might be said of all human motivation—is often different from what they avow. Gorden Allport, the well-known social psychologist, once wrote that piety is often a "mask" which covers prejudices; the prejudices in turn appear to outsiders as being connected with religion. Thus an action may look like a case of religious persecution based on the principles of the persecutor, but actually be motivated by some historical, cultural, personal or social factor. The 1986 United Nations report on religious intolerance cited this view as the explanation for some forms of religious persecution.[4] There is good precedent for this in the crucifixion of Jesus, which was ostensibly occasioned by the religious zeal of the chief priests, but was actually motivated by their envy of His influence (Mark 15:10). In one of the early persecutions against the apostles, the Sadducees acted because they were "filled with jealousy," a motivation that does not appear in the dialogue of the text (Acts 5:17f.).

The persecution of the Old Testament prophet Daniel proceeded from similar motives. Babylonian officials, envious of Daniel's political success, used the religious issue as a means of striking at him. They induced King Darius to issue an edict that would prevent Daniel from worshiping the Lord. They expected, rightly, that Daniel would be unwilling to obey the law, and the king would then oust him from his position of authority (Daniel 6:55f.).

The perversity of this motivation can be seen in the fact that it often follows so closely upon the doing of good deeds. Immediately after Jesus healed a man with a withered hand the Pharisees went out and plotted his destruction (Matthew 12:14). Another of the Gospels tells of this event by saying that Jesus was "grieved at their hardness of heart." Evidently, their envy was a product largely of the validation of Jesus' ministry by his good works, a validation which they could not duplicate; thus His ministry served to discredit theirs. This illustrates the universal temptation to which Allport pointed.

On another occasion the whole synagogue in which Jesus was speaking rose up against Him in wrath and attempted to destroy Him by throwing Him off a hill. The problem in that case was His teaching that the Gentiles too were to be part of God's Kingdom, a statement offensive to the national pride of those who mistook the reason they were designated the "chosen" people (Luke 4:16-30). Nationalism was also the offended principle when Jesus was accused of being a Samaritan (John 8:48). Another complaint the persecutors had against Jesus was that He refused to flatter them. They hated Him "because I testify of it [the world] that its works are evil" (John 7:7). He told them they were lawless (John 7:19f.).

Politicians commonly are responsible for persecutions, and it's helpful to learn from the Biblical precedents that illustrate how they can benefit from persecuting the people of God. We have already seen how Daniel's faith was tested through the agency of politicians who envied his advancement in the king's service. In the trial of Jesus we observe a politician wrestling between a desire to do justice and a desire to solidify his position with the populace by doing their bidding. The crowd finally persuaded Pilate to condemn Jesus to death only after the politician's repeated pleas for them to reconsider (Luke 23:1-25). Later on Herod had James killed, and when he saw that was a crowd-pleaser proceeded to arrest Peter as well (Acts 12:1-3). Still later, the provincial governor, Festus, "wishing to do the Jews a favor"—evidently for his own political benefit—tried to maneuver Paul into agreeing to a trial before himself, only to be thwarted by the apostle's appeal to Rome (Act 25:9ff.).

The New Testament also records occasions when financial benefits impelled the persecutors to act. Judas prefaced his betrayal of Jesus by the demand for silver and agreed only after learning that the price was right (Matthew 26:14ff.). The persecution in Philippi stemmed from the apostles' interference with the income of the owners of a young slave whom Paul freed from an evil spirit (Acts 16:19ff.). And in Ephesus the apostles were mobbed by crowds that the idol-makers incited to riot because they feared that the gospel would convert their customers away from idolatry—"there is danger . . . that this trade of ours may come into disrepute . . . " (Acts 19:24ff.).

It is a mistake simply to take at face value what the persecutors say of their own motivation. That seems to be what Jesus was getting at when he said of the Pharisees that they were opposed to John the Baptist because he was ascetic and therefore supposedly was demonized, whereas they accused the Son of God of being a drunkard (Luke 7:33f.). The meaning evidently is that people oppose God and therefore the church, and when they do so they may give whatever reason they find convenient.

I have put so much emphasis on the personal and self-serving motivation of the persecutors because the numerous Biblical examples make its importance so clear. But it would be cynical to assume that persecutors are never sincere in their devotion to an evil cause. Indeed, Jesus told the disciples that a time would come when "whoever kills you will think he is offering service to God" (John 16:1ff.). In the Islamic persecutions we have the most striking fulfillment of that prophecy.

PERSECUTION MEANS SUFFERING

The suffering that comes with persecution may be of different kinds. When Jesus cured someone who had been born blind, the man's parents denied that they knew who effected the cure. The text explicitly says they did this because a decision had been made to expel from the synagogue anyone who confessed Jesus as the Christ (John 9:22f.). Thus, the terrible fate they feared was ostracism; they were willing to sacrifice almost anything not to be disowned by those who belonged to the power structure. Later on when a number of those in authority believed in Jesus they remained silent about it, and for the same reason. But there is an additional note in the text describing this group which shows why this was so important to them: ". . . they loved the praise of men more than the praise of God" (John 12:43). As in so many other spheres of life, pride is the great stumbling block.

The Bible depicts the servants of God as suffering and perishing by the most brutal means, and yet in many of these descriptions of suffering there is a curious upbeat tone that is mixed with the painful realities.

> We are afflicted in every way, but not crushed; perplexed, but not driven to despair; persecuted, but not forsaken; struck down but not destroyed; always carrying in the body the death of Jesus, so that the life of Jesus may also be manifested in our bodies. (2 Corinthians 4:8-10)

> . . . as servants of God we commend ourselves in every way: through great endurance, in afflictions, hardships, calamities, beatings, imprisonments, tumults, labors, watching, hunger . . . with the weapons of righteousness for the right hand and for the left; in honor and dishonor, in ill repute and good repute. We are treated as impostors, and yet are true; as unknown, as yet well known; as dying, and behold we live; as punished, and yet not killed; as sorrowful, yet always rejoicing; as poor, yet making many rich; as having nothing, and yet possessing everything (2 Corinthians 6:4ff.).

The Christian doctrine of suffering for the Lord's sake has this double-barreled nature cropping up again and again, often embodying the most improbable extremes of suffering and joy. Perhaps the most oft-quoted example of this occurred when in the early days the apostles were beaten and released, after being ordered by the authorities not to preach again.

> Then they left the presence of the council, rejoicing that they were counted worthy to suffer dishonor for the name. And every day in the temple and at home they did not cease teaching and preaching Jesus as the Christ. (Acts 5:40f.)

With this hard-won understanding of rejoicing in the midst of suffering, the apostles taught their own disciples in a way that was commensurate with their experiences:

> Do not be surprised at the fiery ordeal which comes upon you to prove you, as though something strange were happening to you. But rejoice in so far as you share Christ's sufferings, that you may also rejoice and be glad when his glory is revealed. If you are reproached for the name of Christ, you are blessed, because the spirit of glory and of God rests upon you. But let none of you suffer as a murderer, or a thief, or a wrongdoer, or a mischief-maker; yet if one suffers as a Christian, let him not be ashamed, but under that name let him glorify God. (1 Peter 4:12ff.)

Observers have long remarked on the role persecution plays in sparking revival in the church, although there is little consensus on just why that is so. This conjunction of suffering and joy may be one of the reasons for it. For pagan philosophies have no explanation that can make sense of suffering. It all seems senseless, so much so that many people think it absurd to believe there is a God who created, loves and sustains the world. (This is the philosophical problem of theodicy.) But in the suffering and death of Christ, the one of whom it is said that "the world was made through him" (John 1:10), His followers have the great model that provides meaning to their sufferings: ". . . looking to Jesus the pioneer and perfecter of our faith, who for the joy that was set before him endured the cross, despising the shame, and is seated at the right hand of the throne of God" (Hebrews 12:2). It's hard to believe that the apostles were unaware of this principle when after their beating they left the council rejoicing that they were considered worthy to suffer shame in the name of Christ.

SPIRITUAL PREPARATION FOR PERSECUTION

What I have called the double-barreled aspect of persecution—suffering/joy—suggests that there is something about the Christian suffering of persecution that is uncommon. Normally we expect the associated characteristics to be suffering/sorrow or suffering/despair. A recent news story carries the account of an Irish hostage just released from captivity in Lebanon. He describes his experience as "a crucifying loneliness, a silent screaming slide into the bowels of ultimate despair."[5] What is it that could bring *joy* into unpromising circumstances like that? Is it purely a figure of speech that the Irish hostage called his experience a *crucifying* loneliness? Or was he aware of the words of Jesus Christ on the cross: "My God, my God, why hast thou forsaken me" (Mark 15:34)? The cosmic all-encompassing sense of being alone in bearing the sin of the world that Jesus went through may be said to have its pale counterpart in the ordeals that His followers encounter. When the letter to the Hebrews speaks of the suffering of Jesus, it comes directly after the chapter in which the persecution of the Old Testament saints is described—the mocking, torture, deprivation and killing. Then the Savior is depicted, in the passage cited earlier, as "the pioneer and perfecter of our faith, who for the joy that was set before him endured the cross, despising the shame, and is seated at the right hand of the throne of God" (Hebrews 12:2). Thus the joy in the midst of terrible suffering comes from putting the suffering in its true context. And its context is the hope— "the joy that was set before him"—that resides in what it all means. The ultimate eschatological victory of Jesus Christ over all His enemies is shared by His faithful disciples. The difference between hope and despair is not in the degree of suffering, but rather in the meaning of the suffering.

The Apostle Paul expressed a similar idea in one short passage: "Rejoice in your hope, be patient in tribulation, be constant in prayer" (Romans 12:12). This might serve as a shorthand reminder of all the Bible says about the subject to those who are suffering for their faith and have access to no other passage. As in the quotation from Hebrews, joy comes from the hope—which in these passages seems to be more like certainty—for the way it will all come out. The Hebrews passage referring to both the prophets and Jesus makes it clear that this is true even if the persecution should end in the death of the believers. While rejoicing in hope the apostle says to be patient in tribulation; thus patience is the immediate response to the suffering that is being endured. And, the passage continues, prayer should suffuse the believer's whole existence as he patiently endures what he cannot bring to an end. Should it seem fanciful to place this in the context of persecution, it's worth noting that almost immediately after that verse the apostle writes: "Bless those who persecute you . . ." (Romans 12:14). This example of Jesus is to be paramount for those who suffer after Him. "Consider him who endured from sinners such hostility against himself, so that you may not grow weary or fainthearted" (Hebrews 12:3).

Irina Ratushinskaya, after many days of semi-starvation in

freezing punishment cells, found imprisonment as a Christian to be a school for character building. She comments on the motivation of the authorities in imposing the dehumanizing atmosphere of the prison camps: "The camps don't exist to form character, they exist to destroy the persona."[6] And yet they accomplish what the authorities have no intention of accomplishing by contributing to the spiritual strengthening of the Christian inmates. We can think of this as analogous to the process of muscle building, which takes place only as the muscles are forced to strain against opposition. Pain is an inescapable part of the preparation for athletic excellence. The act of being in a setting like that of the labor camps places pressures on the person that either strengthen or destroy him, just as a muscle is built up or broken down by the pressures placed upon it. The apostle said the same in urging the Romans to rejoice in their sufferings because "suffering produces endurance, and endurance produces character" (Romans 5:3f.). The 1 Peter letter, which is full of counsel about suffering, urges the believers to see it as a test of their faith, advising them not to be "surprised at the fiery ordeal which comes upon you to prove you," but—again—to "rejoice in so far as you share Christ's sufferings . . ." (1 Peter 4:13).

MARTYRDOM: SECRET WEAPON OF THE CHURCH

It has become common to attribute the survival and health of the church through the first three centuries of persecution to its willingness to suffer martyrdom.[7] Josef Tson argues that martyrdom is a weapon of the church. He sees it as a means whereby Satanic forces are defeated (Revelation 12:11), the mission of the church accomplished (2 Corinthians 1:6), and the life of the church enriched (Colossians 1:24; 1 Peter 4:12f.). But he thinks that western Christians who have not known persecution are not in a good position to appreciate this. Tson recalls being asked by fellow students at Oxford University what chance he had of success if he returned to Romania after his studies. He smiled at what he thought was a typically western attitude. More appropriate is the idea contained in Matthew 10:16 ("I send you as sheep in the midst of wolves"), and Tson asked them to consider what chance of "success" the sheep had in those circumstances. The question for him was not success but obedience.

During one of Tson's interrogations a *securitate* officer threatened to kill him. Tson answered in this way:

Sir, let me explain that issue to you. Your supreme weapon is killing. My supreme weapon is dying. Sir, you know my sermons are all over the country on tapes now. If you kill me, I will be sprinkling them with my blood. Whoever listens to them after that will say, "I'd better listen. This man sealed it with his blood." They will speak ten times louder than before.

One of his fellow pastors, also undergoing questioning, was told by another officer that they would never fall for Tson's gambit and kill him because it would only strengthen the church. Hearing his colleague explain the officer's statement was a revelation to Tson.

That gave me pause. For years I was a Christian who was cautious and low-keyed because I wanted to survive. I had accepted all the restrictions the authorities put on me because I wanted to live. Now I wanted to die, and they wouldn't oblige. Now I could do whatever I wanted in Romania. For years I wanted to save my life, and I was losing it. Now that I wanted to lose it, I was winning it. Somebody said those words before, but they had not sunk in my mind.[8]

Cardinal Lustiger of France recently made the same point: "The tyrant confuses the victim, whom he overcomes, with the martyr, who really gets the best of him."[9]

After Romanian pastor Vasile Talos was injured in a murder attempt by the police, Tson preached a sermon on the incident that was beamed into Romania. He made the point that the pastor's preaching would have more power because of the visible wounds of persecution, and this deeply affected many people in Romania. That evening when Talos went to church to lead the service people shook his hand, but many drew his head down to kiss the wound. One party member came to church and told Talos that he had heard Tson's sermon on the radio and wanted to know if it was true. When told that it was he replied, "Then I want to be here with my wife." A few months later they were baptized. The regime took a serious blow because of this publicity.[10]

Perhaps this note of martyrdom as victory is one of the meanings that we should infer from the last recorded words of Jesus to the Apostle Peter, when he spoke of Peter's coming martyrdom: "This he said to show by what death [Peter] was to glorify God" (John 21:19).

THE "COURAGE" OF
ESCHATOLOGICAL EXPECTATIONS

Reading accounts of the persecution of the early Christians —and numerous contemporary ones as well—we describe their actions as courageous. But what we are observing is not courage in the usual sense. Rather these people had an eschatological perspective. Their courage, if that is what it was, was based on the firm conviction that they would be raised in the end. Resurrection puts suffering and death in the perspective that made it possible for them to do what to observers looks like courageous actions.[11] Moses left the easy life in the royal household in order to accept the status of outcast because he scorned "fleeting" pleasures and "looked to the reward" (Hebrews 11:25f.). In other words he was oriented to the future rather than to the present. This was also the explanation Jesus gave for His extraordinary statement that sounds common only to those who have heard it repeated often. "Blessed are those who are persecuted for righteousness' sake, for theirs is the kingdom of heaven. Blessed are you when men revile you and persecute you and utter all kinds of evil against you falsely on my account" (Matthew 5:10ff.). This is immediately followed by an explanation that helps us understand how people are able to behave in such unlikely ways: "Rejoice and be glad, for your reward is great in heaven, for so men persecuted the prophets who were before you."

This passage places current persecutions right in the tradition pioneered by the prophets of the old covenant. It thus puts our own tribulations in a long and honorable tradition, and at the same time shows the blessed culmination of the whole bloody business. It is an antidote to both self-pity and the curse of apparent meaninglessness—"Why me, O Lord?"

The British Methodist scholar E. Gordon Rupp begins his book on conflict in church history in this way:

> One of the obvious qualities of the first Christians was their exultant confidence in the presence of evil. You might not like these Christians, but you had to admit they had a nerve. It was this stubborn truculence of theirs which exasperated the Roman magistrates, infuriated the mobs, and yet which again and again drew men and women to their side, even though they were aware that this adherence meant savage torture and sudden death. These Christians proclaimed victory.[12]

The Apostle Paul taught the early church to regard such terrible consequences as a "slight momentary affliction" the purpose of which was to prepare us "for an eternal weight of glory beyond all comparison . . ."(2 Corinthians 4:17). This was in the same letter which he began by describing the experiences of his companions and himself traveling through the province of Asia: "we were so utterly unbearably crushed that we despaired of life itself" (2 Corinthians 1:8).

Carl Henry has examined the theological principle behind this kind of fortitude and acceptance of danger. He finds helpful the study of the word *thlipsis*, usually translated as "trouble." It occurs forty-five times in the New Testament. Henry says that the meaning of the passages that deal with the issue is that the risen Christ enters into the sufferings of His people, and this provides the basis for their overcoming the challenges to the integrity of their faith. "Take heart, I have overcome the world" (John 16:33). This is not a form of self-reliance or a shallow "Keep your chin up." Rather it points to the source and object of the faith of the believer, Christ Himself, and it's often coupled with "stop fearing." Jesus anchored the universal virtue of courage in His victory over the world. "Take heart, I have overcome the world" (John 16:33).[13]

The eschatological element is present in almost every presentation of the Biblical teaching of persecution. Things are difficult now, but it will all be made up to you later. This is not a mindless optimism or a desperate whistling past the graveyard. It is a confidence borne of the faith that brought the believer into the Kingdom of God in the first place, and thus opened up the possibility of suffering for the sake of Christ.

> Jesus said, "Truly I say to you, there is no one who has left house or brothers or sisters or mother or father or children or lands, for my sake and the gospel, who will not receive a hundred fold . . . with persecutions, and in the age to come eternal life." (Mark 10:29, 30)

> "And now, behold, I am going to Jerusalem, bound in the Spirit, not knowing what shall befall me there; except that the Holy Spirit testifies to me in every city that imprisonment and afflictions await me. But I do not account my life of any value nor as precious to myself, if only I may accomplish my course and the ministry which I received from the Lord Jesus, to testify to the gospel of the grace of God." (Acts 20:22ff.)

But recall the former days when, after you were enlightened, you endured a hard struggle with sufferings, sometimes being publicly exposed to abuse and affliction, and sometimes being partners with those so treated. For you had compassion on the prisoners, and you joyfully accepted the plundering of your property, since you knew that you yourselves had a better possession and an abiding one. (Hebrews 10:32ff.)

THE INNER LIFE OR THE WHOLE WORLD

One Russian Orthodox observer, Yevgeni Barabanov, suggested during the hard days of the Brezhnev period that many of the clergy liked the limitations placed on church life because they believed that what the true church does is the liturgy which *is* Christianity. (He went on to suggest that this was a problem not only in the totalitarian countries but throughout the world.)[14] The basic issue is that of the relationship between church and society, and that is always a serious theological matter giving rise to much controversy. Barabanov's suggestion thrusts the issue of the church under persecution in an entirely different direction than is normal in discussing these issues. For he saw the crux of the matter not so much in the state's persecution of the church—although he affirmed that reality—but in the church's refusal or inability to see clearly its true responsibilities. Or at least to interpret those responsibilities in an unduly restrictive fashion, losing sight of its need to evangelize and to bring about justice in the country.

Gennadi Shimanov wrote an open letter on the same subject to Patriarch Pimen in 1976, arguing that the U.S.S.R. was in need of active support by Christians. This would advance not only the church but the whole society, including the state. Shimanov's letter was similar to an ecumenical appeal the same year to the highest level of the Soviet government and at the same time to the World Council of Churches. The writers of this document were twenty-seven Christians from six denominations. Although Shimanov's effort was intended to show the close ties between Russian society and the Orthodox Church, the ecumenical letter encompassed Christianity in general. What they had in common was the point of view that the regime's hostility to Christian faith was not only damaging to the church but to the whole society.[15]

The Russian Orthodox and evangelical Christians who sent the ecumenical letter could collaborate in this way because none of the Soviet churches had a good record in coming to grips with their responsibility to influence society. There was much dissatisfaction about this in small groups of educated people, most of them Orthodox. One such band, called 37 from the number of the apartment in which they met, gathered in Leningrad, the leadership given largely by a young philosophy graduate by the name of Tatiana Goricheva. Their two principles were, first, to bridge the gulf between the Christian church and the world; and second, that the best means of doing so is love. The seminar centered around philosophical and theological issues toward which a wide variety of convictions could be brought to bear. Besides the Orthodox, the group included Protestants, Jews, atheists, pagans, and the inevitable KGB officers. One joke had it that when the 37 group was meeting everyone else could relax because the whole KGB was busy over there. The 37 proceedings included genuine opportunities for exchanges of opposing views, which lent a breath of fresh air to Soviet intellectuals who elsewhere could only express openly the conventional Marxist-Leninist pieties. Some of the unbelievers in the strange mix of participants became Christians. The 37 group published twenty issues of a journal, also called 37, between 1975 and 1981, which was a long run for *samizdat*. The authorities subjected the members to considerable harassment but no jailings. The movement petered out after Goricheva was expelled from the U.S.S.R. in 1980, or at least splintered into a number of groups with specialized interests.

In Moscow about the same time a Christian seminar, composed entirely of Russian Orthodox intellectuals, began meeting. The KGB learned of their existence early on, but did little about it beyond the normal harassment and intimidation. One reason is the Seminar members never constituted themselves as an organization with officers and a program. And they remained so small in number it was difficult for the KGB to infiltrate them. But when they began producing scholarly papers in *samizdat* form under the title *Obshchina*, the kid-gloves treatment stopped. All the members of the seminar were swept off the streets and jailed.

It's not immediately clear why the Leningrad group was treated so much more leniently than the Moscow counterpart, since they were not entirely dissimilar in orientation, both being renewal groups either primarily or completely composed of Orthodox Christians. One issue of 37 contained a favorable review of *Obshchina* and a report of a conversation held with one member of the Moscow group. Jane Ellis has compared the respective writings and concluded that their common ground was a belief in the need for the Christian transformation of culture and society, and particularly of their own generation. They agreed that they were moving towards each other: 37 was the fruit of people in the world of culture turning to religion, while *Obshchina* was moving from religion towards culture.[16]

Speaking with Tatiana Goricheva in her Paris apartment several years after she was forced from the Soviet Union, I asked her why they were treated so leniently in Leningrad compared with the harsh prison and work camp experience of the Moscow group. She replied by contrasting the philosophical, theological, and literary preoccupations of 37 with the societal concerns in Moscow. In the capital they were exploring practical issues relating to social life, a field that inherently has strong political implications. The regime was also especially unhappy with the group's exploration of the history of the martyrs, even though they were studying it during the time of the Tsars.[17]

A few months later (just ten months after he had ended eight and one-half years of torture and misery in a strict regime labor camp) the former leader of the Moscow Seminar, Alexander Ogorodnikov, told me that from the time of his conversion to Christianity in 1973 he was convinced that Christians have to be concerned and active in doing something to help reform the society.[18] Years earlier Ogorodnikov had written in *Obshchina* that the task of the Moscow Seminar was to "transform the world," and he specified that this meant both the inner world of the soul and the outer world of the society.[19] Christians with this outlook can expect the most serious reaction from persecutors.

GOD IS SOVEREIGN EVEN DURING THE WORST OF CIRCUMSTANCES

Josef Tson has written of his attitude toward the persecution in Romania:

> For many years, mainly in the 1970s, as I saw the suffering brought on by Communism, I was groaning and saying, "Lord, why? Why do you allow Communism?" Now I have as the main pillar of my theology the sovereignty of God. The sovereignty of God means Satan at the end always finds out that he just promoted God's cause. All God's enemies combine to destroy His work, and they always discover at the end that they just promoted it. That's the sovereignty of God.[20]

That is why a Biblical philosophy of history has to recognize that God's victories often come disguised as defeats: persecutions, death, destruction of churches and so on. A theology of disaster that is true to a Biblical worldview recognizes the victory lurking behind every external setback to faithful followers of Christ. Western Christians, perhaps jaded by years of immersion in an environment conditioned by rationalism, do not easily credit stories of supernatural intervention. But it's hard to speak long with committed Christians from other parts of the world without becoming aware that other paradigms may be closer to the Biblical message and to the way that God actually works in the world.

In Uganda on April 12, 1978, Idi Amin's soldiers fired automatic weapons at the platform of the Makerere Gospel Mission to Uganda Church in one of the suburbs of Kampala. With bullets ricocheting and tearing holes in the walls and roof, the six hundred people in the church fell to their knees and with upraised arms began to praise God. The soldiers arrested and beat about two hundred of them and dragged them off to the Nakesero State Research Bureau headquarters, where thousands of Ugandans had already lost their lives. There they sat huddled in a circle with gasoline cans placed around them after being told that they would be burned alive. The soldiers said they were only awaiting the order to be given by a high-ranking officer. Later it turned out that the officer had an automobile accident, which the people took as a direct intervention of God on their behalf.[21] Mission literature is full of examples in which Christians become persuaded of God's power and ability to intervene in miraculous ways in the midst of serious persecution.[22]

But there is more to it than miracles. Often a setback is taken by the church as a disaster, but it finds later on that the circumstances served to be a boon. The Malaysian church, for example, had to put up with government restrictions on missionary visa renewals after ten years residence. The government also began turning down visas for foreigners' residence to do jobs that Malaysian citizens could do. These restrictions have hampered the activities of missionaries in the country. But some Malaysian Christians believe that this has strengthened the church. "We have seen in the last twenty-five years or so the development of local leadership which would not have been so rapid or effective had foreign missionaries stayed on indefinitely." At the same time and for the same reason the church has achieved general financial autonomy, which means that foreign missionary efforts can be redirected toward areas in which local capabilities are not present.[23] Thus what we take to be evidence of persecution may need to be interpreted in a deeper way. The hostility could be the means of preventing a healthy mission emphasis from deteriorating into a suffocating paternalistic embrace that serves mainly to keep the indigenous church in a state of perpetual adolescence.

Often churches in poor countries seem better prepared to accept the hard truths of the Biblical revelation than westerners. Christians in Ethiopia began preparing for persecution long before the Marxist-Leninist regime took over in 1974, evidently as a result of their study of the Bible. Some are known even to have prayed for persecution as a means of purifying the church.[24]

Under the Marxist-Leninist persecutions the churches of Ethiopia and Mozambique grew in numbers and spiritual strength. Conversions among the youth were a particular mark of this revival, and some observers believe this fact in particular aroused the wrath of the regimes. Some who were imprisoned for long periods were actually sorry to be released, since it cut short a particularly fruitful preaching ministry in the prisons.[25] Their experience was evidently similar to that of the Apostle Paul who found that prison was an opportunity for ministry:

> I want you to know, brethren, that what has happened to me has really served to advance the gospel, so that it has become known throughout the whole praetorian guard and to all the rest that my imprisonment is for Christ; and most of the brethren have been made confident in the Lord because of my imprisonment, and are much more bold to speak the word of God without fear. (Philippians 1:12ff.)

The pressures of persecution sometimes cement the Christians into a unity that ought to have been maintained in any case, but which eluded them prior to the pressure. In the late seventies the Ethiopian churches formed the Christian Council for Cooperation of Churches. One feature was the inclusion of the Roman Catholic Church, an unusual event in Africa.[26]

Jonathan Chao, president of Christ's College in Taiwan, has worked with numerous mainland Chinese pastors who have spent many years in prison. He reports that their suffering has refined them and made them not only deeply humble, but also fearless. Thus they are having strikingly powerful ministries now that they are out of prison.[27] Perhaps the best known of the imprisoned pastors is Wang Ming-Dao. He began preaching in 1921, and after the communist victory of 1949 refused to join the Three-Self Patriotic Movement. He and his wife were both imprisoned in 1955. After fourteen months of brainwashing and torture he signed a confession that his church had been counter-revolutionary. Afterwards, he concluded that his recantation was wrong. So he withdrew his confession and went back to prison for twenty-one years, until 1980. His wife had been released two years earlier. After Pastor Wang emerged from prison he cited the warning of the Apocalypse: "Do not fear what you are about to suffer. Behold, the devil is about to throw some of you into prison, that you may be tested, and for ten days you will have tribulation. Be faithful unto death, and I will give you the crown of life" (Revelation 2:10). He went on to say that he has not lost because of his suffering, but has gained a greater blessing.[28]

It's typical of people like Pastor Wang that they subsume all that happened to them under the general heading of God's sovereignty, believing that "in everything God works for good with those who love him . . ."(Romans. 8:28). That is clearly the teaching also of the Biblical writers quoted earlier in this chapter.

PROSPECTS FOR THE FUTURE

Gordon Rupp believes that the conditions of the first-century persecutions are being repeated in the last half of the twentieth century. He cites the growing sense of paralysis and fatalism in society, the end of the vision of progress that lasted for at least a century, so that people seem to count for little in comparison with the great impersonal forces that are assumed to control things.[29] There is a convulsion of despair, and people not only throw revelation out the window, but reason as well. Naziism and Communism seemed reasonable because people could not accept any alternative explanation or course of action. And east European countries that have overthrown Communism are still largely socialist in orientation, which means their economic problems will persist. Meanwhile the nihilism of the West has become epidemic, with some people desperately latching on to eastern religions in an effort to find meaning. Thus, forty years after Rupp inscribed his foreboding, the conditions he foretold have continued to bear him out.

THE CHURCH REACTS TO ITS TORMENTORS

*T*hus far we have given most of our attention to the pressures placed on Christians by forces hostile to their faith. This perhaps has distorted the picture by making it seem as if the church is purely a passive actor in the drama, in contrast to the active role played by the persecutors. But unless the persecution is so extreme that the authorities intend to terminate the existence of the church altogether, there are various possible relationships of coexistence—some compatible with the calling of the church and some not. Recent years have seen numerous examples of both.

THE CHURCH CO-OPTED

Under totalitarian rule the state attempts to bring all elements of the society under its control. All institutions—indeed all people—are to serve the purposes of the authorities and in effect become arms of the state. Dependent as it is on propaganda to elicit support or at least toleration from the populace, the totalitarian state is especially concerned to bring under control the institutions that affect people's thinking. Thus schools, printing presses, broadcast facilities and churches receive the closest scrutiny and strictest regulation.

    The totalitarian state pushes the church to echo the government position on all matters. Even on the issue of its own persecution, the church is expected to fall into line and repeat the barefaced lies of the officials who control them. Russian Orthodox Metropolitan Filaret responded in 1976 with the following typical statement to a question by the Soviet Press Agency Novosti:

> No one is persecuted for religious convictions in the Soviet Union. Believers and non-believers in our country form one society engaged in active and creative labour for the good of their Motherland. The attitude of the Soviet State to the needs of the Church is considerate and understanding.[1]

The Metropolitan went on to criticize the western press for slandering the Soviet Union on this issue.

After the illusion of state legitimacy lay in ruins and the duplicity of government spokesmen was exposed even in the official Soviet press, Russian Orthodox hierarchs were still deceiving the public. In 1989 Patriarch Pimen and Metropolitan Filaret both said that between seven hundred and eight hundred confiscated churches had been returned to the Russian Orthodox Church. But Orthodox activists publicly disputed this, saying that the true figure was much lower, and that the returned buildings had suffered such neglect that they were little more than a pile of wreckage and would take years to rebuild.[2] When church officials are privately challenged on the dishonesty of their public statements they typically respond by pointing to the need to preserve the church—survival makes necessary much that they would prefer not to do. Dimitri Pospielovsky, an Orthodox historian who lives in Canada, remonstrated about this with Metropolitan Nikodim, who responded by saying that it was only westerners who were critical of the hierarchs' actions. Nikodim described his own method as one of indirection that was more likely to benefit the church than the straightforward technique (which others would call telling the truth) preferred by outsiders.[3]

Even on purely spiritual matters the hierarchy sometimes tries to overrule the faithful in seemingly arbitrary ways. When in the *glasnost* thaw lay intellectuals in Leningrad began producing a *samizdat* publication called *Choice*, church officials tried to get them to change some of their articles because they presented theological material in a way that was personally relevant. The hierarchy, perhaps acting on behalf of party censors, wanted such matters kept abstract.[4] The censors may have feared the kind of pastoral teaching that would impart a sense of personal integrity and resolution. At about the same time the *Choice* activists were going through those frustrations, Alexander Ogorodnikov circulated a letter in which he said that not only had the

Russian Orthodox Church matured in its spiritual development without the participation of the hierarchy, but in spite of them.

> The Church hierarchy, which has passed through the hard school of compromise, seems to be content with the status quo and does not strive toward greater freedom for religion; for freedom would oblige the hierarchy to engage in true service of the church, to speak the word of Truth to the people—something for which the hierarchy is unprepared, and which it fears.[5]

The obsequiousness of church officials evidently is related to the degree in which the society in general is expected to express such sentiments. They bow before the throne no less deeply than everyone else. Only a few months before the fall of the Ceausescus the Romanian Orthodox Synod wrote to the President:

> We . . . wholly approve of the ardent activity which you, as the greatest and most brilliant hero of peace and tireless fighter for understanding and peaceful collaboration, wage for the victory of mankind's ideals of freedom and progress, and for complete equality in law, respect for national independence and sovereignty, and for the development of the principles of non-interference in internal affairs, i.e. those principles which Romania consistently and determinedly applies to its relations with all the states of the world.
>
> With profound gratitude for your efforts in the cause of the Romanian people's happiness and of world peace, with the greatest reverence, we give our warmest thanks for the atmosphere of complete religious freedom which you have ensured for the religious groups of our homeland, and for your far-reaching understanding towards the Orthodox Church and all believers in the practice of religion and culture.[6]

After the regime fell, the Romanian Orthodox leaders apologized for their fawning behavior toward the dictator.

Richard Wurmbrand, a Romanian Lutheran pastor who spent many years in prison, writes that during the communist takeover an Orthodox bishop put a hammer and sickle on his robes and asked his priests to refer to him not as Your Grace, but as Comrade Bishop.[7] Nor was the Orthodox Church the only one that failed to meet the test. We saw in Chapter 6 that the Romanian Baptist Union, contrary to its own constitution, allowed itself to be transformed from a free association of autonomous churches into a governing body which the regime used as a transmission belt to control the churches. A *samizdat* published in 1988 charged that the Reformed Church had made similar compromises. Of the two Reformed bishops neither encouraged pastors to have a lively ministry that could engender spiritual life in the church, and one of them even punished those who attempted to do so.[8]

After the anti-communist revolution a canon law expert described the Bulgarian Orthodox Church hierarchy in similar terms. Prof. Radko Poptodorov, writing in the magazine *Fatherland* in early 1990, condemned the leadership for "their subservience to the regime, their complete neglect of the Church's statutes, their lust for power, and the corruption prevalent among bishops."[9] In June 1989, two hundred Hungarian pastors and lay activists met in Budapest, calling themselves the Reformed Renewal Movement. They charged that for forty years Reformed leaders betrayed the church by cooperating with communist officials in preventing the evangelization of young people.[10]

THE CHURCH RENEWED

Church renewal is not something that takes place once and for all. It seems to take on the character of the passing seasons, coming for a time of refreshment which is then followed by a kind of weariness and descent into a more mundane existence or worse. This pattern has existed throughout the history of the church, beginning with the New Testament period, and is unrelated to persecution. The descriptions of the apostolic churches in Revelation 2 and 3 show that this pattern has existed from the earliest times.

The renewal in the Russian Orthodox Church began in the late 1950s, coinciding with the start of party boss Khrushchev's anti-religious campaign. Probably the ending of the Stalin myth had something to do with it. Jane Ellis believes that "revival," though commonly used to describe this awakening, is the wrong word. "The reality is a slow, gradual, often painful process of people rediscovering their Christian roots. . . ." She believes it had something to do with a seeking for the culture of the past and the self-identity of the Russian nation. It was at the same time an intellectual movement.[11]

A Catholic priest in Mozambique, Fr. Antonio Panteglini, says of the renewal there that it stemmed directly from the persecution which freed the church of "opportunist members." The ones who are left are genuine, and the quality of their faith has been an effective witness to others.[12] Under the Marxist-Leninist persecutions the churches of Ethiopia and Mozambique grew in numbers and spiritual strength. Conversions among the youth were a special mark of this revival, and some observers believe this aroused the particular wrath of the regimes.[13]

In Vietnam the church boomed after 1975. The revival went on in spite of the difficulties caused by the imprisonment of pastors, along with the government's refusal to allow training or ordination of replacements. One church had a thousand members when the pastor was arrested; some time later it had doubled in size. Another had one hundred members in 1975; by 1987 it had grown to more than a thousand. In 1975 there were no churches with multiple services on Sunday. Twelve years later the Evangelical Church of Vietnam had almost twenty such churches, one of which held four services each Sunday. A Vietnamese church leader in the West says that the key to the revival is the absolute loyalty to Jesus Christ by the Vietnamese Christians. They are devoted in Bible study and prayer meetings held in homes, jobsites and farms. There are thousands of Bible study groups meeting, a number that is continually increasing.[14]

The common saying that a persecuted church becomes strong needs to be qualified. Our earlier examples of grave weaknesses of persecuted churches should be enough to demonstrate that. Still, there must be a way to account for the remarkable strength and zeal in so many places where the church is persecuted. The remark from Mozambique about lukewarm Christians being frightened off leaving the strong ones to inspire a renewal is one answer to the question; house church members in China often make similar statements. The persecution that began anew in Egypt in the early 1980s evidently had something to do with the fact that the leadership of the Coptic church fell into the hands of the newly elected Pope Shenouda III, a dynamic prelate who conducted well-attended Bible studies and became very popular. President Sadat and the Muslim Brotherhood resented the renewal of the church and the increased unity that came with it. Thus the newly energized ministry attracted the enmity of the state and at the same time made it more likely that the church would be able to withstand that enmity.[15]

A Roman Catholic analysis of the persecution in Nepal concludes that the Protestants bear the brunt of the pressure because most of them are evangelicals and believe they have a responsibility to preach the gospel to their neighbors. The few Catholics don't feel that responsibility and for the most part are left alone.[16] (There is no way that one can acquaint Hindus in Nepal with the gospel without violating the law.) As in the case of Egypt, then, a vibrant ministry brings down the wrath of the authorities.

An unusual element of the reform movement in the Russian Orthodox Church is its connection with resistance to the Church's hierarchy. In 1965 two Moscow priests, Gleb Yakunin and Nikolai Eshliman, wrote open letters fanning opposition to the Moscow Patriarchate, which responded by banning them from jobs in the Moscow region. These calls for reformation of the hierarchy had a great effect on the church, spurring others to try their hand in formulating and publicizing similar views. Solzhenitsyn was inspired by the two priests and determined to emulate them. Seven years later he wrote his own open letter to Patriarch Pimen, a blistering one in which he took the position that the church cannot be saved by telling lies. This "Lenten Letter" affirmed that the church's victory comes in its sacrifices, and that no good could come from allowing atheists to rule the church. This was the first public notice that Solzhenitsyn was an Orthodox Christian.[17] Jane Ellis identifies in this and similar exchanges the central conflict in this debate over the nature of the church: it was "between those who believed that the church must be preserved as an institution and those who believed that the church was above all a metaphysical body."[18] If the former, then it must be physically preserved at almost any cost. If the latter, then its preservation would never be in doubt and its moral subversion would be the real danger.

Resolute clergy in restrictive settings can do much besides calling the hierarchy to task. Effective leaders learn how to work in the gray areas between what is allowed and what is not. In the Soviet Union it has been permitted to offer personal spiritual advice to young people but not to instruct them. It would take the wisdom of a Solomon to tell where one leaves off and the other begins, and effective spiritual workers have not been inclined to ask CRA officers to give them the appropriate definitions.

A striking example of this kind of initiative was the case of Fr. Dimitri Dudko. Ordained in 1960, after a period of preparation that included eight years in a labor camp, Dudko's ministry in Moscow in the late 1960s was characterized by realistic interpretations of certain features of everyday Soviet life that everyone knew about but nobody mentioned. Hearers were electrified, for example, when he openly mentioned the presence of informers in the church. In December 1973 he began question and answer sessions after the Saturday evening liturgy in which he dealt with the problems that ordinary people had about Christian faith. One observer tried to account for his popularity: "Father Dimitri's listeners were won over by his sincerity, simplicity and enormous conviction; chiefly by his sincerity. Never, nowhere was there a single false note. All his answers to questions were direct, clear and precise. . . ." And pointed. Here is part of his answer to a question about the cowardice of the hierarchy:

> You see the inadequacies of today's clergy and point to the Patriarch himself, but are you aware that you're looking at things too superficially? Who has fewer civil rights than the Patriarch? They say he's surrounded by thousands of informers. He so much as sighs and it's heard in every government department. Everything he does against his conscience he does under pressure and, of course, out of weakness, like any man. But you don't want to be compassionate. You sit in the judge's seat and pronounce sentence.

Dudko was finally transferred to another parish where it was thought he could do less harm and was later silenced by arrest and imprisonment.[19] But his example shows the possibilities for effective ministry even in the harsh Moscow environment.

   If the clergy do not fulfill their obligations, that does not mean all is lost. Even in sacerdotal churches the laity can and often do stand in the breach that the formal leadership leaves vacant. One Russian Orthodox patriarch privately stated that the clergy was in such bad shape that only the laity could salvage the church.[20] On the same theme, Ogorodnikov claimed that the growth of religious awareness after World War II— especially after the clamp-down on the seminar movement of the 1970s—not only occurred without the officials of the church but in spite of them.

> It is a painful truth that it has fallen to a relatively small number of lay activists to attempt to advance the cause of renewal of church life and greater religious liberty. The hierarchy and a largely timid clergy make no such demands. . . . Thus changes in religious life are coming not from the top, but from the grass roots.[21]

The booming Vietnamese church after 1975 also owed much to its vigorous lay movement which responded strongly during the difficulties caused by the imprisonment of pastors and the refusal to allow the training or ordination of new ones.[22]

STRATEGIC CONSIDERATIONS FOR THE RESISTANCE OF THE CHURCH

Christians hoping to deal effectively with the threats arrayed against them must first have a clear understanding of what it is they face. Tactical or prudential moves will avail nothing unless they are devised in accordance with a right conception of the source of the threat. Persecutions are not fortuitous events, brought about by accidents or by the "luck of the draw," however much they may give that appearance. Rather they come almost naturally as a result of the omnipresent injustices of the world combined with the church's own peculiar being. The nature of the church and its beliefs make it inevitable that unjust institutions strike at it. For it stands as a refutation of the false ideologies that inevitably power those institutions. Economic determinism, statism, utopianism, theoretical lawlessness (or antinomianism), national or racial supremacy, and many more ideologies are naturally hostile to the transcendent faith that Christians believe judges human action on the basis of absolute standards—including the actions of the ideologues.

The practical lesson from all this is that the first responsibility of the church is to be faithful to its own calling. Without that, the striving for "survival," or the making of brilliant plans to circumvent the restrictions placed upon it, will serve only to distract it from its true purpose. Ending a conversation with a Soviet pastor who had just emigrated to the West a few days earlier, I asked him what westerners could learn from his experience should they fall under the same kind of persecution. Instead of passing on practical tips, he said only, "Hold to the teachings of the Bible without fail."[23] In his simple way, he hit upon the very thing that the persecutors fear the most. That is why the Council on Religious Affairs is known to seek candidates for the hierarchy who have moral defects.[24] Little acts of faithlessness are harbingers of bigger ones to come.

Hidden defects in character show up when people come under pressure. Richard Wurmbrand met numerous Romanian clergymen who admitted to him privately that they were informants of the secret police. At his question they said that as much as they despised this activity they were not going to renounce it. The reason they gave was not fear for themselves, but rather that if they refused to cooperate, the church would be closed.[25] But is a church that is kept open at that kind of price of more use to the Kingdom of God than one that is closed down and meets in secret?

Counseling the church to be faithful in order to withstand persecution can be a Catch-22 piece of advice—something like telling a job seeker to gain experience before applying for a job. One of the dangers to a church under persecution is that it is cut off from the kind of influence it needs to keep itself faithful, and is therefore endangered by internal weakness and heresy. In China there is a cult which says that God only answers prayers uttered while standing on one's head. This came from the experience of a man who fell into a well headfirst and became stuck in that position. No sooner had he prayed than he felt a rope looped around his feet and he was hauled to the surface. There is another cult that says that only those hearing the audible voice of God can be saved, an inference from Paul's experience on the road to Damascus. Part of this comes from the background of superstition and shamanism in the rural reaches of back-country China, but it probably owes its existence more to the fact that these Christians are cut off from sound teaching. Another factor is that Qigong, an occult religion, is undergoing revival—sponsored by the government since 1986—at the same time as the revival in the church. Ron MacMillan interviewed twelve pastors in rural China in June 1990, and eleven of them said heresy was the major problem facing the Chinese church. The spread of occultism is abetted by religious visitors from the West who specialize in schismatic and heretical religious teaching but receive a hearing from Chinese churches that are suffering from isolation and lack discernment.[26]

Part of getting back to the basics of the faith includes repenting of sins, and this is true of churches as well as individuals. Istvan Tokes, a theologian in the Reformed Church of Romania, speaks of the extra-legal polity of that church during the 1980s when he was dismissed from his academic and ecclesiastical posts because he criticized the church's submission to the state. He says the way to restore the church from its control by "brutal arbitrary" leaders is to repent and by doing so restore the church to its proper purity.[27] Gleb Yakunin, diagnosing the problems of the Russian Orthodox Church, pointed out that the Church had never repented of its enthusiastic praise for Stalin, not even when Khrushchev's destalinization campaign offered the ideal opportunity.[28]

As in the case of all social, political and religious movements, the intellectuals have a special role to play in the maintenance of the church's faithfulness. Even the ideology that disparages ideas as the cause of societal change in favor of social and economic forces— Marxism-Leninism—was led by intellectuals. Ideas thus can be used for both good and ill. The expansion of Christian movements from the first century, indeed going back to the Hebrew prophets, was also led by people who worked primarily with ideas. In our own day the Christian seminar movement in the seventies and eighties made an incalculable difference in the Soviet Union. Robert Conquest's recent examination of the role of ideas in the collapse of the communist ideal concludes that it was "largely through the efforts of a not very large number of free pens and typewriters that the imposing structure of falsification was eaten away from inside until nothing was left but a hollow shell."[29] The opportunity for influence also introduces a special temptation for the potential leaders of such movements. They have often found it easy to be sidetracked, even bought off, by prestigious, psychologically rewarding, and financially lucrative alternatives to resistance.

But resistance has its own rewards, none of which are obvious to those who are blind to the spiritual side of life. Many of those who participated in the seminar movement in the Soviet Union supported themselves as night watchmen or similar menial jobs, forgoing alternatives in the bureaucracy, research institutes, or the like. Ogorodnikov, as a young official in the Komsomol, could look forward to a normal progression of advancement through the Communist Party organization and a successful career, but instead chose a life that led to eight years of freezing and starving in punishment cells. There are formidable temptations involved in that kind of choice, and there is no end to the rationalizations available to anyone whose sense of honesty is less than compelling. As a class, intellectuals have never exhibited an impressive degree of courage, and the weaknesses of the breed present great disadvantages to a resistance that is necessarily dependent on the power of ideas. The tyrannies, of course, recognize the enormous potential that ideas have to change the relative power of contending forces. So they proscribe theological education entirely or else strictly limit the number of students. And they slip their own candidates in along with those the church desires to educate. In most of these countries known Christians are eliminated from consideration for entry into sensitive fields or else not permitted any kind of higher education. And such publications as the church is permitted to distribute are carefully vetted for dangerous material— i.e., that which would inform Christians about the real nature of their faith and their church. In that way church literature becomes another outlet for official state propaganda.

THE INNER LIFE

Nobody is exempt from constant spiritual struggle, but there are special stresses under conditions of persecution that make the problem acute. Where the dominant ideologies power an aggressive government-promoted atheism or a hostile dominant religion, Christians are bombarded by constant propaganda asserting their inferiority. It would be too much to expect that the believers themselves would be unaffected after having this drummed into them their whole lives. M. P. Kulakov, president of the Seventh-Day Adventists of the U.S.S.R., tells of the effect of not being accepted as normal people, of spending time in prisons and labor camps for one's faith. "These circumstances, under which my family and fellow believers grew up, promoted an inferiority complex."[30]

Persecution does odd things to the psyche. We can sometimes see great courage and inexplicable timidity in the same person. One man who had just come out of the Soviet Union described for me the bold evangelistic tactics his church had been using, despite their illegality and the harsh punishments to which they would be subjected if caught. In the midst of our conversation I asked him whether the KGB officers seemed to be only going through the motions of doing their jobs or whether they seemed to act out of sincere convictions about the ideology. Abruptly he ended that part of the conversation, saying he still had two children in the Soviet Union. I didn't know his name, and I don't see how I could have done him any harm even if I had wanted to, but that wasn't the way he saw it.[31]

Special temptations as well as psychological battering await the believer under repressive regimes. One Russian Orthodox priest tells how when he was newly ordained a representative of the local party organization invited him to renounce his faith. He had tempting offers dangled before him, including the chance for advanced academic study and a good appointment. Whatever form the inducements take, the main thing is that they'll make you somebody in the society. Instead of being part of a despised minority under artificial disabilities, you become respected and important. When he turned the party man down the church rallied to his support. He says this is typical of what happened. He knows only two or three priests who succumbed to this temptation. When the priests refused to give in they found the church people rallying behind them, with renewed life and interest in the church.[32]

Of course, there is a lot of ambiguous ground between being a turncoat on the one hand and a lion on the other. When the quality of faith is weak or uninformed, the church is vulnerable out of proportion to the severity of the pressure arrayed against it. The hammering of Shinto nationalism against the church in Japan was as successful as it was because the Christians there were theologically weak and unable to resist syncretism. The pantheism of the surrounding religion crept into their thinking. Few resisted the patriotic requirement of bowing to the shrines in time of national danger. They had little understanding of the Lordship of Christ over all human authorities, and thus were not prepared to resist the claims of state absolutism.[33]

The strengthening of individual faith runs counter to what is probably the most important part of the strategy of the oppressors. As we have seen, they can control the church structure much more easily than they can the motivations of the people; yet the individual is the ultimate target of the whole propaganda apparatus. George Orwell captured this perfectly in *1984* when he had the Party spokesman tell Winston Smith that the Party doesn't just aim to eliminate its enemies; it intends to change them. The strategy of the believers must be directed toward frustrating the design of enormous state resources intended to make them not only subservient but also uncritical. One pastor reports that in the Soviet Union, Baptists train their children by gathering together in the evening for conversation. They talk and pray together about the problems of living in school, community and workplace. Family devotions are utterly essential. By the time the children begin school they are committed to the faith and ready to stand up under adversity.[34]

In other places too, the psychological and spiritual dangers are more pervasive than the physical. An Indonesian leader warns of the danger of a defeatist spirit in the church in an Islamic environment. The constant pressure makes the church pessimistic about its prospects and then defensive. People turn inward, become preoccupied with their own safety, passive and self-pitying. Paradoxically they may become confrontational and antagonistic toward Muslims, or take on a western orientation and show hostility toward their own national institutions. This is in sharp contrast to the joy one sees in New Testament accounts of the church, a church which also suffered severe persecution. This source believes that the remarkable acceptance of the gospel in Indonesia is due partly to the involvement of believers in all aspects of the society; they have been leaders in commerce, agriculture, politics, education, journalism and the military. But all that can be swept away by inner attitudes of defeat.[35]

MAINTAINING THE UNITY OF THE CHURCH

The strategy for maintaining the unity of the church is something like a mirror image of the state's strategies for promoting hostilities and discord—the *agents provocateurs* planted within the church, the divisive policies such as Khrushchev's successful effort to split the Baptists with the Letter of Instruction, and similar actions detailed in preceding chapters. If all the Christians had to worry about were the persecutors' activities, the problem would be much less serious than it actually is. But even if the authorities let the church alone, there would be plenty of divisiveness to dull the Christian witness; disunity in an environment of persecution accentuates the disabilities that would be there anyway. Mutual hostilities between Christian communions are an offense to the gospel in any circumstance, but in the face of persecution they are especially foolish.

One reason for these hostilities is that, like other organizations, churches—whatever else they may be—are bureaucratic and political structures, and therefore operate on the basis of interests as well as responsibilities. This is quite apart from normal disagreements about doctrine and church polity. "What's in it for us?," suitably disguised under pious obfuscations, often substitutes for "How can we serve?" The notorious complicity of the Russian Orthodox Church with Stalin's eradication of the Ukrainian Orthodox and Uniate Catholic Churches is a prime example of this. Nearly forty years after Stalin's death, the Orthodox Church is still loath to give up its windfall in power and property. In this kind of struggle lay groups, not perceiving themselves as having the same vested interests, are way ahead of the hierarchies in demanding that justice be done. Unofficial Russian

Orthodox groups, for example, are demanding that their church satisfy the just demands of the dispossessed churches.[36]

When the evangelical churches and ministries were banned by the Amin government in Uganda, they initially received no defense from the Roman Catholic and Anglican churches which, rather than showing the unity of the Body of Christ, quietly took satisfaction at this turn of events. Being concerned about "sheep-stealing," they were able to continue as they had been without reevaluating the spiritual state and effectiveness of their ministries.[37] Paradoxically, the small persecuted sects went through the revivifying fires of persecution while the temporarily favored groups continued in their stagnation.

In Islamic countries mutual suspicions cripple the tiny Christian community. Someone will denounce another convert because he fears the presence of government spies, and the unity is broken. In some parts of Turkey only foreign Christian workers are trusted by everyone.[38] Anecdotes abound showing the same mutual suspicions within the church in Bulgaria, where historical factors exacerbate the natural divisiveness of the situation. And in Egypt the religious tensions normally present when Christians live in the midst of an Islamic populace are heightened by economic and social interests which affect not only the hostilities between religions but also the competing interests within the Christian community—even within the same church group.[39]

When a stagnant and unrepentant church leadership refuses to lead or even be moved by a rising spirit of reform, the result can be an open breach in the church. In late 1989, six priests at a conference organized by Gleb Yakunin announced that they were withdrawing from the Moscow Patriarchate and joining the Russian Orthodox Church Outside of Russia, the headquarters of which is in New York. This church had been organized shortly after the Revolution by bishops fleeing from their homeland.[40] Should this movement of schism continue, it will make it all the more difficult to reform the Russian Orthodox Church.

This is one of many areas in which the profoundest of theological principles yields the most concrete practical effects. The prayer of Jesus that His disciples attain to perfect unity (John 17:22f.) finds its echo in the apostles' letters where we read of the importance of "harmony with one another" (Romans 15:5), "unity of the spirit in the bond of peace" (Ephesians 4:3), "perfect harmony" (Colossians 3:14). Where this is lacking it is inevitable that the response to persecution will be blunted and the persecutors' cause aided. At the Islamic onslaught into eastern Europe many centuries ago, for example, the non-Orthodox churches actually welcomed the invaders, whose real nature they did not understand, because they had suffered such serious disabilities from the Orthodox who acted against them through the arm of the state.[41]

The disunity can reach a ludicrous stage in which the weaker party of contending church groups appeals to the erstwhile persecutors for justice! This happened when in 1989 Ukrainian Catholics went on a hunger strike to protest the continuing possession by Russian Orthodox congregations of their buildings that had earlier been seized under the Stalinist oppression. They sent a delegation to the head of the Council of the Supreme Soviet to complain of "heavy" persecution by the Russian Orthodox Church and ask for redress, only to be sent back to the Ukrainian authorities for help. Yuri Khristoradnov, the responsible government official, added that the Russian Orthodox Church was the roadblock to having the Ukrainian Catholics recognized.[42]

Anwar Sadat evidently timed his move against the Egyptian Coptic church as he did because he was able to gain the support of a rival of Shenouda III, Bishop Samuel, whose patriarchal ambitions were dashed by Shenouda's elevation. After Shenouda's arrest, Samuel traveled abroad and convinced people that the whole affair was a personal dispute between Sadat and Shenouda, thus undercutting the call for justice that could have helped the church. He did not act alone in undercutting Shenouda but served as leader of a cabal within the church that did the government's bidding in an effort to gain personal power.[43]

As the pressure against the Egyptian Christians currently mounts, a Roman Catholic priest says that the main danger to Christianity there does not come from the government or the Muslim resurgence, but from the disunity and lack of vision in the churches. The different denominations do little to cooperate with each other, and there is no plan for the future to do something about this. The president of the Protestant churches in Egypt, Samuel Habib (often called the "Protestant Pope"), is implacably hostile to Shenouda and also has close ties with government officials.[44]

One result of the hammering effect of persecution is the split of the church into two segments. This can be overt, as in the case of the Chinese house churches vs. the Three-Self movement and the registered and unregistered Baptists in the Soviet Union; or it can be de facto, as in the Russian Orthodox Church. There the hierarchy is largely discredited among sincere informed believers, both inside the country and outside, but supported by the regime and external collaborationist forces, such as the World Council of Churches. Meanwhile the state's pressure continues on the dissident groups who refuse to collaborate with the persecutors; they are generally supported by small bodies on the outside, mostly either Roman Catholic or evangelical. The irony in this is that the state's successes in capturing the official church for its own purposes spawns an internal church opposition both to the state and its ecclesiastical minions.

When the churches exhibit the repentance that their theology demands of them, it is always possible to set things aright and make restitution for past failures. Romanian Baptist pastor Doru Popa reports that in Arad two Romanian Orthodox priests voluntarily turned their churches over to the dispossessed Uniate church as soon as they could find alternate meeting sites for their own congregations. He endorses the contention of Reformed pastor Laszlo Tokes that church unity is crucial to restoring a sense of amity to the estranged Hungarian and Romanian peoples in the country if peace and stability are to be preserved.[45]

There are also institutional ways in which to foster unity among the churches. In 1985 Roman Catholics and mainline Protestant and evangelical groups formed the Christian Federation of Malaysia as a response to the pressures from the dominant Muslims. It has had some influence even though the Christians in the country make up only 7 percent of the population. What is more, the Federation is a member of the Malaysian Consultative Council for Buddhism, Christianity, Hinduism and Sikhism.[46] This makes it less likely that the government-Muslim combination can play off one against the other as has happened in, say, the U.S.S.R. In the late 1970s a similar organization, the Christian Council for Cooperation of Churches, was formed in Ethiopia as a response to the persecution. Here too the Roman Catholics were included, which is not common in Africa.[47]

In Uganda Idi Amin tried to get the churches to split. He accused the Anglicans of plotting to overthrow him, in an attempt to isolate them and curry favor with others, particularly the Roman Catholic Church. In this he failed, and under the persecution the Roman Catholic, Protestant and Orthodox churches attained a high degree of consultation, overcoming the previous hostility and apathy. This success came even though the Joint Catholic Protestant Council had been limited in effectiveness. The threat to them all evidently made the difference.[48]

In Israel, Jewish and Arab believers are beginning to meet together and establish fraternal relationships under the most difficult circumstances. The Arab Christians are under the threat of attack by radical, militant Arabs; messianic Jews are at risk of possible misunderstanding by the government and charges of disloyalty. This forging of unity is not yet a big movement, but an essential beginning.[49]

Isolation is the preferred method for totalitarian states in dealing with potential dissident groups, and that is why they favor policies of complete individualism, doing away with intermediate institutions that stand between the individual and the state.[50] The Chinese Communist Party, giving advice to its Cuban counterpart, put it this way: "We know full well that when the practice of religion becomes no more than an individual responsibility, it is slowly forgotten."[51]

The mass exodus of German Christians from the Soviet Union raises another thorny issue that is part of the matter of unity. Can it be said that unity has been attained when some people leave a difficult situation and their fellow believers behind and emigrate to where life is easier? This is also an issue in many Muslim nations from which large numbers of Christians emigrate, often for economic reasons. It is unseemly for someone writing a book where freedom and prosperity are taken for granted to lecture to such people, but this is at least something for believers in areas of persecution to face together frankly.

THE PERSECUTED CHURCH AND ITS SOCIETY: WHAT RELATIONSHIP?

The subject we deal with in this section is of particular interest in areas of persecution, but its importance and controversial nature are of much broader relevance. Are the church's legitimate interests purely spiritual, or do they have an earthly dimension that brings Christians legitimately into such supposedly "secular" spheres as economics, art, education and so on? And most important for the kinds of regimes that persecute, does *and so on* include politics? On questions like this we are interested not just in what may not be done (that is, matters of morality and government restrictions), but what *should* be done.

This is an issue on which there is much disagreement among

Christians, and it seems as if totalitarian oppressors may also be confused regarding their strategy. The Soviet Council on Religious Affairs concluded that its best interests lay in coercing the churches away from their spiritual agenda into the materialism of the official ideology.[52] This conclusion evidently was based on the assumption that the authorities would be able to manipulate the church so that it became simply a mouthpiece for the regime in areas in which the state had a strong interest.

But it's possible that the desire to neutralize the church could more profitably be pursued by capitalizing on the church's tendency to neutralize itself, which it does by declaring itself to be irrelevant to the concerns of the society—and the Party. If the church believes itself to be solely otherworldly why should the state not encourage that belief by insisting on the spirituality of the church's mission? This course of action would weaken not only materialism but also concerns about the material world. It would increase the plausibility of the hierarchy's abstention from societal issues, and that in turn could only further the regime's efforts to increase the totality of its control. This is the strategy that has been pursued with considerable success by the program of American humanists, as we saw in an earlier chapter, one that has led to a "naked public square." It's hard to imagine a program more suited to the totalitarian state, and it would have the further advantage of bringing applause rather than condemnation in the free countries. Conversely, a church that intended to frustrate this intention of the state to consign it to irrelevance could emphasize certain Biblical themes that all too often are ignored. The command of God to Adam was to "have dominion" over everything on earth (Genesis 1:28), which suggests that the church's mandate is much broader than the narrow "spiritual" interpretation often given. Writing to the exiles from Judea, taken captive to Babylon, Jeremiah told them to work for the improvement of that society: "seek the welfare of the city. . . ." He also said that the prophets who taught otherwise—spiritualizers, we might call them—were false prophets (Jeremiah 29:4-9).

Normally persecution takes place in a repressive society in which there is no redress for the injustice. How can such a society be reformed? One Indian Christian who has considerable personal acquaintance with the persecution of a Christian minority in his country says that preaching is often the path to reform, citing the prophetic literature. He argues that the charge to Jeremiah was just such a mission. In the midst of injustice the prophet was to proclaim the word of the Lord and so bring the society to repentance (Jeremiah 1:10).[53] But that requires a broader understanding of the church's mission than many Christians have.

One protest letter to the Patriarch argues that eliminating the legal disabilities of restrictive legislation will benefit the Soviet state as well as the society "because it will liquidate the soil in which anti-Soviet attitudes sprout and will attract millions of Soviet patriots to the side of a harmonised Soviet State." The letter, however, ties this eventuality to "the thousand-year-old moral roots of Russia." But if such morality indeed came to be dominant, the institutionalized immorality of the Soviet state would not be tolerated for long. In fact, that is one of the reasons for the present delegitimation of the regime in the minds of so many of its citizens.

In the celebrated 1988 interview of CRA chief Konstantin Kharchev—which reportedly cost Kharchev his job—both the bureaucrat and his interviewer speak of the contributions religion makes to culture, and why religious intolerance impoverishes the whole culture.[54] This is true as far as it goes, but in a way it reveals less insight than Stalin had shown because it does not recognize the inescapable political ramifications when a people places its loyalty above the state. Such loyalty means that even the terror of death threats are not ultimate because people have the conviction that there is something beyond death. It makes the state a secondary authority, precisely what totalitarianism cannot abide. Thus a renewed and invigorated Christian presence will do wonderful things for the society, but nothing at all for the totalitarian state; indeed, just the opposite.

When Christians fail to recognize their responsibilities for cultural transformation, this is not a function only of theology, but also of their concrete circumstances. One effect of persecution is to force its victims into a tight little knot, closed not only to hostile and dangerous elements of the culture but to every part of the culture. The theology of separatism reinforces the tendency that is natural to the situation. The separatist Baptists of the Soviet Union have had no interest in changing their society, apart from the direct effects of repression, being content to live as best they could in a hostile environment. Thus they posed the least threat to the regime. But they suffered constant harassment because of their refusal to register and thereby put themselves under the official Baptist organization, which they considered an arm of the atheistic state. This made their existence an offense to the totalitarian authority which insisted that all communal life be under the control of the regime. Still, their otherworldly theology, their lack of education, and their rejection of secular culture make them objectively very little threat: since even a democratic and just society which put no pressure on them would be out of the will of God, being "secular," there would be little motivation to bring about such a change. There might be analogously little threat to the regime from traditional Orthodox piety—highly spiritualized, monastic, habitually subject to whatever regime might be in power—had not the Marxist-Leninist ideology found the persistence of religion intolerable to its assumptions. But when after the death of Stalin and very much increasingly during the Brezhnev period small groups of young intellectuals began taking seriously the implications of Christian faith, the regime lost little time in subverting or destroying the movement.[55]

Such divergences account for the surprising attack of the respected Moscow archpriest, Vsevolod Shpiller, on Alexander Solzhenitsyn. His complaint was that Solzhenitsyn had made the church too worldly, derogating from its spiritual character. Mikhail Agursky, a recent convert to Orthodoxy, characterized this disagreement as "the conflict between two types of faith which have co-existed in Orthodoxy for a long time."[56] We can detect a similar disagreement in virtually every type of Christian church.

If Christian faith rightly has an interest in and responsibility to influence the course of the society, that still requires an evaluation of the legitimacy of each activity that is allegedly based on such a position. Activism cannot be its own justification. A recent statement by a spokesman for the Soviet Council on Religious Affairs, admittedly not the most objective of sources, echoes the concerns of many believers. He describes the hierarchy as being motivated more by fears for its influence and opulence than by any genuine concern about its responsibilities. He says the leadership is "ambitious," seeking principally "influence," that their fears are chiefly responsible for Kharchev's loss of his job as head of the CRA; they don't want their perquisites to be *perestroika*ed out of existence, and they can even be expected to press for the Russian Orthodox Church becoming the state religion as the Soviet state continues to unravel.[57] This may be an extreme case, but we have seen enough to want to exercise caution about temptations to the wrong kind of worldliness.

In contrast to both legitimate and illegitimate social concerns, there is widespread belief among Soviet evangelicals that they're living in the last days, and they think the emigration of Soviet Jews to Israel is part of this. Eschatology is a major concern of their Bible study.[58] This is true in many parts of the world. The Bible society representative in Kathmandu, Loknath Manaen, says that the evangelicals are unable to take part in the reconstruction of Nepalese society because of their isolation; they suffer from a psychology of persecution so that they have no vision. But there is a degree of comfort in their ghetto, Manaen continues, which is to some extent self-constructed. The changes coming in Nepal will create many opportunities, but the Protestants are not prepared to take advantage of them.[59]

The same was true in Hong Kong at the time of the Beijing massacre of 1989. One pastor spoke of the salutary effect of the shock, in that it enabled the Christians of Hong Kong to prepare for what is ahead of them in 1997 when the Beijing regime takes over. People are now becoming more serious about their faith. The disaster also revealed a serious weakness: "We lack a theological basis for dealing with political issues." But that is beginning to change.[60] Such examples suggest that social experience combines with theological perspective in bringing about a change of view. A recent doctoral dissertation reports that when the Soviets took over in East Germany at the end of World War II they treated the confessing church gently, acknowledging the part it played in opposing Naziism. They also wanted to avoid unnecessary hostility to the new order among the Germans. "In the process, the church accepted a non-political role and tacitly took her place on the fringe of society." That is why even though the German Democratic Republic constitution of 1949 did not prohibit the church from making statements on public policy, the church still remained silent on such issues.[61]

In some cases evangelical churches have recognized the danger of being marginalized and made irrelevant to the society. When immediately after the war in Vietnam, Ho Chi Minh told the Evangelical Church of Vietnam to form an Evangelical National Salvation Committee in common with other committees that were to be formed, Pastor Le Van Thai requested that the ECV not be required to do so. When Ho asked him why, he replied:

> Every church member belongs to his or her social or professional organization. Please let them keep their own place in those organizations such as youth, laborers, workers, the civil servants, the teachers for each of these organizations has its own National

Salvation Committee. If we form the Evangelical National
Salvation Committee we should pull back church members from
their own organization and should cause trouble and division.

Ho agreed to the proposal, which shows that sometimes the most hostile of regimes offer opportunities for negotiation.[62]

Some of our examples suggest that the most important changes do not come as a result of slow incremental movement—the evolutionary model—but as a result of sudden catastrophe. The aftermath of the 1989 Tienenman Square massacre in China finds the church there in a strong position in spite of the fact that the persecution has become more vigorous. There have been many conversions, and the Christians have become bolder. A house church leader in Xiamen put it this way: ". . . we Christians have become a curiosity . . . we are the only group in this society that still has hope for the future . . . everyone else lost hope on June 4, and they want to know why we are not depressed at the prospect of a less prosperous China." There has also been a deepening of faith by believers who had pinned too many of their hopes on the economic resurgence of China.[63]

As is so often the case, the increased effectiveness of the Christians has provoked greater vigilance by the authorities. A year after the massacre the Chinese leadership issued a document linking the events of eastern Europe with Christianity. It singles out Romania and says that Christians brought about the fall of the regime. It goes on to speak of foreign enemies in China as teachers, students, and businessmen whose real motive is the spread of Christianity.[64] The implication of all this is plain: The Chinese regime assumes that a vigorous church means trouble, even though the house churches that are its main concern have shown little or no interest in politics.

Economic prosperity is not normally a problem in societies that persecute, but other temptations are more common. Dissident religious movements are sometimes associated with nationalism. The continuing strength of the Roman Catholic Church in Poland and Lithuania, for example, and the Ukrainian Orthodox and Uniate (Roman Catholic) churches are bound up with feelings of national identity as opposed to Soviet imperial rule. Christians may wish to take advantage of such non-religious congruences, but they shouldn't mistake nationalist or other motives for Christian discipleship. When the communist persecution of the Polish church recedes further into the past, will the old Catholic repression of Protestants resume, fueled by the ancient conflation of "Polish" and "Catholic"? We are already hearing expressions of concern about this from Polish Protestants.

No examination of the relationship of the church to the society should ignore the opportunities for evangelism. These occur in the most unlikely places. One priest reports that some of the KGB officers assigned to the seminary as students when he was there were converted to Christ and resigned from the service.[65] In Egypt some Christians regard Islamic fundamentalism as an opportunity because it makes moderate Muslims more open to a consideration of alternatives, including Christian faith.[66] Alexander Ogorodnikov, as we have seen, reports how as a young Komsomol officer he turned toward the faith. Dostoyevsky, he said, "reached my heart."[67] There should be Christians around such people who are able to help them.

THE CHURCH STRIKES BACK: THE PRACTICE OF RESISTANCE

TACTICAL RESPONSES TO PERSECUTION

We turn now to a number of practical measures that have proven useful to the persecuted church in various places. This is far from a complete catalog, but no one has ever attempted a comprehensive survey of the church's experience under persecution. The present overview should be of help in focusing attention on fruitful areas for further investigation.

When we speak of practical considerations in the church's dealing with oppression we encounter a dilemma that many deal with by impaling themselves on one horn or the other. One must stick to principle and not compromise, it is said. Or else, one must not rigidly follow principles that may become outmoded, but rather seek ways to accommodate oneself to the actual situation. Both positions have been adopted with terrible results. The first has led to ineffectiveness and unnecessary suffering, and the second has led to a collaborationist church. There are ways in which one can be both faithful and effective, and the discipline by which we find them is called practical wisdom. One of the best ways to arrive at practical wisdom is to learn from what others have done. Thus much of this chapter examines the experiences of people who have dealt with oppression.

Malaysian Christians have been conscious of the balance required to navigate in these gray areas. They are willing to negotiate, but they also know how to be tough in a position of weakness. Daniel Ho, executive secretary of the National Evangelical Christian Fellowship of Malaysia, describes their approach in this way: "We try as much as possible not to adopt a confrontational attitude right away. We try to work through meetings and dialogues with them. . . . But if after taking all these steps we fail, then we say we have no choice but to challenge it."[1]

One lesson that emerges from the African experience is that it is possible to prepare for persecution. Christians in Ethiopia began doing this long before the Marxist-Leninist regime took over in 1974. Some even prayed for persecution as a means of purifying the church. In Uganda, on the other hand, there was little preparation for what was to come. There spiritual vitality in the 1960s led to many conversions and spiritual growth. But Ugandans, Daniel Kyanda says of his own countrymen, were unwilling or unable to recognize that people were being killed for their faith. In the generally deplorable human rights condition of the country Christians failed to see that the pattern of killings was heavily weighted among their number.[2] Kyanda has urged that Christians prepare diligently for the pressures that he believes inevitably descend on a faithful church and to do so by conforming to the principles of Christian discipleship. "There is no way you can put together a crash program once it comes. Before persecution occurs we have to practice truth in relationships and living honest lives."[3]

Leadership has proven to be an essential element in the way the churches respond to persecution. That was true throughout the whole period of the Muslim domination of Jewish and Christian communities, and nothing has happened recently to suggest that anything is different now. In her study of the *dhimmi*, Bat Ye'or found that whole congregations might allow themselves to be forced to convert to Islam if the leadership was at all shaky on the issue.[4]

The organizational context in which the leadership is offered also is a matter of some importance. Centralized systems are more vulnerable to manipulation by oppressors who can focus their attention on subverting the leadership. When liturgical worship is the heart of a church's activities the congregation is dependent upon a church building, which is easy for the authorities to control. A congregational polity is the most able to deal with the control issue, which partially accounts for the vitality of many of the Baptist churches in the Soviet Union. Still, the members of the hierarchical churches, given the right leadership, can break out of their limitations and accomplish a great deal. One of the reasons the Soviet authorities had so much difficulty coping with the Moscow Seminar movement at first was that it had no organization or officers. When the authorities catch on, it may be advisable to decentralize even further. A member of the 37 Seminar in Leningrad told me that they deliberately broke the seminar up for security reasons and replaced it with a variety of groups meeting together on various concerns: e.g., literature, politics, preservation of historical monuments. They met informally, and the ties between the groups are based only on friendships, not on organizational accountability.[5]

Where the repression is so complete that it prevents the church from meeting openly at all, there is no alternative to small groups except a complete atomization of believers, which would mean there is no church at all. In one North African country, people meet in small groups in houses or apartments. They vary the meeting place from week to week. Sometimes a group of three or four families will meet in the woods.[6] House churches have also been vital in sub-Saharan Africa.

The Baptists in the U.S.S.R. have used the small fellowship model of the church for defensive purposes, something to which the congregational model is well adapted. If someone doesn't come to a meeting they find out why. They ask a prospective member to pray with them, and they've found that police informants normally are unable or unwilling to do so. If someone is turned by the police, that fact is revealed in close relationships. They watch closely for personal weaknesses, because the police make use of them; if a man commits adultery and the police find out, they use it for blackmail. These people stress being strong, not giving to personal weaknesses that jeopardize the whole community.[7]

A universal problem of the churches under persecution is the difficulty of training people to do the work of the ministry. But determination and courage have done wonders in some places. We have one report from China which tells of forty or fifty people living together for more than a month in courtyards or even caves. The "theological students" rise at 5 A.M., pray until 8, and then have four classes, each lasting three hours until 10 P.M. One time when they lit a gas lamp in a cave a dozen students were nearly asphyxiated because of poor ventilation. Sometimes these classes come under surveillance and participants end up in prison. The organizers try to maintain secrecy, but it's difficult to do so when you have several dozen people together for weeks at a time.[8]

Some churches have found an effective outlet for service in forming alliances with non-Christian movements where there are common interests. In the Soviet Union two such movements are those favoring democracy and nationalism. The rising civil rights movement has attracted many people with no obvious religious commitment, and there are opportunities for Christians to work fruitfully with them.[9] Of course, there is always the danger of the church losing its distinctive message and embracing (or be seen as embracing) positions that are antithetical to its own traditions. That is always going to be a potential source of danger when one leaves the extreme of maximum separation from the culture.

One of the most important tactics of the persecuted churches has been their development of ties to the free countries. In that respect, the Helsinki agreement was a big help to Christians in the U.S.S.R. One pastor reports that it had the effect of legitimizing the teaching of religion to children in the home, even though such activity remained formally illegal. Christians who disputed with officials about such things always referred back to Helsinki to legitimate their practices. The same informant says that when the churches in his area (the Ukraine) had pressure put on them in the late 1970s, they would take advantage of the fact that the President of the United States was a Baptist. They would say, "If this keeps up we'll tell our brother Jimmy Carter what is happening," and the officials would often withdraw in frustration.[10]

Appeals to international bodies are effective because many repressive regimes exhibit paranoidal tendencies when their reputation is at stake; lacking any real legitimacy, they try to gain through propaganda whatever they can of that scarce commodity. The regime's publicity at the time of Dmitri Dudko's recantation evidenced almost complete preoccupation with the way the West was reacting to his imprisonment. *Izvestiya* headlined, "The West Is Seeking Sensations." This was after Dudko had spent five months in prison in complete isolation and under constant interrogation.[11]

The hunger strike is effective for prisoners of conscience because when news of it reaches the West it galvanizes public opinion and therefore political pressure. Ogorodnikov puts it this way: "They can persecute only in the shadows." He went through hunger strikes for

689 days of his more than eight years in the labor camp, mostly for the right to have a Bible. He had it only six months before it was taken away. When I asked him why the regime cared whether or not he starved himself to death, he replied that such an event would be a disastrous propaganda blow for it, one to be prevented at any cost.[12] Prisoners known in the West are invariably force-fed when their lives are endangered during hunger strikes.

In 1976 the Christian Committee for the Defense of Believers' Rights in the U.S.S.R. was set up in close consultation with the Helsinki monitoring group in Moscow. Initially its membership was exclusively composed of Russian Orthodox people. The organizers said they wanted to atone for the past persecution of other churches by their own. The Committee produced eleven volumes of Russian and one of English text and addressed many letters to outside church leaders, including the Pope. It was able to get reports out quickly because its Moscow base allowed easy access to foreigners. The example of this group prompted similar committees in Lithuania and Romania. For the first three years the Committee had only six members, and no more than four at any one time. The Committee announced that if anyone was arrested there would be others ready to step in. By 1980 the three founders were gone, and the transmission of documents almost ceased.[13] There is no way to calculate with any precision the effectiveness of this marshalling of documentary evidence of persecution and its transmittal to the West, but it was almost certainly very great.

Christians under great pressure in Turkey have decided to take advantage of the country's attempts to gain full membership in the European Common Market. They are aware that the European parliament is demanding an improved human rights record as the price of entry. Thus they want to substitute foreign pressure for the failure of their constitutional rights to protect them: "Turkey cannot afford adverse reports concerning treatment of minorities," one church elder said.[14] Their leaders acknowledged that this approach would not work overnight, nor would it prevent arrests and harassment. But they expect that a legal framework for their protection eventually will come into being.[15]

The Malaysian Christians reacted to the repression by their government by highlighting the damage done to the reputation of the country elsewhere. "Our image is in tatters." There follows a description of articles in various Asian, European and American newspapers and magazines and extended quotations covering three pages.[16] This is a legitimate technique showing that the persecution harms not only the Christians but the whole country.

When Romanian pastor Peter Dugulescu began having a fruitful ministry, government officials regarded him as too dynamic and tried to push him out of town. In order to stay he formed an alliance with an organization in England that places obsolete medical equipment in poor countries. They offered an X-ray machine to the local hospital, but only on condition that Dugulescu remain on the scene in order to administer the gift. When the local medical people asked Dugulescu to handle the transaction, he replied that he couldn't because he was being ordered to leave town. The hospital staff went to the police to protest this action, and the upshot was that he stayed. The lesson is that you have to find out what makes the local situation tick—the pressure points, the desires and needs—and find ways to play on them, gaining the most leverage from foreign contacts.[17]

Persecuting regimes are more or less lawless, which is to say they put the will of officials above any written statute. But that does not mean the law is useless; such an assumption could make the situation worse than it has to be. Often people have been able to take advantage of even the meager protection offered by a lawless state. When the Apostle Paul was to be taken to Jerusalem for trial, possibly to be assassinated on the way, he took advantage of his legal rights by appealing to Caesar (Acts 25:10f.). In the Soviet Union the lawlessness was so blatant that it was very difficult for anyone to obtain a copy of the 1929 law that regulated religion. So believers didn't know their legal responsibilities and their rights. Mathematician Igor Shafarevich was able to get a copy of the law and also access to a secret volume called *Legislation on Religious Cults*, which was intended for use by officials. This provided information that was of practical use to Christians confronted with state oppression.[18]

When the political situation makes the law useless, international bodies may be able to provide redress. The Christian Association of Nigeria (CAN) plans to take the military government to the International Court of Justice in The Hague over the setting up a pro-Muslim pilgrim's commission; their contention is that the law is discriminatory. The Nigerian supreme court said it couldn't rule on the case because the legislation specified that no court in Nigeria could take jurisdiction over the law. The judge ruled that, contrary to the government's argument, the law is discriminatory, but because of the legislation he could not enforce the ruling. So the CAN is taking the case to the World Court.[19]

Josef Tson has said that if he had known the law that related to the confiscation of his library in the early 1970s he would have had it back almost immediately instead of having to wait until foreign pressure made the authorities return it. Earlier the law was meaningless as a means of securing rights; the regime was convinced of the superiority of Communism, and saw no need to worry about the opinion of outside countries. But by the time of the confiscation the law had become important because the failure of the system was evident, and so was the need for western economic help. The West had begun to condition everything it did on human rights, so when the U.S. told the Romanians to solve a particular human rights case or run the risk of losing Most Favored Nation trade status, the problem was solved. The urge for the appearance of legitimacy gave great leverage to governments and individuals in other countries.[20] This leverage finally proved to be intolerable, and a couple of years before his death Ceausescu renounced MFN status and the pressures that went along with it.

In Malaysia Christians have been released after appeal to the courts for relief from unconstitutional arrest and mistreatment.[21] Of course, this will not work when the authorities do not make a pretense of being lawful. The authorities may not even know the law, much less be inclined to follow it. In Turkey the general opinion even among police is that Christian witness is not legal, even though freedom of worship is guaranteed under the constitution.[22]

Totalitarian settings are among other things bureaucratic settings. This means, contrary to some stereotypes, that personal relationships, personality quirks, self-interest, and various private motivations often determine the decisions that are made. In one sticky situation, a pastor quoted Lenin to an officer of the CRA as saying that it's foolish to fight Christians on religious grounds. This relieved the pressure.[23]

Some are especially skilled at such activity—in the army people like this are called "guardhouse lawyers." One pastor in the Soviet Union read an article in *Science and Religion* (the official magazine of atheism) when on a trip to Kiev, and noticed a speech by the head of the CRA on the occasion of the fiftieth anniversary of the Soviet Revolution. The next day he was called in to the local CRA office and asked to hand over a list of the members of his church. He refused to do it. The officer became very angry and told him that he was the only pastor in the region who would not comply. He replied that if others wanted to break they law they could do so, but he would not do it. At the officer's look of amazement, he asked, "Have you read the latest *Science and Religion?* Your boss said in that magazine that the Soviet Union does not keep a list of believers in the country. Who do you think you are to ask me to disobey the law?" The officer got out his copy of the magazine but couldn't find the passage. So the pastor found it for him and explained that if he handed over the list they would both be breaking the law.

The same pastor baptized young people, which was a violation of the law, and the officials challenged him on it. But he replied by asking if baptism is a religious rite. At the affirmative answer he asked, "What does the law say about church and state? If anyone denies a believer the right to practice his religious beliefs he is in danger of breaking the law." The pastor also argued that a parent whose child he refused to baptize could sue him for refusing to exercise his responsibilities as a religious leader. This silenced the CRA man.[24]

Of course, there are few people with the combination of gifts to carry out that kind of tactic. But the fact that it's possible to be successful at so bold a method in a repressive society suggests that the range of activities that can be employed is wider than the timid would imagine.

PRACTICAL ADVICE

There are innumerable examples of practical wisdom that Christians have used in coping with persecution. Unfortunately this information, bought at the cost of much sacrifice and many mistakes, seldom gets transmitted to people in other parts of the world who could profit from it. This section collects some of those bits in order to suggest the kind of information that is available. But this cannot make up for the lack of a systematic collection of practical wisdom with a view toward disseminating it on a wider scale; this remains a task for the future.

Public ceremonies: In most countries of repression public religious expressions, such as evangelistic meetings, are forbidden outside of church buildings. But often ceremonies such as weddings and funerals can be held in outdoor facilities, like front yards and public parks, and Christians in eastern Europe and the Soviet Union became adept in preaching the gospel to bystanders. Some weddings in Romania are reported to have attracted as many as 3,500 onlookers. Surprisingly, believers in Vietnam learned about this practice and began doing the same thing; for them a birthday party turns into an evangelistic rally.[25]

Youth training: The strategy of the totalitarian regimes has been to allow what expressions of Christian faith the requirements of public relations dictate—for the old people—while strangling the passing on of the faith to the youth. An East German theologian called this strategy "toleration to the vanishing point."[26] The counter move entails instruction in the family, in illegal Sunday schools, and in activities that capture the interest of young people, such as youth bands and choirs.

Publishing: With all legal publishing under control of the state, Christian nurture is severely hampered by the lack of Bibles and other literature. In the Soviet Union unregistered Baptists set up an illegal publishing house several years after the split with the registered Baptists in 1961. Their leaders announced the existence of the Khristianin publishing house to the Soviet government in 1971, saying that it was intended solely to satisfy the dearth of Christian literature. They asked the authorities not to hinder the operation of this press or to regard it as illegal. The regime ignored these pleas, and there followed years of systematic search for and closing down of the presses, with numerous workers ending up in the labor camps.[27]

Mutual help: Selfishness is never a good Christian response, but in cases of persecution it is a disaster. We have numerous reports of Christians sharing food with each other in times of privation or caring for one another's children when parents are jailed.

Act, don't ask: This advice comes from a number of sources. Asking permission to do something will usually evoke a negative response, if only for the reason that officials need to cover themselves from criticism or censure. The motto in Turkey at the beginning of the twentieth century went like this: "Whatever is done is permitted; whatever is asked is forbidden."[28]

Place people in key positions: In 1977 Idi Amin banned twenty-seven Christian groups, excepting only the Anglican, Eastern Orthodox and Roman Catholic churches. In just a few days thousands of house churches came into being. One of the organizers, Ben Oluka, worked as a double agent in Amin's office and tipped off leaders before their church was to be raided. He even established one in his own house at the time he was supposed to be helping Amin stamp them out.[29]

Learn to use sympathetic officials: It's surprising that even in some of the most hostile situations, believers have found individuals here and there who are sympathetic enough to help them. This is in addition to the corrupt officials who abound in many countries and can be persuaded to take a message for some favor or other.

After his dismissal as head of the Council on Religious Affairs, Konstantin Kharchev spoke to a conference in London about the difficulties he had in taking over the helm of an organization whose main responsibilities had been to make it impossible for the church to function as it should. He said that as he studied the documents of the office he came to understand that the original theory of Marxism-Leninism was "distorted" after Lenin's time by Stalin, the party, and the bureaucracy. "With this new understanding came a crisis of conscience. How could I continue working?"[30] The answer to that question was that Gorbachev's *perestroika* program allowed him to continue working. Since this revelation could not have increased his disfavor with the current line of the Soviet regime, we may take it all with a grain of salt. And yet, if we are not willing to be naive let us also not be cynical. People in totalitarian regimes are created in the image of the God in whom they do not believe; they know the difference between right and wrong, no matter what they say. There is no reason to doubt that even hardened bureaucrats have human emotions and values and can be reached in some way.

Reuven Brenner, a Canadian economist who emigrated from a communist country, thinks such regimes are held together by fear on the part of the bureaucrats. They are frightened by the possibility that their actions will in the future be regarded as criminal and that retribution will be taken; this makes them resist a loosening that could presage the revolution that ends their power—and their protection. He thinks the best way to make change possible is to give these officials a stake in a new and just regime.[31] To put the same thing in theological perspective, we might say that we should forgive those who sin against us and let them know that we are not bent on revenge.

Not only are people different from each other, but so are regions. In both the Soviet Union and Vietnam the authorities dealing with Christians may be tougher on them in one place than in another.[32] Sometimes *far* tougher. In Siberia the Christians in the town of Barnaul were treated to horrifying repression, including murder, over a number of years, in a period when the Stalinist horrors were supposedly over.[33] It is worth studying carefully the people you have to deal with to see what they are really like. Dissident Anatoli

Krasnov-Levitin told of numerous occasions when fellow prisoners, guards and soldiers would speak to him about alternatives to the repression under which they all lived. His jailers would express disappointment at being forced to leave duty during the midst of a lively discussion, and some would secretly shake hands with him.[34]

From this, however, one should not infer that it's all right to take at face value every expression of sincere regard made by an officer. Apparently Dmitri Dudko's downfall came when his KGB interrogator was able to establish a personal relationship with him. Dudko referred to him as his brother. Jane Ellis comments on this:

> Many prisoners who have survived Soviet secret police interrogations, from Stalinist times to the present day, have testified that their only hope of maintaining their personal integrity was to remain obdurate to all suggestions, refusing to concede even the slightest degree to their interrogators. Once Dudko had made a small concession, the skilled KGB interrogator knew how to exploit it.[35]

Relationships with officials often become complex, and when people are able to negotiate the terrain with skill and understanding, much can be accomplished. Josef Tson tells of the time his church decided to expand its building. He went to see one of the top Romanian Party officials in the region, a former Baptist, and asked for permission to build a barn. The man asked Tson to tell him what he had in mind. Tson frankly told him his plans for expanding the church in such a way that from the outside it would look like a barn. When the official was convinced it would not look like a church he issued the necessary permit. Tson says the local official may be more sympathetic to the church than to the central authority, but you have to figure out a way to do what you want so that he will not get into trouble. "It all depends on the relationship you establish with the official."[36]

On occasion, it's possible to get something done by having a relationship not with the officer causing trouble but with a higher official. When one CRA man put extra pressure on an unregistered church, the people thought it was because he was trying to get promoted. This officer both filed complaints and conducted the required hearings himself, which was against regulations, and he levied heavy fines. The church was able to get this stopped because the officer's superior was having his car serviced by one of its members who complained to him about the illegal proceedings.[37] The Soviet Union is a place where things don't work right, and official channels are often bypassed to get them fixed. In such countries it pays to have skills and to learn how and where to use them to best effect.

Sometimes persecutors recognize that a lessening of hostility does not serve their purposes and therefore try to keep the tensions high. Baruch Maoz, a Christian pastor in Israel, reports that someone spoke to a local chief rabbi who was harassing the church and said to him, "Why don't you meet Mr. Maoz. He is rather a nice man." To which the rabbi replied, "That is precisely the problem." Maoz continues: "I think that they fight getting to know us because it's psychologically easier to fight a caricature, a non-entity, than someone that they actually shook hands with and smiled at."[38]

Christians under pressure can exploit differences between officials with whom they deal. In one Soviet factory there were disputes between the party organs and the factory managers. The former wanted to put pressure on the Christian workers in order to make themselves look good with higher party officials. But the Christians were the best workers, and the managers couldn't afford to get rid of them. So there was a standoff from which the Christians benefitted. Still, the party saw to it that bonuses earned by the Christians did not get paid.[39]

A former manager in the Soviet Union, one of the few evangelicals who was well educated and attained high positions, says that a part of practical wisdom is discerning the motivation of the officials. It's almost impossible to get any place with a CRA man if a KGB man is present and vice versa. If they're alone it may be possible to reason with them, and it may be possible to play one off against the other. They have a lot of discretion and within limits they can do as they please. It's necessary to figure out a way for them to satisfy the church's needs without damaging their careers.[40] Richard Wurmbrand says that even in the worst days of the Romanian regime there were secret believers in the Romanian government—including the secret police. And some who were not believers were secretly trying to help. The state newspapers knew of and complained about this.[41]

PREPARING FOR CHANGE

In at least one respect living under persecution is little different from any other way of life: people become accustomed to the *status quo* and are unprepared when it changes. One Soviet intellectual put it this way: "In many respects the church is more conservative than the state. Fear has conditioned them."[42] People thus described find it difficult to cope with changed tactics by the oppressors and especially difficult to conceive of the possibility that something they might do could bring about favorable change.

In addition to the changes wrought by the regime, Christians may have to face other changes that the regime is helpless to halt. With the accelerating breakup of the Soviet empire as this is being written, Christians in some parts of the country may be confronted with the breaking away and independence of several of the predominantly Muslim republics. At that time persecution could take a radically different form, such as to make them long for the gentler days of beatings and hard labor camps. The lesson from this is to be mentally alert and supple of mind, ready to change strategies as the situation changes and to begin planning for change before it actually arrives.

CONCLUSION

At the unofficial and much-harassed Human Rights Seminar in Moscow, held in December 1987, one participant said that if rights were guaranteed in accordance with the Helsinki accords that would not be sufficient to produce a just society. It would be a necessary condition but not a sufficient condition. Needed in addition would be a true revolution in thinking—in other words, a cultural revolution.[43] This is what the Christians should be striving for, something that many of them recognize, although doubtless it is only a small minority. Rights pertain to human beings as a result of their creation in the image of God. People who do not believe that (or cease believing it) lose contact with the transcendent and permanent. When that happens any guarantees about justice that may exist are based on subjective or pragmatic considerations and are therefore subject to nullification. Christian discipleship should be understood to include recognition of the relationship between Christian faith and justice. Otherwise, Christians are almost as likely as others to participate in the destruction of rights.

The revolution that took place in the communist world as the 1980s drew to a close had nothing to do with any sudden benevolence on the part of the rulers. Rather, the various disabilities that are integral to those repressive regimes, from their false ideology to their economic futility, robbed them of whatever legitimacy they could once claim. Their manifold failures and lack of public acceptance took away the self-confidence that was necessary to continue the repression. When the people saw that the rulers could no longer retaliate, they took over themselves. The power these politicians had from the first was not the power of guns or prisons, but the internal and external moral force that made people obey them—both those with guns and those facing the guns. It is the glory of the church that so many of its members were not cowed by the prospects of imprisonment or death, and whatever the failings of individuals, the strength and conviction of their roots and underpinnings were such that ultimately these sad travesties of governments did not prevail against them.

That great monument of cynicism, Stalin's reputed question about how many divisions the Pope possessed and its assumption that power comes only from the barrel of a gun, has its answer in the church that remains after the failure of the guns to destroy it. After great destruction of Christian property through Muslim rioting in Nigeria, with seventy-two churches leveled and two left standing in his town, a missionary said, "If Christians react . . . positively, if we move in compassion rather than retaliation . . . . then out of these ashes things are going to grow."[44] Such a statement underscores the fact that how the church does under persecution is a function not of its tactics, but of its faithfulness to its own teachings—which is to say to the commandments of its Lord. Forgiveness is not likely to be found as a normative principle in textbooks on political tactics, but a church that develops politicians without developing disciples is not going to do well, whether it's living under persecution or not.

Christians need to have a long view of time. The intense individualism, with its concomitant self-centeredness, of contemporary western culture is detrimental to the kind of mind-set which can stand up to persecution. This culture's high need for constant gratification works against the long time perspective that is part of Christian doctrine. The most fruitful kinds of activities, from growing a tree to raising a child, can take the greatest amount of time. But for one who places high value on the gratification of desires, time is the main commodity not to be sacrificed for other ends.[45] The passing years take on an entirely different meaning if we recognize that their significance comes from conforming their use to the will of God, who has a right to them, and to the community of which we are a part. That recognition makes it acceptable to have fewer and harder years, because they are better years. Better in the sense that the years are used for their true purpose.

This is especially important to keep in mind when Christians are persecuted because the time frame is often long, longer than just a life-time. The Israelites spent forty years in the wilderness, and the generation that began that trek was all gone by the time the nation marched into Canaan. And even that was only a tithe of the centuries of exile in Egypt, awaiting the call to the Promised Land. The Soviet Christians who remained faithful but suffered and died in the 1920s, 1930s, and 1940s perhaps never even imagined the results of their steadfastness. But in the late 1980s their children and grandchildren reaped the fruit of their faithfulness.

In the Biblical economy people don't live for seventy years only, whatever the worldview of our culture says. They live forever, and thus the true time frame of our actions in the here and now is eternity. There is no way to come out of persecution well without this under-standing. Otherwise one becomes a pragmatist and rationalizes the worst sorts of misbehavior in order to "preserve" the church. What that in fact preserves is not worth preserving, an ersatz church. It is like refusing to plant a tree unless it produces shade within three years. That is a time scale that is not appropriate to the subject. One never gets shade with that idea. And one never gets a faithful church and the blessings that come from it without a time scale in keeping with its nature.

RESISTANCE AND ACCOMMODATION

Some years ago Canon Trevor Beeson of the Church of England published a study of the churches of eastern Europe which he entitled *Discretion and Valour*. Since then it has been convenient to regard the two opposite reactions to persecution in these terms. But this conception is misleading, even apart from the limitations imposed by its use of a euphemism. Elements of the church have exhibited lamentable weakness, even cowardice, that should not be prettified by a term like "discretion." The bipolar division also does not adequately convey the ambiguities and legitimate difference of opinion that operate in this sphere, as in so many others. Both bravery and cowardice there are in the persecuted church, and in abundance, but there is much more besides.

In the recent literature on the subject there have been few defenses of subservience to the persecutors. Normally such defenses are given on the grounds that only such a stance would allow the survival of the church.[1] The advantages of compliance can be substantial. In some cases where one church is relatively pliable and another more resistant the regime will favor the former at the expense of the latter. In Mozambique, for example, the persecution was strongest in the predominantly Roman Catholic south and relatively mild in the Anglican north. The Marxist-Leninist Frelimo regime perceived that the Anglican churches were more favorable to the revolution and allowed them relative freedom, while concluding the opposite of the

Catholic Church. Almost all the Catholic churches were forcibly closed.[2]

In addition to collaboration there is a position that seems closer to Canon Beeson's term *discretion*. Several African church leaders have expressed respectful disagreement with Ethiopian Christians who went to their deaths rather than shout slogans supporting the Marxist-Leninist regime. They do not believe that such compliance amounts to a denial of their faith.[3] Although there are few defenses of an accommodative stance toward persecuting authorities, outside of conciliar Protestantism, there are many attacks on it and not all from people safely ensconced in free countries. These include the aforementioned open letter of Solzhenitsyn.

If the authorities are willing to settle for something less than the complete eradication of the church, which is usually the case, then there is a tacit tradeoff in the church's response to the pressures. The church will be allowed to persist in relative peace if its image, its teachings and its activities do not conflict radically with the regime's demands. The *Journal of the Moscow Patriarchate*, for example, has not been allowed to convey to its readers that the church has any part to play in society; the party holds the monopoly on such a role.[4] This highlights the cost of submission: it is not a question only of compromising in order to settle for, say, 50 percent of the church's true mission. Rather, the church allows the regime to redefine radically what it is and what it stands for. This raises the question of the extent to which it can be considered a church at all. The famous Yakunin Report viewed the hierarchy as having become so flabby in its acquiescence that it was unable to give any form to the inchoate renewal of Christian faith in the Soviet Union.

Even the simple act of registration may not be the mere formality that many westerners think it is. It can carry with it not only the implied necessity of the permission of the state for the church to exist—which is serious enough—but also may come to control the teachings of the church. Pastor Lin Xiangao, a veteran of many years in Chinese prisons, in describing why he refused to join the Three-Self Movement even while much pressure was being applied against him, said in early 1990: "I am free to preach the whole Bible while I am unregistered! If I were part of the Three-Self I could not teach creation, it would have to be evolution; I could not teach the Second Coming [of Christ], it would have to be the 'Four Modernisations.'" Shortly afterwards, the government closed his church down, amid rumors that he would soon be executed. The likelihood is that he was spared imprisonment (so far) only because of his worldwide reputation. Similarly, a pastor in Bucharest told me that the Romanian regime would not permit preaching on eschatological themes because the hope of the people had to be centered on the party, not in something that could be brought about only by God.

Josef Tson has been very blunt about those who too easily do the bidding of the authorities, and sometimes it seems as if he is questioning whether the compromised churches can even be called churches. He writes of his own church in Romania that it was wrong to allow the state to overturn the Baptist form of governance and thereby substitute the rule of men for what they believed to be the rule of God.[5]

Writing from the perspective of the church in North India, Vishal Mangalwadi associates religious persecution with the corruption of the whole society. He believes there will inevitably be conflict between the forces of economic oppression and any institution that stands for justice. Having been active in both church extension work and economic development, he views oppression directed against the Christians as a function of the vested interests being challenged by work on behalf of the poor masses. Thus in that context the authenticity of Christian faith in its outward expression necessarily goes hand in hand with persecution. Why necessarily? "Because in an oppressive society if a group stands up to take care of the little lambs, it automatically stands up against the wolves. . . . [Christ] knew that one cannot serve the sheep realistically without infuriating the vested interests—the wolves."[6]

This is important to consider on two counts. First, the persecution of the church may take place in such a way that it seems directed not against religious practices, but social and economic ones. But that is only the appearance; Christian faith is inseparable from action, and to be persecuted for the action is to be persecuted for the faith. In some cases, the question of persecution will not even arise until the church begins being true to its calling. Second, the faithfulness of the church in such a context often comes prior to any question of persecution. Mangalwadi's experience in India suggests that churches willing to accept the existence of injustice and oppression will often remain unharmed. But he has seen a Christian community burned out, believers beaten, jailed and even killed, and has been on the receiving end of some of this treatment himself.[7]

Some of the persecuting governments have recognized the loss to their own side when resorting to harsh measures to win their way over the churches. Speaking when the power and prestige of the Polish Communist Party had badly slipped but before it was overthrown, government spokesman Jerzy Rydlewski of the religious affairs ministry said: "Persecution clearly increases [the church's] prestige and authority."[8] Violence has proven counterproductive in other situations as well.[9] Thus, resistance can pay off even when on the surface it appears to fail.

When the church seems hopelessly compromised, the courageous activity of individuals or small groups can still offset the unfaithfulness to some degree. Letters written by the two Moscow priests, Gleb Yakunin and Nikolai Eshliman (see Chapter 9), engendered publicity abroad and the start of public opposition to the subservience of the Moscow patriarchate. Both priests lost their jobs, but there was a great effect upon the church and Solzhenitsyn was inspired by the effort to make his own contribution.

The quiet witness of believers can be powerful in ways that are far from public notice. In difficult situations there have been many conversions to Christ of jailers, orderlies, doctors, nurses and secret police through the steadfast witness of believers. Solzhenitsyn himself dates his conversion to the quiet witness of a doctor in the *gulag* who was beaten to death a few hours later. Soviet pastor Mitko Mateev tells of the miserable suffering of himself and four other pastors undergoing torture until one of the supervisors of the torture named Gavulov said to him, "Mr. Mateev, I listen to your singing and praying even for me. Tell me, how can you do it? Where does such strength come from? The other pastors have it too." And then: "Mr. Mateev, I want to become a Christian. I want to believe and become as strong as you and the others. What must I do to become a Christian?" Later Mateev heard that Gavulov was brought to trial for collaborating with prisoners and executed at secret police headquarters.[10]

Some church leaders are openly calling for a bolder stance by Christians even in the most restrictive Muslim countries. British analyst Clifford Denton believes that foreign workers witnessing for Christ on their off hours ("tentmakers" in the common parlance) should become openly Christian. "I think it is time both at home and overseas, tempered with wisdom, that we spoke plainly about the message of Jesus and brought ourselves into the open in Christian witness and clear intent."[11] Secrecy hurts Christians in ways that may not be easily perceived. In a North African country one man spoke of his astonishment when the police rounded up suspected Christians in every town in the country, because he learned thereby how many there were: "To our great surprise, the police had more record of Christians than we knew existed. This caused us to rejoice greatly."[12] The secrecy increases the isolation of believers and exaggerates their feeling of being alone.

A small number of Afghan Muslims have become Christians in the refugee camps in Pakistan. Although many have suffered severely, some even being put to death, and others have kept their faith secret, some have boldly spoken of new life in Christ and found that their families were not as hostile as they expected. In some cases a father would be a secret believer and speak of his faith in Christ only upon finding a newly-converted son with a Bible.[13]

People respond to a demonstration of Christian faith that is relevant to life, and in many environments of persecution that is not possible without exceptional courage. Father Dimitri Dudko enthralled many people who would not otherwise enter a Russian Orthodox church. They flocked to hear him because he told the truth about Christian faith and its relationship to life. Prepared for this ministry by eight years of imprisonment, he spoke mostly about basic Christian doctrines. Some of his sermons were simply passages he read out of books that he possessed but his hearers did not. This was unique in the Soviet Union. One observer remarked:

> Why does he do it? I don't understand how he continues. He is quite different from Solzhenitsyn. I have spoken to them both. Solzhenitsyn simply was afraid of nothing and nobody, but this man is afraid all the time. Yet he carries on.[14]

Something of the same quality was present in the Christian Committee for the Defence of Believers' Rights.

One fact that has become clearer recently is that courageous actions by Christians can affect not only the church but the whole society. Pastor Laszlo Tokes of the Reformed Church in Romania had been harassed by the secret police for years, and they stepped up the pressure after he appeared on Hungarian television on July 24, 1989. There he spoke of the regime's violation of religious freedom and ethnic minority rights. He was especially critical of the Ceausescu plan to demolish as many as seven thousand of Romania's thirteen thousand villages. The regime ordered the church leadership to transfer

Tokes to a tiny village in the hinterlands of northern Transylvania. Meanwhile they subjected him to continual police questioning. On November 4, 1989 four men broke into his residence, evidently intending to kill him. With the help of a visitor Tokes fought them off, but suffered a knife wound to the head. Arrest threats were constant. His ration book was taken away, which meant he could not buy food or heating fuel for the house. The authorities shut off his phone, but turned it on periodically for the purpose of issuing death threats. Because he refused to leave the church his bishop, under orders from the government, induced a court to order his eviction. But when officials came to enforce the order, they were met by a human chain of church members as well as Christians from elsewhere in the city. Non-believers also joined them.

On December 16 the crowd began getting out of control, took over Communist Party headquarters in the city and burned pictures of Ceausescu. Soldiers fired blanks to frighten them. The next day an enraged Ceausescu threatened to execute officials who did not use live ammunition. Two days later the military was sent in with orders to shoot to kill. Three officers refused to order the killings, and the *securitate* killed them out in the open square. Security forces then fired into the crowd. There was great slaughter, with protesters arrested, taken to remote areas, tortured, killed and buried in mass graves. Tokes and his wife were arrested shortly after that, but the new provisional government released them after the Ceausescus were executed.[15] There was a frightful carnage, but the Romanian revolution began with Tokes's brave resistance.

Romanian Baptist pastor Doru Popa, speaking in London, reported that some church leaders had gained respect among the population in general by refusing to compromise with the government. In some towns without political opposition these people served as "symbols of resistance" to the regime. Some of them came to have influential positions of leadership in the National Salvation Front because of their example and the respect they had earned.[16]

A few weeks after Tokes's ordeal, the Communist Party of China issued a document called "Wen Jian" for distribution to all universities and research institutes, in which it warned against all foreigners teaching in China on the grounds that many of them are Christians who must be watched carefully. Suspicious activities must be met by expulsion from the country. Evidently the Chinese communist leadership, which was close to Ceausescu, was shaken by the influence of the churches in the Romanian revolution as well as elsewhere in eastern Europe.[17] Some observers believe the churches played a similar role in the fate of the butcher of Uganda. Idi Amin had ordered the invasion of Archbishop Janani Luwum's residence on February 12, 1977 and his abduction in the middle of the night, and this was followed four days later by the archbishop's murder. The fifteen Anglican bishops protested to Amin, and this was the turning point in Uganda. The murder and the protest concentrated opposition to Amin both within and outside of the country; resistance continued to mount, and he fell two years later.[18] The same year Amin killed the archbishop he banned twenty-seven Christian groups, excepting only the Anglican, Eastern Orthodox and Roman Catholic Churches. Rather than meekly accepting the decision of a tyrant who had already murdered many thousands of people, the Christians immediately formed thousands of house churches and carried on corporate worship as they had been accustomed.[19]

During the immense persecution in the Soviet Union during the 1920s and 1930s the visible church in many regions simply disappeared. But that did not mean the church ceased to exist. One contemporary account described what happened:

> When the last church building has been closed in a town, then they take their staff and go from place to place. They teach everywhere, in the villages, in the houses and in the stables, in the forests and under the open sky in the field. They look pale and miserable, and often their clothing is torn. A few crumbs of bread are their only nourishment. In their little sack they carry a Bible, their most precious belonging. They are warmly received by the people, but woe to them if they fall into the hands of the stool-pigeons of the police.[20]

That kind of courage provides an interesting and unexpected counter to one of the most useful and least-understood tricks of totalitarian regimes. Their propensity to atomize people into complete isolation by breaking down all forms of association—family, church, community, voluntary organization—leaving nothing between the individual and the state, is countered by a new unity based on common suffering. Anatoli Krasnov-Levitin wrote a letter to Pope Paul VI in which he spoke of the great hostilities between the churches in the 1920s; they were often so bitter that it seemed they would never be transcended. But the Soviet regime unwittingly devised a way to overcome that difficulty. After these Christians suffered together in the labor camps and prisons, endured the same squalor, beatings, and semi-starvation, hatred gave way to mutual understanding and love. They were one in Christ. "Thus an ecumenicity in living religious practice is taking place in Russia," said Krasnov-Levitin. "It does not consist in conferences, official meetings, and pompous banquets, as in the case of [the World Council of Churches]. It is obvious which of the two is the more authentic."[21]

But the advantages of courageous leadership do not accrue to timid attempts to keep up with trends lest one be left too far behind. On May 23, 1989 Chinese Bishop Ting of the Three-Self Patriotic Movement lauded the Christians who were taking part in the demonstrations at Tienenman Square. He joined forty other members of the National People's Congress in proposing an emergency meeting of the Congress, and he expressed gratitude for the demonstrations in Hong Kong in support of those in Beijing. Bad timing—ten days later the massacre took place. Ting's influence with the government disappeared—indeed his safety was assured only by his visibility abroad—and there was no noticeable support for him from Christians either within China or abroad.[22] His earlier opportunism had not won respect, and Ting's long record of complicity overcame his belated support for the democratic movement.

Numerous examples of resistance "paying off" should not be taken to mean there is a formula to be followed whereby risks do not lead to real losses. Where the church engages in spiritual warfare there will be casualties, and the church must accept that. George Otis, an experienced mission observer and executive, argues that to refuse to regard the cause of Christ as of greater importance than the individual is sentimentality, which he defines as compassion not ruled by discipline. The kernel of wheat must fall into the ground and die in order to bear fruit. Otis thinks the problem is that the individualism that dominates in western cultures has invaded the church with alien ideas, and its members therefore are not inclined to accept individual sacrifice for greater benefits to the whole Body of Christ.[23] Josef Tson has concluded similarly, arguing both from Biblical exegesis and his own experiences both in Romania and the West.

Otis believes that the fear of risk obscures the fact that there are also risks in playing it safe. The Parable of the Talents illustrates that a conservative, risk-avoidance strategy risks losing all. "The very steps taken to alleviate loss in fact *promote* it." He quotes Freeman Dyson to the effect that saying "no" addresses visible costs, but it tends to discount the hidden costs of doing nothing.[24] A 1988 letter from a remote part of Shaanxi province in China illustrates Otis's point. Many young Christian teenagers came under strong pressure from the police about that time. Some were thrown into toilet pits, and others were beaten with electric stun batons, some so badly they could only crawl. A few gave information to the police, but they received jail sentences. Those who refused to speak were released for lack of proof.[25]

Jerusalem pastor Baruch Maoz, who has known years of harassment, thinks that the psychological factors are very important, that showing weakness and fear encourages the opposition to step up the intimidation because they see the manifestations as signs of their own success. Maoz's experience suggests that standing up fearlessly tends to forestall future pressures. He mentions an event when his wife was out walking with their small child. She approached the house behind three of their opponents, one of whom said, "This is where the missionary lives." Another replied, "Yes, we really need to get him out of town." The third said, "You know, the problem is, it doesn't matter what you do to him. He doesn't respond. He doesn't react. He doesn't show fear. You might as well not do anything." Maoz comments on his church's attitude toward all this:

> We refuse to go underground. We refuse to have a secret telephone number in order to escape the harassment. We aren't going to be pushed around. We're not doing anything we should be ashamed of. They're the ones who should be ashamed of themselves. What these people are doing is a form of terrorism, and it won't continue if you don't feed it with your response.

Maoz goes on to say that this defiant stance does not apply when a church is in danger of its very life.[26]

A North African woman, living in an atmosphere of extreme repression far different from that of Maoz, echoes some of his convictions. She says that Christians speaking boldly to the police who question them win their respect. "They crack down on the weak."[27]

Trevor Beeson notes that the practice of strength has had similar results in communist countries. The lesson is that resistance often produces improvement.

> Faced by the persistence of religious faith and the apparent ability of some religious institutions to flourish under persecution, a

few of the Communist regimes have modified their policies and are now seeking to co-operate with the churches and other religious bodies.[28]

"Co-operate" has different meanings, but the point is that while the regime's intention is to modify the church's behavior, the church can do the same favor for the regime. The question is, What is the best strategy to bring about the desired modification? And the answer will vary by time and place.

One of the best illustrations of how pugnacious thinking and acting can rescue a church from near extinction is afforded by the Lithuanian Catholic Church. By the mid-1950s it was on the ropes, in such bad shape that Albert Galter wrote this in a book published in 1957:

> Of the external life of the Catholic Church, so flourishing in Lithuania before the persecution, there remains very little sign today. Of her 11 bishops there remains only one, and his powers have been severely curtailed. All Catholic schools have been despoiled, and religious instruction is banished from every kind of educational establishment. The Catholic press no longer exists, and public opinion is constantly being turned against the clergy. The Soviet Union, while proceeding by stages and avoiding as far as possible all impression of conducting a violent persecution, has succeeded to an alarming degree in making religion a purely private affair and in reducing the Church to an institution for the "exercise of worship" in such buildings only as the State still allows for such a purpose.[29]

A dismal picture, indeed, but one that became largely obsolete long before the Soviet empire began unraveling. The Lithuanians rallied in a quiet defiance that forced the Soviets' hand and led to a severe reaction, including the killing of priests in staged auto "accidents," a favorite KGB method. One of the crowning achievements of this revival of the Lithuanian church was the longest running *samizdat* in Soviet history, and a most useful one that has given people in the West a continual insight into the state of the church in Lithuania. It also gave the KGB fits, as security agents constantly arrested people involved in the production and distribution, but could never stop the publication. This *Chronicle of the Catholic Church in Lithuania* circulated not only among Lithuanians but for many years has been smuggled out of the country, translated into English and published in the United States.[30]

The nub of the resistance-accommodation question with which this chapter deals is not the valor-discretion dichotomy. To regard it in that way is to secularize an essentially religious issue. Christians are not called upon to be brave so much as they are called upon to be faithful, which is a much more exacting standard. One can be brave and faithless, in the sense that Christ is not regarded as Lord and the standards of faith and fruitfulness do not dominate the life. A defiant prisoner in the labor camps, refusing to work and exhibiting hatred and contempt for his persecutors is exhibiting courage, but there may be little in his existence which manifests faithfulness in any Christian sense. Similarly, a church that allows itself to act as mouthpiece for an evil regime should not be thought of as "discreet." Its leaders may even be brave, acting to insure the church's survival, they suppose, but doing so without understanding that the requirements of faithfulness are a higher value than survival. Do such leaders know that survival is in the hands of the Lord of the church and not in the hands of politicians exercising force or church officials trying to stave them off?

Chapter 8 argued that the early Christians may be said to have courage when we see their actions, but it was not courage in the usual sense. Rather, their courage was based on the firm conviction that they would be raised in the end. Resurrection puts suffering and death in the perspective that made it possible for these people to do what to observers looks like courageous actions.[31] One scholar attributes the survival of the church through the first three centuries of persecution to "its clear and uncompromising idea of martyrdom." He believes this comes in a straight line from the Old Testament with its record of bloody persecution of the prophets. The death of Stephen by stoning, for example, is put by Luke in the context of the killing of both the prophets and Jesus. Paul considered such suffering a "single continuous story."[32] And he stated an important conclusion about his own captivity that has been borne out in recent times:

I want you to know, brethren, that what has happened to me has really served to advance the gospel, so that it has become known throughout the whole praetorian guard and to all the rest that my imprisonment is for Christ; and most of the brethren have been made confident in the Lord because of my imprisonment, and are much more bold to speak the word of God without fear. (Philippians 1:12ff.)

And the upbeat assessment that Paul made of his ministry as a prisoner (Philippians 1:12ff.) is not to be taken as a prediction of the effect of boldness and imprisonment, but rather as a notice of the possibilities. There are plenty of examples showing that punishment can intimidate onlookers—*pour encourager les autres*, in the pungent French maxim—and we must give more attention to the incentives to bold action.

To speak of conflicts with the state authorities is necessarily to bring up the issue of whether it is legitimate to disobey the law. Or rather, since it is more complex than a yes or no answer permits, under what circumstances is it legitimate to disobey the law? If we were to say "never," we would make the state the final authority over us, a position only God legitimately occupies, and thus be guilty of idolatry. We know from the Biblical texts that the early church often stood opposed to the state. The starkest expression of this is the apostles' forthright statement, "We must obey God rather than men" (Acts 5:29).

Few modern Christians have considered this question as deeply as the Dutch minister who goes by the name Brother Andrew, who for a generation has led a ministry of Bible transporting and pastoral care for the benefit of Christians whose governments restricted both. He concludes not only that we can break the laws in certain cases, but that we *must* because it is the only alternative to breaking the Law of God.[33] Andrew believes it is self-defeating to have more scruples than is required by God's Law, since the forces that are arrayed against the believer then become overwhelming. Therefore, obedience to lower sovereignties must always be conditional and qualified.[34]

What justification is there for disobeying the restrictions placed upon us by legally constituted authorities when the Bible teaches that governments are ordained by God and thus have divine legitimacy? Andrew argues that rulers are not justified in doing whatever they wish, but only in those activities which are part of the divine purpose for them.[35] Anyone who appeals to Scriptural commands regarding obedience to constituted authorities must also consider Biblical descriptions of the legitimate powers which are to be obeyed. The former limit our right to do as we please; the latter limit the right of our rulers to do as they please. Thus are checked the evils of both individualism and statism; both kinds of lawlessness are shown to be evil.

In practice Christians with a strong sense of calling—as distinct from those who are demoralized and cowed—have often dealt with the illegitimate restrictions placed upon them by doing what they can get away with. To ask permission is to invite a negative response—or worse. With the breakup of communist morale and authority in the Soviet Union, many actions were taken that were formally illegal and that a short time before would have been severely punished. For example, children were being taught in Sunday schools, even though that activity was prohibited.[36] The general principle resembles the military doctrine of "leaning into the fires." This describes attacking infantry being supported by artillery fire until the very last moment before closing with the enemy defenses; the supporting fires are continued to the point of beginning to cause casualties to friendly forces on the grounds that the losses will be less than if the support ends too soon. In the same way Christians in these circumstances press ahead into the danger zone, taking some casualties in the form of harassment or imprisonment, because too much timidity may be more dangerous.

Ideally, the church's principled response to attempts at intimidation will be unified, everyone acting in concert. In the event, that seldom happens. People differ in their courage, their circumstances, and their convictions. Sometimes the more venturesome will be forced out of the church and become dissidents not only with respect to the state but also with respect to the church. So the seeds of the state's failure are found in its success: the repression may compromise the integrity of the official church but spawn an external resistance that will not bow to the church officials through whom the regime exercises control.

The church may adopt an overly compliant attitude toward its oppressors for reasons other than opportunism and cowardice. Sometimes the ancient traditions cause it to lean in that direction. Eastern Orthodoxy, for example, has had a long tradition of subservience to political authorities which encourages its adherents to obey the state passively.[37] In most of the countries of persecution the statist, often socialist, nature of the society makes people deeply pessimistic about ever being able to effect change or even to think about how things might be changed. Marsh Moyle, a westerner with long experience in eastern European countries, observes that the educational system discourages independent thinking. There is much frustration over the low quality of life, continual anger, and the endless temptation to be dishonest in private life because all of public life is built on lies. In the church people tend to do nothing to change their situation because they are conditioned to expect that someone else will lead. Morality, having become relative in the society, is too often regarded similarly by the church. The whole environment is artificially made into a moral twilight zone. Moyle recounts an incident in which a western Christian speaking to an east European counterpart refused to take a gift because he would have to lie to the border guards. The easterner was amazed, and said: "You are spoiled in your moral life. You live in moral luxury."[38]

Sometimes the pressure to compromise is so great that bringing it about appears to be the sole purpose of the authorities. If so, there is good reason for them to do so, namely the extent to which it increases the difficulty of future resistance. Moyle concludes:

> Some have tried to find justification for compromise within scripture. Once one has compromised with a clear conscience, it is hard to go back; one compromise leads to another. For some it is a slow descent from rigourous objections through silent acquiescence, to open compromise. Once someone is compromised he is weak. It is hard to return and there is little forgiveness. . . . Those who fail to meet the standard are sometimes treated harshly. For others the issue is swept under the carpet, depending, sadly, on the connections the person has.[39]

The Soviet law of 1929 regarded religion as a sentiment, and therefore purely personal, not as a statement of truth. Many Christians, through long conditioning, fell into the same habit of thinking. It's vital that Christians not regard themselves as guardians of something purely subjective. Once they come to think that, it makes no sense to stand against persecution, since the faith has no transcendent referent. It seems much better to bend with the tide and not suffer for the sake of something that is purely interior. For one with that perspective, there is no point in resisting the pressures to conform.

Although someone like Solzhenitsyn will always be a rare and outsized character more than a role model, it's nevertheless instructive to see his perspective. One can call him a "survivor" in that he survived, but his autobiographical writings make it clear that he was not primarily interested in surviving but in changing the course of history. He refers to his forced isolation when the Writer's Union and the literary publications would have nothing to do with him. This did not make him weaker, as evidently everyone expected, "but on the contrary, only more independent and stronger, since I no longer had to account to anyone, and was not tied by any secondary considerations."[40] He did not think it a foregone conclusion that the power of the mighty had to triumph: "Ever since 1917, we had always, all of us, surrendered everything; it seemed to make life easier. So many had succumbed to this error—of overestimating the *other side's* strength and underestimating their own."[41] He thought this timidity, far from insuring safety, actually increased the danger.

> During my time in the camps I had got to know the enemies of the human race quite well: they respect the *big fist* and nothing else; the harder you slug them, the safer you will be. (People in the West simply will not understand this, and are forever hoping to mollify them with concessions.) . . . In spite of the granite facade that our government showed the world outside, *internally* the initiative was always in my hands. From first to last, I behaved as though *they* simply did not exist. I ignored *them*.[42]

We have seen enough to make us doubt some of the common generalizations about the persecution of the church. A church may or may not be strengthened and made more effective by being persecuted. Possibly in every case some parts of the church—some people—are strengthened while others collapse spiritually. Some show valor, and others are "discreet" to the point of timidity or worse. But great ambiguities also abound, and it is not wise for foreigners to judge too hastily. In the gray areas it is well to remember that God is the judge and not we.

It is also true that not every kind of courage is healthy. George Otis has expressed concern about a lack of courage in some parts of the persecuted church—while being much more critical of outsiders who encourage such timidity with their paternalism—but he also finds that an untoward bravado is common and unwarranted. The church's ministry is blunted by a tendency to react to circumstance in terms of either security concerns or else crusades and causes. In the first instance important opportunities are sacrificed unless they can be accomplished without risk. In the latter it is the opposite: confrontation is welcomed and "statements" made that will embarrass the authorities and call attention to the situation. The two poles are *survival* and *sacrifice*. Both have been detrimental, but the survivalist much more so. As evidence for this, Otis cites the numerous places of persecution where evangelism is almost nonexistent compared with the very few places where persecution has driven the church out of existence.[43]

In her survey of the church in eastern Europe, Janice Broun concludes that the best stance for the church to take towards the state is "critical support." She argues against a pietist approach that is found in some Orthodox and Protestant communions, a withdrawal and disinterest in "worldly" matters: hence the "support" she advocates. But the support is to be *critical*, which is to say fearless on issues in which the church's concern is central.[44] Perhaps a better term would be *critical engagement*. In the sense I intend, *critical* refers both to the way we regard the regime and the way we regard our own perceptions and strategy, with a heavy dose of practical wisdom; and *engagement* is a military term that means we recognize that a struggle is taking place.

There is a related issue that is now becoming more acute. A mass exodus of Christians is taking place from some places of persecution, leaving behind small numbers of increasingly vulnerable believers. Many thousands of Christians have left the Soviet Union, and many more in its Islamic areas are moving to where it is safer. Thousands of Christians have left Muslim countries, including Lebanon, which not only increases the danger for those who remain, but also the vulnerability elsewhere in the region. Gabriel Habib, Secretary General of the Middle East Council of Churches, has said: "If the position of Christians in Lebanon is shaken, it will confirm the second-class status for the fourteen million other Christians in the Arab world and there will be little hope for them to get equal treatment."[45]

Similar pressures are bound to erupt elsewhere, and the cause of Christ is not likely to be advanced any place from which Christians are retreating. Yet it will not do for the comfortable and safe merely to offer gratuitous advice on this matter. There will have to be ways of sharing both danger and opportunities.

EXTENDING
A HELPING HAND

*T*he prime responsibility for assisting persecuted Christians lies with the church in free countries, a task it has accomplished imperfectly. This should not surprise anyone since churches, like all human societies, are composed of people who are both sinful and limited in their knowledge and understanding. The New Testament contains passages that are hardly less critical of the early church than the statements of its adversaries, and the same is true of the Old Testament prophets concerning the religion of the Temple.[1]

THE FAILURES OF THE CHURCHES
IN FREE COUNTRIES

The churches' strengths and deficiencies with respect to ministry to persecuted Christians have been a function of their general health and vigor. This is to be expected, since the difficulties of responding to persecution in other lands can be addressed usefully only by church bodies which are faithful, healthy, and willing to pay the price. Some churches, because of their internal weaknesses, have been nearly powerless to confront those who are destroying believers elsewhere. One member-critic of the French Catholic Church, Sergiu Grossu, captures the broad sweep of issues in which many other mainline churches are failing, noting that his church in effect is committing treason against its Lord, contradicting by its actions its own governing documents and standards:

This explains the appearance of the theology of violence and revolution; the disastrous tendency to "politicize" the Gospel and
"demythologize" the Bible; the story of the emotional approach,
the anti-evangelical drift of many priests and bishops toward the
enemy of Christianity; indeed, even the desire to collaborate with
the French Communist Party. . . .[2]

That judgment relates more to the activities of certain scholars and
prelates than to the central authority. In Rome officials have had little patience with state attacks on Catholicism and have a good record
of defending the church against its persecutors.[3]

Mainline Protestant leaders have had a much worse record
understanding the travails of the persecuted church. The activities of
the Chinese regime have been especially troublesome for them to
interpret properly. Near the beginning of the Great Proletarian
Cultural Revolution, a calamity that would claim millions of innocent
lives before it ran its ten-year course, John C. Bennett, president of
Union Theological Seminary in New York and active in the leadership
of the National Council of Churches (NCC), said: "The Chinese revolution . . . calls for awe initially rather than condemnation.
Communism needs to be seen as the instrument of modernization, of
national unity, of greater social welfare."[4]

In 1987, just as the regime had begun permitting a dose of free
enterprise—an implicit rejection of socialism—a professor of theology
at a conservative Protestant seminary told me that socialism had not
been proved to be a failure in China; he gave the astonishing reason
that the people were well clothed and fed. When I began to point out
evidence that might call into question this theologian's idyllic notion
of the Chinese "prosperity," he cut me off. Some such process evidently accompanies all these evasions of reality. It's as if they don a
mental raincoat to protect them from facts that might dissolve their
illusions.

The NCC has not always been this way. Early in the post-war
years the organization sponsored the Research Center for Religion
and Human Rights in Closed Societies, whose main outlet has been
the journal *Religion in Communist Dominated Areas*. But as the NCC
allowed a political mission to dominate its agenda the Center became
an embarrassment to it, and the connection was severed.

During a much-ballyhooed NCC trip to the U.S.S.R. in 1984
two women stood up in the balcony and waved signs during a worship service at the Moscow Baptist Church, obviously for the benefit

of the foreign guests. One of the signs read, "Pray for the persecuted church." Evidently the women hoped the visitors would carry back to the U.S. the pleas of a church that was being persecuted by the Soviet government. Fat chance with the NCC running things. None of the Americans who went to the pulpit following the incident mentioned it. In front of the church after the service Intourist guides separated the protesters from the visitors. One of the Americans, a minister, had this to say: "I find it disturbing to have worship interrupted by any kind of group. . . . Just because people do something to grab media attention doesn't mean that's the best way to settle things." Bruce Rigdon, a Presbyterian minister and seminary professor and the NCC delegation's leader, opined that the authorities handled the situation better than it would have been done in the U.S. He also called the Council on Religious Affairs an example of "cooperation" between the church and the state, which is like saying that the chicken and the fox cooperate to see that the latter has a good meal.[5] This series of statements could be the paradigm for NCC reactions to persecution in the totalitarian world: make excuses for the persecutors and their collaborators and denigrate your own country.

On December 8, 1987, NCC General Secretary Arie Brower thanked Communist Party chief Mikhail Gorbachev at the Soviet Embassy in Washington for salvaging the reputation of the Council. Brower believed that Gorbachev's work in renewing the Soviet Union was lending credibility to what the NCC had been saying for so many years.[6] That evening I watched Gorbachev and Reagan on the flickering screen of an ancient black and white television set in a Leningrad apartment and spoke with my hosts, a Baptist family, about church life in the Soviet Union. Too bad Brower couldn't be there, for he would have learned of other things to say to the Soviet party chief.

In the latest fiasco of mainline Protestantism and the communist world, Presbyterian bureaucrats in league with NCC officials have been promoting the North Korean tyranny in its unification drive. They even hailed on the platform representatives of the show church in Pyongyang. This was vigorously opposed by South Korean Christians, mainly Presbyterians, as well as Korean-American Presbyterians.[7]

For the most dramatic exposition of the spiritual climate which these church leaders have been so busy defending, we turn to one of the successors of the deposed leaders of the communist regimes. Czechoslovakian President Vaclav Havel in his 1990 New Year's address tells of the spiritual and moral vacuum in his country, the principle legacy of the communist decades:

> . . . we are living in a ruined moral climate. We have been taken ill morally because we have grown accustomed to saying one thing and thinking another. We have learned to believe nothing, to pay no attention to each other, to care only for ourselves. Concepts like love, friendship, compassion, humility or forgiveness have lost their range and content. . . .[8]

Why did we hear nothing about this from the NCC? If the Council had been saying such things through the miserable years of oppression, there would have been no need to seek absolution through the efforts of the leader whose lot it became to try to paste together the pieces of the disintegrating Soviet empire, who has gained the increasing contempt of the Soviet people.

It should not be thought that the myopia of mainline Protestantism is a function solely of its propensity for the left. When I spoke with the NCC's main specialist on Muslim-Christian relations, he was at a loss to suggest any sources of information on the Muslim persecution of Christians, so rare had such events been. He knew of no current cases. When there is trouble, he says, it is usually because of economic and political factors. He claims to believe that Muslims have a better record on human rights than Christians do in modern times as well as in the past.[9]

Another expert, the NCC's specialist on Islam, views the problems of Christians living in Islamic lands as not very different from those of anyone living where another religion is dominant. The problem for him is that Christians in the West have a negative predisposition toward Muslims and do not consider what Christians do to Muslims. He is concerned that stereotypes about Muslims are being perpetuated and points out that in places like Syria and Iraq Christians are not persecuted; rulers even parade their Christians. He says this is because they regard themselves as secular states.[10] Of course, if they are secular states rather than Islamic states, you cannot use them to show how beneficent Muslim rule is toward Christians. Does it occur to this expert to ask himself why Muslims living in London attend the mosque and send their children to Muslim schools, whereas Christians in, say, Morocco worship furtively—and illegally—with a few friends in their homes?

After five Coptic Christians were shot to death upon emerging from church in Alexandria in May 1990, twenty-three Copts were arrested at the funeral. They could not secure representation because the Egyptian authorities threatened the lawyers with reprisals. This incident followed the death in prison after repeated torture sessions of an evangelical Christian, which itself followed the burning of five Coptic churches and a number of Christian-owned businesses. Byron Haines, Middle East area associate for the Presbyterian Church (USA), urged that there be no publicity on these matters and stressed that the Protestants of Egypt were trying to maintain their good relationship with the government. He spoke as if the difficulties in Egypt stem from the allegations of the Copts.[11]

It's more difficult to account for this kind of blindness than it is in the case of the communist lands. In the Soviet Union and China, westerners associate with collaborationist church leaders; it may said that the NCC officials are victims—however much they contribute to their own victimhood—of the regimes' disinformation. But in few Muslim lands is there anything analogous to that. A Church of Pakistan bishop provides one possible explanation. He notes that there are affinities between liberal Christian theology and the Muslim doctrine of God, and that may provide the clue we seek. Both emphasize the humanity of Jesus but shy away from his Deity. Muslim scholars are aware of this and point to the similarities between their beliefs and those of some Protestant theologians. Those similarities may, in turn, make Islam seem more worthy of sympathy to the Protestant holders of such a theology.[12]

Even in less sensitive places the mainline churches have a curious reluctance to speak out. The last few years have seen vicious outbreaks of repression against Protestants in Mexico, often by quasi-Christian followers of animist faiths. One group of six hundred Mexican Presbyterians in some two dozen congregations was forced to flee from their homes. Officials of the Presbyterian Church (USA) knew of this series of incidents but, apart from "our" bureaucrats talking to "their" bureaucrats, did nothing about it. When pressed by members of their own denomination to do something, the American Presbyterian leaders temporized and, finally, sat on their hands.[13]

Even mission agencies have become willing disseminators of lies when it suits their political interests. According to one agency Nepal "is one of the most tolerant countries in the world when it comes to religion, especially between Hindus who make up 90% of the population and Buddhists who number approximately 7%." But the next page hints at a different story. "The law of Nepal thus seeks to guarantee that people—Christians included—shall be free to practice their *own* religion but are not free to try and induce others to leave the religion they were born into for another religion."[14] This misstates the case. Nepal citizens who are Hindus are free to induce anyone else to leave their religion, but nobody else is free to induce a Hindu to convert. And no Nepalese Hindu is free to convert himself to another faith; such conversions are subject to prison terms, the state then nullifies the conversion, and after release from prison the whole cycle of conversion, imprisonment and nullification can be repeated without end. The United Mission to Nepal, which published this misleading information, is permitted to operate in the country only on condition that it refrain from preaching the Christian message to the populace. When I visited its hospital in Kathmandu, I saw no sign that it was a Christian mission—not so much as a cross on a wall; in fact there was a Hindu idol in the courtyard outside the premises. Yet the Mission feels free to say that the country "is one of the most tolerant" in the world. It's hard to believe that this willful lie is unrelated to the mission's desire to remain in the country. Praiseworthy motivation no doubt, but one that is dishonored by the means chosen to attain its fulfillment.

FAILURES OF THE WCC

Is the worldwide ecumenical movement any better in these matters than its U.S. component? Not so you would notice. Two priests of the Russian Orthodox Church appealed to the delegates of the fifth Assembly (1975) of the World Council of Churches in Nairobi, Kenya. Gleb Yakunin and Lev Regelson, in asking for assistance from the WCC, recalled the help given by the worldwide Christian community in the early 1920s.

> Although about 10,000 priests, monks and nuns were nevertheless executed, the growing indignation of the world forced the wave of repression to ebb after a few months and achieved Patriarch Tikhon's release from detention, which was of decisive importance for the Russian Orthodox Church.

Yakunin and Regelson "remind" the WCC of the worldwide prayer organized in 1930 for the repressed Russian Orthodox Church and the "shameful" denial of persecution by the leaders of that Church.

But now, they said, the Christian community had not fulfilled its earlier promise. Along with the legitimate issues the WCC has addressed, "the matter of religious persecution failed to occupy the place it deserves—although it ought to become the central theme of Christian ecumenism."

> The world did not hear the World Council of Churches raising its authoritative voice when the Russian Orthodox Church was half destroyed; that voice was not heard, either, even when in that vast country, China, Christianity was made illegal; no indignant protest was heard from the WCC even when religion was completely crushed in Albania—and the WCC still remained silent even after a priest was shot in Albania for having baptized a baby.[15]

Even when the WCC meets in the very place where the church is persecuted, it resolutely shuts its ears to the cries of those surrounding the meeting. The executive committee of the organization, meeting in Odessa in 1964, ignored protests from anonymous believers in the city. The committee neither discussed nor publicized the issue. The Russian Orthodox Church was hosting the conference on its territory *at the moment it was under severe attack by its own government*. Critics have pointed out that the development of the church's international role (that is to say, its *political* role) came most rapidly when it was suffering the pains of the anti-religious campaign. It became obvious that one purpose of the international role was to draw the world's attention from that campaign.[16] And the WCC walked blithely into the trap.

More recently, a campaign by groups funded by the WCC and NCC advocates the withdrawal of U.S. aid from the Aquino government in the Philippines and advances openly the interests of the New People's Army (NPA), a communist-organized guerrilla group that, among other things, has been murdering Filipino pastors and destroying churches. An Open Letter of Concern advocating this campaign signed by fifty American missionaries was sent in 1986 to more than one thousand churches in the U.S. This is probably not unrelated to the strategy outlined in a 1982 Philippines Communist Party document entitled "General Orientation of Our Work Within the Church Sector," which advocates the standard national front strategy of forming alliances. This strategy requires the recruitment of church people who may be unsympathetic to Communism, but who can be persuaded to support humanitarian movements under the control of the party. That was the reason the "Letter of Concern" supported the National Democratic Front and had little to say that was critical of the murderous activities of the NPA. In fact it described the activities of the NPA in terms of community health services and protection from government intimidation. Associated organizations receive funds through the NCC, the Methodist Church, the United Church of Christ, and possibly others.[17]

A current witness from the oppressed church assesses the role of the churches living in freedom in a way that is little different from Yakunin and Regelson fifteen years earlier. Romanian Reformed pastor Laszlo Tokes told a Norwegian journalist that foreign church bodies did nothing to help the persecuted church in his country. When he almost lost his life resisting the regime in late 1989, the WCC and the World Alliance of Reformed Churches showed a "total lack of support," an "unwillingness to fight for the truth."[18] Tokes has also put the matter to the western churches in starkly Biblical terms: "I want to ask the international church bodies whether the time has not come to repent and ask for forgiveness."[19]

An imprisoned Romanian Orthodox priest, Father Calciu, has similar criticisms:

> The WCC holds . . . receptions where church leaders embrace atheistic Communist ministers expressing brotherly love while millions of people die of famine in Communist camps. These "missionaries" and collaborators have to ask themselves if they are drinking wine, or the blood of martyrs whom they are sacrificing for an illusory peace with Communists. [20]

About as close to the repentance Tokes is calling for that we are likely to see any time soon was a statement that packed all the punch of weak tea. Emilio Castro, WCC General Secretary, said, "We didn't speak strongly enough, that is clear. That is the price we thought we needed to pay in order to help the human-rights situation inside Romania." An official message of the Romanian Orthodox Church similarly expressed "regret" that the church had not "publicly acknowledged the hidden pain and suffering of the Romanian people." Bishop Teoctist defended the church's position as necessary to "prevent the church from obliteration." He resigned the month following the ousting of the Ceausescu regime.[21] (The state of the Romanian Orthodox Church may be inferred from the fact that shortly afterwards he returned to office.) Other Orthodox leaders expressed regret at failing to show "the courage of the martyrs," but at the same time included self-congratulatory phrases about their "positive achievements." The reality was much worse than is suggested by such remarks. In fact, while the communist regime was in power Romanian Orthodox leaders threatened to leave the WCC if the organization spoke out against abuses in their country.[22] Their most positive achievement may have been assisting the WCC in its dereliction of duty.

The WCC, in its hostility to U.S. policy in Southeast Asia, has ignored the atrocities of the communist regimes in the area. Even when the churches have been the victims of the most brutal policies the organization has kept its peace, has been "understanding" and patient. Even the Cultural Revolution in China, which wiped the visible church off the earth, evoked little reaction from the Council. And its Commission on World Evangelism and Mission, meeting in Bangkok in 1973, issued a statement emphasizing "the need for a theological and ethical understanding of the transformation of Chinese society and its implications for other societies." Some of the delegates opined that Maoism was akin to the realization of the Kingdom of God. A few years later, when the government of Taiwan arrested a politically active Protestant minister, the General Secretary, Philip Potter, sent a telegram to the president advising of the Council's "great shock and grave concern." The Council is grieved at the arrest of one individual in a capitalist country and unwilling to say anything about the murder of millions in its communist counterpart. Nor is the Council's effort limited to propaganda; it gives money and political support to totalitarian African guerrilla groups that murder Christians.[23]

Perhaps the co-founder of the Research Center for Religion and Human Rights in Closed Societies summed it up best in a recent statement:

> If the leadership of international religious organizations interceded for the oppressed, it did so timidly and reluctantly; it was always eager to accept assurances of Communist governments and collaborating church leaders that the dissident believers were in fact law-breakers or chronic complainers. However, the same organizations did not feel any hesitation when protesting against violations of human rights in South Korea (but never

North Korea), South Africa and Latin American states (naturally, except for Nicaragua and Cuba).[24]

The WCC cannot plead ignorance. Theologian Harold O. J. Brown recently recalled a conversation he had many years ago with Eugene Carson Blake, the American Presbyterian leader who was then the Council's General Secretary. Brown asked him why the Council was criticizing the discrimination against atheists in western countries while turning a blind eye toward the vicious treatment of Christians in the communist countries. Blake cited prudential reasons, arguing that the Soviet government would simply be enraged at criticism and crack down on the Christians even harder. Brown is not convinced that Blake was telling the real reason, and he points out that the conciliar bodies acted as if they were ignorant of what, under *glasnost*, would later be freely admitted by official Soviet sources.[25]

FAILURES AMONG THE EVANGELICALS

The false responses of Christians do not end with the conciliar movement. Along with sterling work done by many evangelical churches and mission agencies there has also been considerable unconcern as well as lack of discernment. Billy Graham made an astonishing remark in a visit to the Soviet Union when he said he had not witnessed any religious persecution there. That may have been formally true, which is to say that since he saw what his Soviet hosts wished him to see he saw no persecution. But even at that it seems less than honest, since he spoke to the Pentecostal family that was holed up in the U.S. Embassy, part of a community that had suffered terrible treatment for their faith.[26] Valeri Barinov, an evangelist and rock musician from Leningrad, comments on Graham's statements:

> I was in prison when Billy Graham visited the Soviet Union, and I found it hard to understand how such people could come to our country and remain silent about the persecution of their brothers and sisters. Perhaps he spoke privately, but I considered such moves to be powerless gestures. I was disappointed that he appeared to make no effort to signal his public support for the persecuted church.[27]

Graham is not the only spot on the evangelical record in supporting the persecuted church. Evangelical intellectuals have a way of riding the conciliar train when it comes to this or that program area. One of them, laboring under the theory that Communism is reforming itself, makes an almost comical attack on Kent Hill's history of the church under Soviet rule, *The Puzzle of the Soviet Church*. Thus Hill is said to be "trashing" the moribund conciliar movement and "throwing tomatoes" at Billy Graham while failing to recognize the capacity of the Soviet regime to reform itself. But if Communism is reforming itself then so was Humpty-Dumpty when he took a tumble off the wall. Internal collapse and universal condemnation are what the communist regimes have been experiencing, but to big-council people and their apologists this is self-reform. This reviewer accuses Hill of slander for criticizing the whitewashing of the Soviet regime by church officials in the U.S.S.R. with this extremely odd— for him—explanation. "He seems unaware that these men trusted their audience to have sufficient wisdom to read between the lies."[28] The oddity is in the fact that it is the reviewer's friends in the NCC and WCC, whom he here defends against Hill's arguments, who have proven singularly incapable of doing much more than repeating the lies. That is the burden of Hill's complaint, and the reviewer does nothing to show where he went wrong.

Silence is evidently considered to be golden in many circumstances that cry out for exposure. Bucharest pastor Vasile Talos was almost killed when the van in which he was riding was deliberately hit by a Romanian army vehicle. The Romanian authorities bungled the attack in more ways than one, including the fact that an American minister was with Talos at the time. I telephoned the American later on to discuss the incident, but he denied knowing anything more than that it was an accident. When I asked him what Talos's opinion was on that subject, he said he hadn't discussed it with Talos. *He and Talos had almost been killed together but he hadn't discussed it with Talos*—incredible dissembling. I mentioned to him another Bucharest pastor who had told me the incident was a deliberate attempt at murder, but he wouldn't comment further.[29]

Afterwards I discussed this conversation with an expatriate Romanian minister who keeps close tabs on what is happening in the country. He gave me detailed evidence for the deliberate nature of the attack and said that the American had a fruitful ministry in Romania that he didn't want to jeopardize by being associated with a report critical of the Romanian government. This is precisely the justification often used for Billy Graham's silence about the persecuted church.

They all want to preserve their access to these countries. They think the gospel is going to be served by furthering the promulgation of lies. Remain silent about persecuted Christians and you'll serve God. This is literally a hell of a theological position.

DOING IT RIGHT: THE CHURCH MAKES A DIFFERENCE FOR THE BETTER

The foregoing may suggest that the church's record in assisting those undergoing persecution is uniformly bad. But that is not true. Ministries of carrying the gospel through radio and personal witness, material help of many kinds, pressures exerted on politicians and diplomats, literature shipments, and other forms of help have been extended by Christians throughout the world. In this section we consider some ways in which we can maximize our contribution to the suffering church.

First on the agenda is to get the motivation right, for without that there is little hope of undertaking the material and personal sacrifices that are necessary to make a difference. Jean Daujat, laureate of the French Academy and the Academy of Sciences, puts it this way:

> If I am a Christian, it means that Jesus Christ communicates his life to me and actually lives in me; the same life of Jesus Christ in me exists also in my brothers. Since we then share the same life—that of Jesus Christ—my brother's life is no longer apart from mine. And that means that I must consider all that happens to my brothers as though it were happening to me. . . . I must consider any need of theirs that I encounter in circumstances willed by God as a call from him that I serve that need.[30]

Daujat's appeal is to faithfulness to God as a consequence of the organic unity between believers in Jesus Christ. There is no point in talking about this kind of faithfulness in action unless it accompanies a faithfulness of doctrine. The growing syncretism of the conciliar churches makes their lack of faithfulness in serving persecuted Christians almost inevitable. If less difference is perceived between Christian faith and its alternatives, there is considerably less urgency in protecting Christian victims from the promoters of the alternatives. Influential voices in the churches tell us that the teaching of Jesus are similar to those in Buddhism or Hinduism or Marxism or humanism, but that His message was distorted or perverted by His followers. The problem here is not outright repudiation of Christian faith; that would be more honest and less harmful. Instead these people express alien ideas while claiming them to be Christian. For example, a British physician says: "India's sacred literature, such words as the Vedas, the Upanishads, the Gita and the sayings of Buddha, have thrown more light for me personally on the gospels than has any teaching from a Christian source."[31] Similarly, a scholar of Buddhism writing from what he thinks is a Christian perspective speculates that Buddhism influenced the thought of Jesus and thus is a source of Christian faith. Thus he concludes that there are not only similarities in "lifestyle" between Jesus and Buddha, but that the teachings of the two are compatible: "the message is one."[32]

There is an analogous bit of syncretism that makes it more difficult for churches in free countries to safeguard religious liberty at home. Where the separation of church and state is taken to be not only a constitutional principle but an overriding one, it becomes increasingly difficult to prevent separation from turning into hostility toward religion by the state. The slightest recognition of the church's position with respect to public policy evokes charges of anti-constitutional entanglement of church with state, whereas voices and policies hostile to the church are legitimate. Thus "no establishment" overrules "free exercise," and too many churches are unable to recognize what has happened.

GETTING THE STORY STRAIGHT

If the church is to do right, it must first learn to think right. It is the same relationship that foreign policy has to intelligence. Information must be gathered and then must be rightly interpreted. That is not as easy to do as it may sound; the errors of the past ought to be evidence enough of that. As in the case of foreign policy, wishful thinking combines with deception by persecutors to lead astray the unwary or careless. After the communist takeover of Poland, for example, there was a two-year period in which, despite isolated attacks, the regime maintained a formally correct position toward the church.[33] An interregnum like that sets the stage for wrong expectations and a misleading set of assumptions that tend to be discarded only with great difficulty after much disillusionment. The lesson is that we must look at both the avowed principles and the justice or injustice of the regime and not just the narrow question of whether one can prove that it is persecuting the church at the current moment.

It is also dangerous to pay much attention to the media and other cultural pace-setters because they are often ruled by a sentimentality that can only lead us astray. The French Protestant social critic Jacques Ellul has pointed out how such thinking has deceived many French intellectuals who tend to regard Muslims as "oppressed people," which means that criticism of what they do is beyond the pale. All the allegations of cruelties to non-Muslims and to their own women are regarded as false. Intellectuals believe and spread exaggerated claims about the value of Islamic culture, especially in relationship with Europe and Asia. They praise the supposed toleration of Islam (as we have already seen in the case of the NCC experts) and buttress the arguments of those who express the highest contempt for Christianity.[34]

Some such reason must be responsible for the complaint of Sudan Roman Catholic bishop Paride Taban who has said that the Christians of southern Sudan are victims of not only a civil war but also a relentless and long-running government Islamization campaign, and feel worthy only of death because their plight is ignored by the whole world.[35] This is hardly different from what happened in the communist world, where western intellectuals became the apologists for regimes that exemplified the socialist ideals they themselves valued and so flummoxed many people in their own countries, including much of the church. The western view of Islam has always been based on a combination of solid factual information and gross distortions.[36]

One way to avoid this is to learn from what has happened in similar circumstances elsewhere. Josef Tson believes that you can predict the course of many events in the communist countries by knowing what happened elsewhere. He saw the situation in Nicaragua as bearing similarities to earlier periods in eastern Europe. Those regimes often gave more religious freedom at the beginning and then cracked down later on. The earlier period gives them the opportunity to distinguish potential collaborators from those they would have to crush. And so it proved to be the case in Nicaragua.[37]

If too much benefit of the doubt is given at the inception of totalitarian regimes, a similar mistake is made as they collapse. Years after the celebrated *glasnost* began in the Soviet Union the KGB was still murdering Christian dissidents. This continued long after NCC officials were thanking party chief Gorbachev for vindicating their support for the regime. During this period western church delegations fell all over themselves hailing the humanitarian instincts of the regime. Soviet history has seen other such thaws. Of course, they did not take place amid the general collapse of the Soviet Union and indeed the whole communist structure of eastern Europe. It's difficult to imagine the Soviet empire being resurrected in anything like its former power, but it's hard not to feel a sense of disquiet at replays of the former periods of euphoria by western church officials.

As if disinformation from the persecuting governments and collaboration by some of the churches were not enough, the United Nations has issued reports that have been little more than whitewashes. A 1986 paper by the UN's Special Rapporteur on Religious Discrimination was based on only sixty-four replies to a questionnaire—and they came mostly from the nations involved as well as from the governments under investigation! That's why the rapporteur could make this astonishing statement: "Fortunately, relatively few immoderate manifestations of such intolerance and discrimination have been brought to light in recent years, and only one or two of these have involved systematic killing, persecution, or physical or mental torture." This is after she admitted ruefully that efforts to eliminate discrimination based on religion "have not met with much success."[38] Thus the special rapporteur knows that there has been little success in ending religious persecution, but she can rejoice that few such cases have been "immoderate" (whatever that means); and this good news comes from information that the governments—some of them, at any rate—*themselves* supply! In other words, the UN labors under the same sort of self-deception that has for so long been the bane of the mainline churches. This report further makes the erroneous statement that ". . . outbreaks of intolerance and discrimination based on religion or belief have proven to be totally unpredictable."[39] No, they are exceedingly predictable, as her own analysis shows. It is highly unlikely that governments guided by Marxism-Leninism or controlled by staunchly committed Muslims or backed by powerful factions committed to Islam will *not* commit gross violations of human rights based on religion. This is almost a given.

The 1986 report was evidently too much even for the hardened bureaucrats of the UN to take seriously (or to cover up sufficiently), for two years later a newly appointed special rapporteur, a Portuguese lawyer, issued another report, one which has received much praise from civil liberties groups. Even so, this report is full of mealy-mouthed diplomatic niceties about "allegations" of events "said to have taken place." In the conclusion, the special rapporteur says he has launched a new phase of his work—having dialogues with the governments alleged to have committed violations, transmitting information to them, and asking them to clarify the allegations. He says he is satisfied with the answers he has so far received; he likes "the openness shown by certain countries," and this encourages him to believe in the efficacy of his method. Even if this is so, it is hard to have any hope for the future in a document and a process whose recommendations are little but the typical bureaucratic boilerplate of the diplomatic establishment.

> Also at the national level, States should endeavour to take measures to facilitate the formulation of international standards through adequate internal preparations and, at the same time, pending the availability of such a binding international instrument, to guarantee the respect for the standards currently applicable, thus preventing or penalizing incidents and measures inconsistent with the standards concerned.[40]

It takes a good deal of imagination to suppose that a regime bent on imprisoning and torturing its citizens will be deterred by this kind of verbiage.

R. T. Davies, president of the Research Center of Religion and Human Rights in Closed Societies, recalls an incident from the 1950s, probably during Khrushchev's vicious anti-religious campaign, when he was working in the U.S. Embassy in Moscow. Someone threw a stone over the Embassy wall into the courtyard. Around it was wrapped a petition addressed to the UN Secretary General asking that help be given to a Moscow church which was forcibly closed by the authorities. The Embassy staff sent the petition on to Washington, and the State Department forwarded it to the UN in New York. Several weeks later the Embassy received a notice from the U.S. mission to the UN that, in keeping with its usual practice, the UN Secretariat had sent the petition on to the Soviet Mission in New York. In the Embassy they were horrified by this action, because of the likely reprisals that would be taken against the people who were desperate enough to try to ask for help in the only way they knew how.[41]

Analysts who point out the realities behind these diplomatic absurdities can expect to be treated roughly by western intellectuals, including those in the churches. Solzhenitsyn-baiting was the West's method of cutting down this man who had exposed not only the tissue of lies that had held together the Soviet power within the U.S.S.R., but also the lies that held together the delusions of the western intelligentsia about the Soviet Union and about the West itself. The object of these intellectuals was not so much to protect communist tyrants from this assault on the truth, but to protect themselves from this assault on the truth. So they charged Solzhenitsyn with being a naive idealist; a proponent of an arms race, a cold war, a hot war; a Russian nationalist; a reactionary who wants to turn the clock back; someone who "does not understand" the West.[42]

SHOWING SOLIDARITY WITH THE PERSECUTED CHURCH

One of the clear lessons from the experience of the last couple of generations is that no matter how physically isolated persecuted Christians seem to be, their fellows on the outside can have an enormous effect on their well-being. The effects can be for the worse as well as the better. Several Russian Orthodox intellectuals have speculated that the Soviet authorities were emboldened to arrest Fr. Dudko because Russian language periodicals in the West had recently been critical of him for his favorable statements concerning Tsar Nicholas II. Apparently this criticism was thought to mean that Dudko's arrest might not be vigorously protested in the West.[43] Such was not in fact the case, but the significant point here is that it was possible to correlate Soviet actions with expected reactions from the free world.

We can match every horror story with its opposite. In November 1989, after the Soviet crackup had reached an advanced stage, longtime *Gulag* prisoner Alexander Ogorodnikov spoke to the French Christians who had helped free him:

> It is thanks to the type of action that you have undertaken on behalf of human rights that the Soviet government felt constrained to free the prisoners of conscience. We owe our freedom not to Gorbachev's good will, but to the pressure of your activities that constrained the Soviet government to free most of the prisoners.[44]

Christians from many other countries have done as much. Prisoners in the *Gulag* report experiences that seem miraculous, and many of these accounts speak gratefully of help from the West. Sometimes they come out after years of the most brutal treatment with joy undimmed by their experiences, in fact with stories of exaltation. Anatoli Levitin, writer, historian, and one of the early champions of the Soviet civil rights movement, entered the prison in 1970 at the age of fifty-five. When he finally emerged from the camps he spoke of the sense of well-being of which he was conscious—"I left [prison], strange as it may seem, with stronger nerves, although I had been subjected to very bad conditions the whole time"—and attributed the quality of his experience to prayer from the outside.[45] The Christian poet Irina Ratushinskaya had similar things to say upon her release.[46]

Brother Andrew, the Dutch minister who is known chiefly for his work in literature transportation, does not believe that such activities can be the sole concern of outside churches.

> . . . our main thrust is the total care of the suffering Church, and that includes the ministry of encouragement, physical help, and instruction as well as distributing Bibles, Christian literature, and hymn books. . . .
>
> Before our Open Doors courier teams go on a trip, we invest in a tremendous amount of research, something we consider absolutely vital. A research team is sent to discover the real needs of the believers inside. . . .[47]

Andrew goes so far as to blame the moral collapse of individuals in the persecuted church on those living in freedom. "I think we all have a responsibility to help our suffering brethren get up off the floor. I see the collapse of people in prison like Wang Ming-Dao and Father Dudko as the result of our failure. They should not have suffered that much."[48]

One of the reasons people on the outside can be so helpful is that persecuted believers suffer much more than deprivation of freedom and physical maltreatment. Often the inner struggle is worse than the overt persecution. A Tunisian woman, speaking recently in my hearing at a small consultation in a free country, told of the inner struggle for a convert in an Islamic sea. "How can all these people be wrong and me right?" Of inestimable benefit to her was the encouragement of two expatriate Christian families in her city. Were the churches to concentrate on being helpful in that way it could work to their own benefit as well as to those they are assisting. In a recent book on the role of Catholicism in American society, George Weigel suggests that parish life could be revitalized were it to focus anew on the restoration of religious liberty. He calls attention to a quarter of a million Jews on hand to protest when in December 1987 Gorbachev came to Washington, and wonders why his church cannot show that kind of solidarity. He thinks Catholics might regularly adopt prisoners-of-conscience, or devise advocacy programs such as that of Amnesty International.[49] It hardly needs to be said that Protestant churches could perform similar deeds and might also enjoy some of the same benefits.

If close contacts between western Christians and their counterparts in countries of persecution are possible, that opens many opportunities for assistance—and many opportunities for serious mistakes. It is the old story of cultural differences that are badly understood and therefore lead to great damage. For the most part these cases have not been well studied, or else the studies are locked up in academic journals and are not widely known.

One unpublished study that has received some private circulation among mission groups working in eastern Europe shows how westerners who understand poorly the cultural traits of the people they are helping have done much damage with material assistance. Money coming in without adequate checks engenders distrust and has the effect of squelching generous giving among indigenous church members. The lack of trust has then further poisoned relationships and caused churches to stagnate. This study does not question the motives of western mission efforts, but rather urges that better understanding be gained before plunging into ill-conceived or poorly administered projects.[50]

The new Soviet openness to foreign business partners as a consequence of the collapsing economy evidently seems to some of the partners to be spelled glanot. But Christians ought to be tempering legitimate expectations of mutually profitable contracts with an insistence on doing business in a way that is commensurate with the moral demands in which they believe; and they can persuade others to do the same. The Slepak principles are one attempt to codify those demands. Named after Vladimir Slepak, one of the founders of the original Helsinki monitoring group in Moscow, these principles state that American firms 1) will not supply the Soviet military, 2) will not purchase goods produced by forced labor, 3) will protect their Soviet employees who are discriminated against by reason of their politics, religion or ethnic status, 4) will not participate in an enterprise that takes place in a confiscated religious building, 5) will not participate in activities that pose a danger to workers, neighbors or property, 6) will not make untied loans to the Soviet Union which can be used to subsidize non-peaceful activities, 7) will give preference to joint activities with private cooperatives rather than those owned by the state.[51]

The temptation to paternalism will always be present when working with counterparts in poor or oppressed countries. The collapse in eastern Europe was followed by an influx of Christians who wanted to help but many of whom were all too ready to take charge. Manfred Kern, executive secretary of the Evangelical Alliance of East Germany, explained the problem: "Our American friends especially find it difficult to understand that people who drive a Trabant [the tinny, smoke-belching East German car] are full persons. But there are a lot of good Christians in small Trabants. Our Western friends should understand this."[52] They should also understand that the common courtesies they extend to their own countrymen are due as well elsewhere and for the same reasons. In several east European countries visitors who thought they were helping overwhelmed their hosts with constant demands on their hospitality. One Romanian church leader put the problem this way: "Since the revolution I've become nothing more than a glorified taxi driver for western visitors."[53] There is often more than a little self-aggrandizement in these visits—in the form of photo opportunities and fund-raising appeals—that the hosts know about and view cynically.

NO MORAL COMPROMISES

Moral actions have consequences which often last long after they take place. We strive to do right not because we'll pay for doing wrong, although that is exactly what we'll do, but because the Law of God is eternal and we cannot maintain that we serve the Lord while we flout His commands. The high pitch of hatred directed against Christians by militant Muslims is due in part to memories of the Crusades that are almost as vivid for them as they were for their ancestors centuries ago—ancestors who fought to defend their homes against Europeans marching under the banner of the cross. When these Muslims consider Christians in their midst, including converts among their own people, they look on them as "crusaders." This is not just posturing, although there is plenty of that too.

If we don't work toward justice in the Biblical sense we could sow the harvest of disaster for Christians in succeeding generations. The suffering of the church in Ethiopia may be due in part to the fact that when it was dominant in society it had no commitment to the service and betterment of the society in which it had a privileged place. The church even resisted beneficial reforms that Haile Selassie was attempting, aligning itself instead with feudal landlords and corrupt bureaucrats.[54] There were occasions in the past when Christians were given authority because of their wisdom and sense of justice and did not abuse that trust—even in Muslim countries.[55] The same principle holds on the domestic scene. Christians have sometimes mistakenly supported restrictions on unpopular groups they do not like. This provides a weapon that may someday be turned against them.[56]

Russian Orthodox priests Gleb Yakunin and Lev Regelson in 1975 proposed a course of action to the WCC along with a forthright condemnation of the organization's inaction. Here is a program that is worthy for all churches to consider.

1) Christians all over the world should learn about what their persecuted brethren are suffering. Information should be disseminated through all the mass media, and church and interfaith groups should also take a hand in this.

2) The leadership of all Christian communities should hold regular prayer meetings for persecuted Christians. In addition to prayer, this should include sermons, meditations, and discussions for action on behalf of those who are persecuted.

3) There should be personal contact between Christians living in freedom and those living under persecution, using business and tourist trips and the mail.

4) Christians should capitalize on the unwillingness of persecutors to have their deeds known to the world. Each person should write one letter a month to the persecutors, as well as appealing to public opinion in his own country .

5) These efforts should be extended on behalf of those of other religions as well as Christians, in recognition of the image of God in all human beings.

6). Christians should protest the illegal use of psychiatric hospitals as means of torture and intimidation.

7) Christians should support attempts to emigrate by those who are persecuted for their faith.

8) The WCC should do something about the inability of Christians to get copies of the Scriptures in the Soviet Union.[57]

There should also be continuing research on the history of the persecution of the church and the responses to it, with training being organized to take advantage of the lessons from the past.[58] The Open Doors with Brother Andrew organization has begun to train churches in this vital area *before* they fall under the power of a hostile state. In this way the church can learn from the lessons of others instead of building up basic knowledge solely through costly suffering.

DIPLOMATIC HELP

A powerful circumstance in the hands of Christians in free countries is the almost universal sensitivity of persecuting regimes about their reputation elsewhere in the world. At the time of Dudko's recantation the Soviet authorities showed intense preoccupation with the reactions of the West. When *Izvestiya* reported the party's line on this celebrated case, it headlined "The West Is Seeking Sensations." This was after Dudko had spent five months in prison, in complete isolation and under constant interrogation.[59]

It's doubtful that sufficient attention is given to the vulnerabilities of persecuting countries. In 1989 the US gave Nepal $15 million in aid, which was a significant portion of the national budget of this small nation. U.S. law bans aid to governments guilty of gross violations of human rights, but sanctions have not been directly threatened, much less imposed. This in spite of the fact that the annual State Department Human Rights reports, required by law, shows Nepal to fall far short of any minimally acceptable standard. The report for 1988, for example, describes the penalties for conversion from Hinduism and tells of numerous cases of legal persecution, indictments, convictions, refusal to grant bail, and torture. It quotes from a speech in which the Minister of Home Affairs affirms the government policy of taking "strong action" against both conversions and preaching Christianity.[60]

Meanwhile, the Nepalese public relations machine continues its blatant lies. The Ministry of Tourism recently published a book entitled *Nepal: Destination with a Difference* which says: "Religious tolerance and harmony such as is found in Nepal, is perhaps a unique example to the world."[61] We can hope that with the ending of the cold war the nations will be willing to consider moral violations that are not related so directly to foreign policy interests, although the western reaction to the Persian Gulf crisis of 1990 suggests there may always be reasons of state that will be taken to justify siding with the most brutal of regimes.

When a foreign government considers repression to be a legitimate reason for a policy response and takes appropriate action, it can make a great difference in the actual conduct of the offender country. U.S. policy toward Romania is a good example, even though it never made the Ceausescu regime a paragon of virtue.[62] I write this with reports in front of me too numerous to detail here of successful efforts by the free countries in relieving the oppressed in Turkey, the Soviet Union, Malaysia, Egypt, Vietnam, and elsewhere. But these happy occurrences seldom happen without interested people, churches and human rights organizations pushing hard to get their own governments to act. And without a concerted *policy* effort in democratic countries success will come in individual cases rather than in lessening the overall repression.

There are plenty of failures to go along with the successes. The contrast between China's treatment of Muslims compared with Christians provides a convenient example. The Chinese authorities act much more favorably toward the former than the latter in spite of the communist hostility toward all religions. The difference is partly a response to the Chinese assessment that Islam is an indigenous religion and Christianity an imported one, but it is largely due to the foreign policy benefits of being perceived favorably by Muslim states, which brings China both diplomatic and economic rewards. The Chinese government has required that organizations and airlines provide special foods for Muslims working or traveling in them, and government inspectors insure that specified slaughterhouses prepare meat in a way consonant with Muslim law. It also withdrew from circulation the Chinese version of *The Satanic Verses* when Muslims protested against Salmon Rushdie's book.[63] The evident difference is that Muslim countries are more willing than western governments to confer rewards and punishments on the Chinese authorities for perceived treatment of co-religionists.

Apart from the moral difficulties of a *realpolitik* foreign policy that does not consider adequately the ethical foundations there may be concrete losses. Pragmatism often sacrifices real interests and opportunities in an effort to secure short-term gains. When a country's ideals are ignored in an effort to avoid trouble, the people suffering from their governments are likely to remember that their tyrants have been accommodated. Even in Islamic countries, which often appear to be monolithic in their opposition to anything but an extreme pro-Muslim stance, the unity can be misleading. Some of these countries have sizable minorities or even majorities that oppose the Muslim Brotherhood type of policy, and a strong remonstrance about the persecution of Christians can stiffen the resolve of a government that has no use for the Brotherhood and its devotees. Algeria is an example of a country in which that kind of internal disunity could be exploited by a principled foreign policy.[64]

Christian commitment of politicians and diplomats sometimes makes an enormous difference even where the official policy of the country is more reserved. The Chief Whip of the Liberal Party in Britain, David Alton, has long been known for his efforts in the religious liberty area, having intervened in many cases, including the Siberian Seven in the U.S.S.R., Christians in Nepal, and Soviet rock musician Valeri Barinov.[65] Four North African Christians who were released from an Egyptian prison after intense international pressure were about to be sent back to Tunisia and Morocco where they might have been killed. At the last moment the French ambassador, a devout Catholic, intervened with the Minister of the Interior, and the four were allowed to settle in France.[66] David Funderburk, former U.S. ambassador to Romania, often went out on a limb—going much further than his official brief—in standing up for the rights of oppressed Christians. And Frank Wolf of the U.S. House of Representatives is one of several legislators who have been tireless in seeking to help oppressed Christians in other countries.[67]

We might do better at learning to affect repressive officials if we had a better idea of how they work. Often the harassment of Christians comes from pressures placed upon the officials by superiors or by political or religious groups in their country. They take the course of least resistance in harassing Christians and by so doing relieve themselves of pressures. When they do not receive opposition from foreign governments or other outside groups, persecution makes life easier for them. The reason we on the outside participate in letter-writing campaigns and other forms of counter-pressure is to let such officials and their political masters know that they cannot solve their problems at Christian expense without paying a price. Our goal should be to make the price as high as possible, and thus give the persecuting authorities the most incentive to change their policies.

CONCLUSION

The present moment in history is one in which an enormous fact has just become evident, one that the media have missed. Seldom has the voluminous commentary about the remarkable transformation of the communist world in 1989 and the months following said anything at all about this momentous fact: *The three-quarter-century attempt of Communism to eradicate Christianity has failed.* Even in Albania, which almost alone dropped the pretense of maintaining religious freedom, and which ruthlessly punished even home prayer, the church is sending up a few green shoots to test the atmosphere. Even where, as in the Soviet Union and China, the horrors included mass murder, the church is still alive and in many cases flourishing beyond almost anybody's anticipation. And even in North Korea, where there is no open church at all—with the exception of those two pitiful showpieces in Pyongyang that fool nobody except western ecclesiastical officials—groups of believers secretly meet in homes or in the woods. The communist plan has failed utterly. They terrorize, they torture, they imprison, they kill, and with all that they fail. It is hard to imagine a surer proof of the falsity of materialism than this display of the powerlessness of the material over the spiritual. Or a more convincing confirmation of the words of Jesus: The gates of Hell will not prevail against the church (Matthew 16:18). There is a similar idea in the Apocalypse where the vision is of the enemies of God committing aggression, to an inevitable bad end. " . . . They will make war on the Lamb, and the Lamb will conquer them, for he is Lord of lords and King of kings, and those with him are called and chosen and faithful" (Revelation 17:14).

Jean Dauja questioned "how those who remain indifferent to the Church of Silence, who even smile upon its persecutors, dare to call themselves Christians."[68] Four centuries earlier, during the persecution of the Protestant church, another Frenchman, John Calvin, wrote to the chief persecutor of his country and denounced "moderate men" who were content to allow the church to suffer, who were "ashamed" of the gospel.[69] This is an admonition we should take to heart.

It would be a serious error to whitewash the checkered record of the church under persecution, but it's hard not to marvel at the numerous evidences of constancy and faith that have made such survival possible, even with the understanding that God's sovereignty lies behind it all. All this suggests a continuing dual responsibility of the church. One task is to prepare ourselves—spiritually and intellectually—for the persecution the church will inevitably suffer in the future. The other is to continue to recognize our identity with fellow members of the Body of Christ and redouble our efforts to help them.

HELPING THE PERSECUTED CHURCH

Several organizations devote their efforts solely to helping the persecuted church. This is a partial list that will get interested people started. Denominational identification is only for information; all these groups are interested in assisting all Christians living under persecution.

PROTESTANT

CREED (Christian Rescue Effort for the Emancipation of Dissidents)
787 Princeton Kingston Rd.
Princeton, New Jersey 08540

Christian Solidarity International (This is the U.S. office of an international organization based in Switzerland.)
P.O. Box 70563
Washington, D.C. 20024

China Ministries International
P.O. Box 40489
Pasadena, California 91114

Open Doors with Brother Andrew
P.O. Box 27001
Santa Ana, California 92799

Slavic Gospel Association
P.O. Box 1122
Wheaton, Illinois 60189

Romanian Missionary Society
P.O. Box 527
Wheaton, Illinois 60189

Institute on Religion and Democracy (The IRD exists to move the
NCC churches to a more balanced position. They serve as a clearing
house for organizations within the mainline denominations that
have the same purpose.)
1331 H St. NW—Suite 900
Washington, D.C. 20005

ROMAN CATHOLIC

Puebla Institute
1030 15th St. NW—Suite 300
Washington, D.C. 20005

Lithuanian Catholic Religious Aid Society
351 Highland Blvd.
Brooklyn, New York 11207

GREAT BRITAIN

Jubilee Campaign (Works with Members of Parliament on religious
liberty cases)
P.O. Box 80
Cobham, Surrey KT11 2BQ
England

SWITZERLAND

Christian Solidarity International
Forchstrasse 20
Post fach 52
8029 Zürich

N O T E S

CHAPTER ONE : *Persecution and Civil Rights in the Twentieth Century*

1. Interviews by the author in Moscow, December 13-15, 1987.
2. Interview by the author in Beijing, February 17, 1988. This and the remaining biographical accounts in this chapter may be read in extended form in Herbert Schlossberg, *Called to Suffer, Called to Triumph* (Portland: Multnomah Press, 1990).
3. Interview by the author in Kathmandu, February 6, 1988.
4. Interview in Paris by the author, September 1988.
5. Robert F. Drinan, *Cry of the Oppressed: The History and Hope of the Human Rights Revolution* (San Francisco: Harper & Row, 1987), p. 1. Elsewhere, perhaps overcome by a twinge of realism, Drinan declines to speculate on whether public morality with respect to human rights has improved over the last forty years (p. 187).
6. Jane Ellis, *The Russian Orthodox Church: A Contemporary History* (Bloomington, IN: Indiana University Press, 1986), p. 3.
7. Wassilij Alexeev and Theofanis G. Stavrou, *The Great Revival: The Russian Church Under German Occupation* (Minneapolis: Burgess, 1976).
8. Kent R. Hill, *The Puzzle of the Soviet Church: An Inside Look at Christianity and Glasnost* (Portland: Multnomah, 1989), pp. 121ff. A revised and enlarged edition of this book is scheduled for publication in 1991 under the title *The Soviet Union on the Brink*.
9. *Ibid.*, pp. 126f.
10. Herbert B. Workman, *Persecution in the Early Church: A Chapter in the History of Renunciation*, 4th ed. (London: The Epworth Press, 1923 [1906]).

CHAPTER TWO: *The Persecution of Christians by Islam*

1. *New Memo*, No. 3, March 1989. Published by the Institute for Demographic Studies, Souldern, England. No pagination.

2. For example, the *World Christian Encyclopedia*, ed. David B. Barrett (Nairobi: Oxford University Press, 1982), p. 527, gives these figures for Nigeria in 1980: Christian, 49 percent; Muslim, 45 percent.

3. Scott Kraft, "Churches, Mosques, Feel Flames of Religious Violence in North Nigeria," *Los Angeles Times*, July 18, 1987, Part II, pp. 20f. An article in *Christianity Today*, July 10, 1987, p. 43, cites evidence that the rioting was premeditated, with churches, businesses and homes targeted for burning beforehand and rioters being paid and given gasoline and matches for the destruction that followed.

4. Goh Keat-Peng, "Church and State in Malaysia," *Transformation*, July-September, 1989, p. 18. There is additional on this in *World*, November 28, 1988, pp. 8f and *World Evangelization Information Service*, November 1, 1988, p. 4.

5. Jubilee Campaign news releases October 27, 1989, October 27, 1988, October 5, 1988, April 14, 1988, April 5, 1988. Jubilee is an organization in London which works closely with Members of Parliament for the preservation of religious liberty around the world.

6. Barbara G. Baker, "Believers in Turkey Claim Their Legal Rights," *Christianity Today*, April 7, 1989 p. 44; *Pulse*, January 26, 1990, p. 1; news releases of the Committee for Religious Freedom (Palisade, Colorado), November 15, 1989, March 29, 1988, April 15, 1988. For good background information see Paul Dumont, "The Power of Islam in Turkey," Olivier Carré, ed., *Islam and the State in the World Today* (New Delhi: Manohar Publications, 1987), pp. 76-94.

7. *Mission Frontiers*, January 1988, p. 29.

8. *The First Freedom* (Puebla Institute), September-October 1988, pp. 3-5; Paul Marx, *HLI Reports*, January 1989, pp. 1f.; Paul Vallely, "Sudan's Best Hope for Peace," *Wall Street Journal*, December 6, 1988, p. A22.

9. *News Network International*, March 14, 1990, pp. 4f. Hereafter cited as *NNI*.

10. Haim Shapiro, "Bethlehem Baptists Barricaded Behind Barbed Wire," Jerusalem *Post*, August 4, 1989.

11. Emmanuel Sivan, *Radical Islam: Medieval Theology and Modern Politics* (New Haven, CT: Yale University Press, 1985), p. x.

12. Khurshid Ahmad, "The Nature of Islamic Resurgence," *Voices of Resurgent Islam*, ed. John L. Esposito (New York: Oxford University Press, 1983), pp. 218-229.

13. Sivan, *Radical Islam*, pp. 130-133.

14. Shawky F. Karas, *The Copts Since the Arab Invasion: Strangers in Their Own Land* (Jersey City: American, Canadian and Australian Coptic Associations, 1985), pp. 131f.

15. Nadia Ramsis Farah, *Religious Strife in Egypt: Crisis and Ideological*

Conflict in the Seventies (New York: Gordon and Breach Science Publishers, 1986), pp. 1f.

16. Karas, *The Copts Since the Arab Invasion*, pp. 124f.

17. *Ibid.*, p. 85.

18. Daniel Kyanda, "A Theology of Persecution: The Development of a Biblical Strategy for the Church Based on First Peter with Case Studies from Ethiopia, Uganda, Burundi and Mozambique," M.A. thesis, Nairobi International School of Theology, 1988, p. 16.

19. Bat Ye'or, *The Dhimmi: Jews and Christians Under Islam*, rev. ed., trans. David Maisel and Paul Fenton (Rutherford, NJ: Fairleigh Dickinson University Press, 1985), pp. 48-65. This has become the standard work on the subject.

20. Farah, *Religious Strife in Egypt*, pp. 4f.

21. Interview by the author of an Arab Christian who is active in ministry in Arab countries. Minneapolis, April 1989.

22. This opinion was reported by W. H. T. Gairdner, "Islam Under Christian Rule," *Islam and Missions*, ed. E. M. Wherry *et. al.* (New York: Fleming H. Revell, 1911), pp. 196f. This volume consists of papers presented at the Lucknow conference January 23-28, 1911. The woman from Russia is not named here, but it may be Jennie von Meyer, whose essay "Islam in Russia" is found in the same volume, pp. 249-272. The following passage is included in her essay: "Not only civil authorities do not care for missions among Moslems for fear of arousing their discontent and provoking their fanaticism, even the Church itself seems to stand in awe, doubt, and dismay before the compact mass of twenty million [Muslims], who ever more and more unitedly rally around their one religious leader, their one creed, and begin to realize and bring into being the religious and political ideal called pan-Islamism. The Church in Russia stands like David and Goliath; but this David had not the same faith in the all-powerful God who could make the stones in his sling an efficient weapon against Goliath's mighty sword!" (p. 263)

23. Gairdner, "Islam Under Christian Rule," pp. 197f.

24. *Ibid.*, pp. 200-205.

25. Nicholas Urban (pseudonym), "Christian Missions and Freedom of Religion Within Islamic Societies," *World Perspectives*, January 17, 1989. Published by NNI.

26. Hassan Turabi, "The Islamic State," *Voices of Resurgent Islam*, ed. Esposito, p. 241.

27. Samuel M. Zwemer, "An Introductory Survey," *Islam and Missions*, ed. Wherry *et. al.*, p. 9.

28. Letter from a missionary who spent many years in North Africa, May 25, 1984.

29. Sivan, *Radical Islam*, p. 36.

30. Thomas Naff, "Towards a Muslim Theory of History," *Islam and Power*, ed. Alexander S. Cudsi and Ali E. Hillal Dessouki (Baltimore: The Johns Hopkins University Press, 1981), p. 28.

31. I have been told informally by an informed source that there is a growing eschatological hope among Muslims, especially Shiite Muslims, and even the expectation of a coming Messiah. I have not seen anything like this in the literature, but that may be only because it's difficult to obtain information on the Muslim world.

32. Michael Youssef, *Revolt Against Modernity: Muslim Zealots and the West* (Leiden: E.J. Brill, 1985), 5f.

33. Quoted in John Laffin, "Islam's Clandestine Operations," Project File: *The Challenge of Islam* (Souldern, England, n.d., no pagination). Further to this see S. K. Malik, *The Quranic Concept of War* (Lahore: Wajidalis, 1979), which includes material on the use of terror for political purposes. Malik is a Pakistani general.

34. Quoted in John Laffin, *The Intentions of Islam*, No. 4 of the Project File Series, *The Challenge of Islam*, Banbury, Oxon, England, October 1988, no pagination.

CHAPTER THREE: *The Islamic Offensive*

1. Nadia Ramsis Farah, *Religious Strife in Egypt: Crisis and Ideological Conflict in the Seventies* (New York: Gordon Breach Science Publishers, 1986), pp. 25-38 and *passim*. Notice the limitations of her argument, which suggest the care that must be used in reading these books. "The change in inter-communal interactions was essentially prompted by the ideological offensive of the post-Nasserite ruling elites. Using Islam as an ideological means to constitute a social base supporting the policies of Egypt's reintegration in the international economic system, they capitalized on one of the trends in Egyptian politics: Islamism . . . A tacit alliance was formed between the ruling elites and the Islamic groups, mainly the Muslim Brothers." "The confrontational attitude of the church accelerated the attacks on the Copts by both the regime and the Islamic groups. What was at stake in this conflict was not only the rights of the religious minority, but the whole strategy of reintegration in the world system by the ruling elites. The protracted nature of the conflict deepened religious antagonisms and signalled a clear deterioration of Muslim-Coptic relations . . . what started as political strategy of ideological mobilization gained its own momentum as a separate issue of religious antagonism. The religious strife became the manifestation of deteriorating Muslim-Coptic relations." *Ibid.*, pp. 37f. The jargon is typical of such treatments. She can speak of "religious strife" but she means it in only the communal sense. This is a reductionism that reduces religion to its social and political determinants and effects and ignores completely the religious factors themselves.

2. Anne Dexter, *View the Land* (South Plainfield, NJ: Bridge Publishing, 1986), p. 26.

3. Kraig Meyer, *A Clash of Swords: The Sword of the Spirit vs. the Sword*

of Islam in the Land of Turkey (Grand Junction, CO: Friends of Turkey, 1986), pp. 52-56.

4. Interview by the author, northern Israel, October 25, 1988.

5. Suad Joseph and Barbara L. K. Pillsbury, *Muslim-Christian Conflicts: Economic, Political, and Social Origins* (Boulder, CO: Westview Press, 1978).

6. Amir Taheri, *Holy Terror: Inside the World of Islamic Terrorism* (Bethesda, MD: Adler & Adler, 1987), p. 214.

7. John Laffin, *The Intentions of Islam*, No. 4 of the Project File Series, *The Challenge of Islam*, Banbury, Oxon, England, October 1988, no pagination.

8. Karas, *The Copts Since the Arab Invasion*, p. 103.

9. Goh Keat-Peng, "Church and State in Malaysia," *Transformation*, July-September 1987, p. 16.

10. *Pulse*, July 15, 1989, p. 5.

11. Youssef, *Revolt Against Modernity*, p. 11, n. 1.

12. Goh Keat-Peng, "Church and State in Malaysia," p. 19.

13. Youssef, *Revolt Against Modernity*, pp. 134ff., 178f.

14. Interview with an Arab Christian by the author, Minneapolis, April 1989.

15. Ali Merad, "The Ideologisation of Islam in the Contemporary Muslim World," *Islam and Power*, ed. Alexander S. Cudsi and Ali E. Hillal Dessouki (Baltimore: Johns Hopkins University Press, 1981), pp. 44f.

16. Jean-Claude Vatin, "Religious Resistance and State Power in Algeria," *ibid.*, pp. 122f.

17. *NNI*, March 14, 1990, pp. 8f.

18. *Ibid.*, December 13, 1989, p. 26-29.

19. Michael Nazir Ali, *Frontiers in Muslim Christian Encounter* (Oxford: Regnum Books, 1987), p. 25.

20. *Human Rights in Islam*, No. 10 in the WAMY series (World Assembly of Muslim Youth, Riyadh, Saudi Arabia), no pagination.

21. Emmanuel Sivan, *Radical Islam: Medieval Theology and Modern Politics* (New Haven, CT: Yale University Press, 1985), pp. 77f.

22. Khan Bahadur Khan, "The World of Islam," *Church-State Relations and the Freedom of Conscience*, Proceedings of the Third World Congress on Religious Liberty, July 23-26, 1989.

23. Hassan Turabi, "The Islamic State," *Voices of Resurgent Islam*, ed. John L. Esposito (New York: Oxford University Press, 1983), p. 250.

24. *New Memo*, No. 1, January 1989, no pagination, published by the Institute for Demographic Studies in Souldern, England.

25. Djibril Samb, "A Muslim Majority and Religious Minorities in a Secular State: The Senegalese Experience," *Church-State Relations and the Freedom of Conscience*, pp. 39-46.

26. Christian Coulon, "State Construction and Islamic Action in Senegal,"

Islam and the State in the World Today, ed. Olivier Carré (New Delhi: Manohar Publications, 1987), pp. 261-273.

27. Denys Lombard, "Islam and Politics in the Countries of the Malay Archipelago," *ibid.*, pp. 236-239.

28. *Pulse*, January 26, 1990, p. 4.

29. *Ibid.*, August 11, 1989, p. 3.

30. J. Stewart Crawford, "Political Changes in Turkey," *Islam and Missions*, ed. E. M. Wherry *et. al.*, (New York: Fleming H. Revell, 1911), pp. 100-105.

31. Interview by the author, Jerusalem, October 1988.

32. Harold O. J. Brown, "A Curious Silence," *The Religion and Society Report*, November 1990, p. 3.

33. Samuel Wilson, "Human Rights, Christianity and Islamic Societies," *World Perspectives*, Vol. 2, No. 5, no date.

34. Taheri, *Holy Terror*, Chapter 14.

35. *Rapprochement* (Newsletter of The Conner Center), March 1990, p. 3.

36. From an unpublished paper written by a person in western Europe known by the author to be informed and reliable.

37. Dilip Hiro, *Holy Wars: The Rise of Islamic Fundamentalism* (New York: Routledge, 1989), p. 284.

CHAPTER FOUR: *The Persecution of Christians by Other Religions*

1. *NNI*, March 14, 1990, pp. 6f.

2. *National and International Religion Report*, October 5, 1987, pp. 1, 19.

3. *Ibid.*, July 27, 1987, p. 2.

4. *NNI Special Report* on Nepal by Ron MacMillan, February 15, 1990.

5. Author's interview with a Thai pastor, Oxford, England, January 1990.

6. C. V. Mathew, *Neo-Hinduism: A Missionary Religion* (Madras, India: Church Growth Research Centre, 1987), p. 6.

7. Quoted in *ibid.*, p. 8.

8. Ebenezer Sunder Raj, "The Constitution and the Laws of Conversion," *Kristiya Drishthanta: A Christian Viewpoint*, ed. Motilal Pandit, Kathleen Nicholls and Vishal Mangalwadi (New Delhi: TRACI, 1987), pp. 125-151.

9. Mathew, *Neo-Hinduism*, p. 62.

10. Sunder Raj, *The Confusion Called Conversion* (New Delhi: TRACI, 1988), Chapter 25.

11. *Nepal: Religious Repression in the Hindu Kingdom* (Washington D.C.: Puebla Institute, 1990), pp. 26ff. No author given.

12. Prem Bahadur Shakya, "The Wonder of Nepal," *Church-State Relations and the Freedom of Conscience*, Proceedings of the Third World Congress on Religious Liberty, July 23- 26, 1989, p. 83.

13. Sometime even those who are in the struggle against persecution err in giving too much credence to the claims of the persecutors. Australian civil rights worker John Smith, in his appeal on behalf of Christians in Nepal, noted what he thought was a paradox in that Nepal was practicing bru-

tality against Christians as a Hindu state, whereas the religion espouses "the absence of intolerance, compassion . . . freedom of thought and conscience, and freedom from fear." Of course, the religion "espouses" what it thinks it needs to espouse in order to get what it wants. What it practices is of more import than these contrived espousals. Smith referred here to the repeated affirmations by Nepal of the Universal Declaration of Human Rights. International Association for the Defense of Religious Liberty, Statement to the United Nations Human Rights Commission, February 1990.

14. Author's interview with a pastor in Jerusalem, October 1988. There is a conspiracy theory in Israel which says that a mysterious organization called "The Mission," based either in Jerusalem or Rome, depending on which report is believed, exists in order to convert Israel to Christianity. It is said to have unlimited funds and to operate by fraud, deceit and bribery. According to the rumors, the Mission is worse than Hitler, who only destroyed Jewish bodies, for it destroys Jewish souls. Some Christians speculate that the national Ministry of Religious Affairs funds some of the anti-Christian activity, but there is apparently no evidence for this. See Anne Dexter, *View the Land* (South Plainfield, NJ: Bridge Publishing, 1986), pp. 146f.

15. Interview with Kenneth Crowell by the author, Tiberias, October 26, 1988. There is an extended account of Crowell's experiences in Tiberias in Herbert Schlossberg, *Called to Suffer, Called to Triumph* (Portland: Multnomah Press, 1990), Chapter 9.

16. Baruch Maoz "Israel in a State of Economic, Political, and Religious Flux," *Pulse*, February 16, 1990, p. 4.

17. Dexter, *View the Land*, pp. 68f.

CHAPTER FIVE: *The Totalitarian Persecution of the Church*

1. Pierre Courthial, in Sergiu Grossu, ed., *The Church in Today's Catacombs*, trans. Janet L. Johnson (New Rochelle, NY: Arlington House, 1975), pp. 126f.

2. *The Persecution of the Catholic Church in the Third Reich: Facts and Documents Translated From the German*, no editor (New York: Longmans, Green & Co., 1942), p. 481. The title of the chapter from which this citation is taken is "The *Ersatz* Religion." The fact that it describes a "substitute" religion should not be taken to mean that it is not a real religion, however mistaken it may be in its choice of gods.

3. J. S. Conway, *The Nazi Persecution of the Churches: 1933-1945* (New York: Basic Books, 1968), p. 328.

4. Sociologist Thomas O. Cushman has argued that the totalitarian nature of the Soviet regime is due partly to the authoritarianism of the Russian Orthodox Church which became part of the Russian heritage assimilated even by the revolutionaries who repudiated the national past. His unpublished paper "The Orthodox Ethic and the Spirit of Communism: An

Exploration Into the Religious Bases of the Soviet State" was presented at a meeting in Monterey, California, in January 1988, where the thesis did not meet with general acceptance. But even if Cushman overstated the case his assumption that the heritage of the past has present implications, even for those who consciously reject the past, is surely true.

5. Jonathan Chao, "Church and State in Socialist China, 1945-1988," *Transformation*, July/September 1989, pp. 6-8.

6. A U.S. State Department publication concludes of the suppression but continued underground existence of the Uniate Church in the Ukraine that it is "the strongest and most representative exponent of cultural and spiritual ties with the West" (because of its allegiance to the Pope) and that it "remains an obstacle to the Soviet goal of creating a single Soviet people." Bureau of Public Affairs, U.S. Department of State, *Soviet Repression of the Ukrainian Catholic Church* (Special Report No. 159), January 1987.

7. Daniel Kyanda, "A Theology of Persecution: The Development of a Biblical Strategy for the Church Based on First Peter with Case Studies from Ethiopia, Uganda, Burundi and Mozambique," M.A. thesis, Nairobi International School of Theology," 1988, p. 21.

8. *Ibid.*, pp. 22f.

9. *Ibid.*, p. 20.

10. Jane Ellis, *The Russian Orthodox Church: A Contemporary History* (Bloomington, IN: Indiana University Press, 1986), pp. 270-273.

11. *Ibid.*, pp. 47ff.

12. *NNI*, March 14, 1990, p. 14.

13. There is an interesting account of the events surrounding this in Wassilij Alexeev and Theofanis G. Stavrou, *The Great Revival: The Russian Church Under German Occupation* (Minneapolis: Burgess, 1976).

14. Keston News Service #326, May 25, 1989, p. 14. This source will be referred to hereafter as *KNS*.

15. Interview by the author, June 2, 1987, Wheaton, Illinois. Tson's name also appears in publications as *Iosif Ton*.

16. A new law governing religion was approved in late 1990, too late for analysis here. A cursory reading reveals it is far superior to the earlier statute. We will not know for some time to what extent the liberalized provisions are honored. The forthcoming publication of Kent Hill, *The Soviet Union on the Brink* (Portland: Multnomah Press, 1991) will have a detailed analysis of the new law and the process by which it came into being. He reports that reality has already bypassed the new law as some of the constituent republics have enacted more liberal statutes and even abolished local branches of the Council on Religious Affairs. I am indebted to Kent Hill for furnishing galley proofs of parts of his book.

17. Quoted in Ellis, *Russian Orthodox Church*, p. 43.

18. Interview by the author, December 8, 1987, Leningrad.

19. Ellis, *Russian Orthodox Church*, pp. 442f.

20. Kyanda, "A Theology of Persecution," p. 38.
21. Albert Galter, *The Red Book of the Persecuted Church* (Westminster, MD: The Newman Press, 1957), p. 33. Theater and especially opera as revolutionary propaganda were also important features of the revolutionary movements of the eighteenth and nineteenth centuries. See James H. Billington, *Fire in the Minds of Men: Origins of the Revolutionary Faith* (New York: Basic Books, 1980), pp. 60, 152ff and *passim.*
22. Galter, *Red Book*, pp. 76f.
23. *KNS*, No. 334, September 21, 1989, p. 14.
24. Galter, *Red Book*, p. 425.
25. Interview by the author with a Soviet German Baptist pastor in West Germany, August 28, 1987. The *Letter* was issued by the officially-recognized All Union Council of Evangelical Christians and Baptists. It is not clear who actually drafted it, but the AUCECB later admitted that the regime had forced it to issue the document. See Walter Sawatsky, *Soviet Evangelicals Since World War II* (Kitchener, Ontario: Herald Press, 1981), pp. 277ff.
26. From a letter written in 1988, in Overseas Missionary Fellowship newsletter, July-August 1989, p. 3.
27. Ellis, *Russian Orthodox Church*, p. 264.
28. Interview by the author with Father A., Leningrad, December 7, 1987.
29. Galter, *Red Book*, pp. 74ff.
30. *Ibid.*, p. 218.
31. Letter of nineteen Latin rite Roman Catholic priests to their bishop in August 1988. *Religion in Communist Lands*, Winter 1989, pp. 361f.
32. Kyanda, "A Theology of Persecution," p. 26.
33. Galter, *Red Book*, pp. 225-240.
34. Ellis, *Russian Orthodox Church*, p. 443.
35. *Ibid.*, p. 428.
36. For an extended example of how the Soviet authorities discredit the leadership of an effective clergyman see the story of Fr. Dmitri Dudko in *ibid.*, pp. 409ff.
37. Josef Tson, *Marxism: The Faded Dream* (Basingstoke, Hants, England: Marshalls, 1985 [1976]), pp. 51f.
38. Galter, *Red Book*, p. 15. The statute by which this was done affirmed the policy of religious freedom.
39. *KNS*, #326, May 25, 1989, p. 5.
40. Appendix 6: "The Reich Youth Leader, Baldur von Schirach's Appeal to the German Catholic Youth," March 15, 1934, in Conway, *Nazi Persecution of the Churches*, p. 359.
41. Ellis, *Russian Orthodox Church*, p. 487.
42. *Ibid.*, pp. 100-113.
43. Typescript interview with a knowledgeable Romanian observer by Forbidden Fruits, 1984-85.
44. Ellis, *Russian Orthodox Church*, pp. 155-160.

45. *Persecution of the Catholic Church in the Third Reich*, p. 483.

46. Ellis, *Russian Orthodox Church*, pp. 23f.

47. Quoted in *NNI*, December 13, 1989, p. 32.

48. Grossu, *Catacombs*, pp. 60f.

49. *National and International Religion Report*, January 15, 1990, p. 2. This is from an interview with Baptist pastor Ilie Tsundrea of Bucharest. When I spoke to Pastor Tsundrea in his study in 1987 it was after taking a round-about route to his church while shaking off a man who was following my companions and me from our hotel. We felt pleased about our skill in doing this until Pastor Tsundrea informed us that the church was always under surveillance. Even as we talked we were already recorded in a *securitate* notebook.

50. Interview by the author, Leningrad, December 8, 1987.

CHAPTER SIX: *Totalitarian Control of the Church Structure*

1. Albert Galter, *The Red Book of the Persecuted Church* (Westminster, MD: The Newman Press, 1957), pp. 3-6.

2. Josef Tson, *The Christian Church Under Communism in Romania*, leaflet (Malton, North Yorkshire, England: The Romanian Aid Fund Ltd., 1983), no pagination.

3. *Ibid.*

4. Jane Ellis, *The Russian Orthodox Church: A Contemporary History* (Bloomington, IN: Indiana University Press, 1986), p. 172.

5. *Ibid.*, p. 4.

6. Galter, *Red Book*, pp. 78f.

7. *Ibid.*, pp. 296, 312f.

8. *Ibid.*, p. 377.

9. Stephen Mungoma, "Case Study on Persecution in Uganda," *Destined to Suffer* (Orange, CA: Open Doors with Brother Andrew, 1979), pp. 57-62, in Daniel Kyanda, "A Theology of Persecution: The Development of a Biblical Strategy for the Church Based on First Peter with Case Studies from Ethiopia, Uganda, Burundi and Mozambique," M.A. thesis, Nairobi International School of Theology, 1988, pp. 25f.

10. Iosif Ton, "The Present Situation of the Baptist Church in Romania," *Religion in Communist Lands*, Supplementary Paper Number 1, November 1973, pp. 5f.

11. Ellis, *Russian Orthodox Church*, pp. 60f.

12. *KNS*, No. 298, April 14, 1988.

13. Galter, *Red Book*, pp. 270-273.

14. *Ibid.*, p. 25.

15. Jonathan Chao, "Church and State in Socialist China, 1949-1988," *Transformation*, July-September 1989, pp. 6-8.

16. *Ibid.*, pp. 10-14.

17. *Ibid.*, p. 6.

18. *European Background Brief* (Open Doors), No. 64, March 1990, pp. 5-9.

19. *KNS*, No. 326, May 25, 1989.

20. Harold O. J. Brown, in *The Religion and Society Report*, September 1989, pp. 7f. Brown took this material from the Zurich doctoral dissertation of former East German pastor Juergen Seidel.

21. In May 1988 seventy-eight priests in Slovakia sent a letter to the diocesan administrator. They disavowed Pacem in Terris, and accused it of being "a stumbling-block to the unity of the priesthood and consequently also the unity of believers." They said few priests in the diocese belonged, but those who do receive favors from the state and "hold almost all key positions in the diocese." A papal decree in 1982 banned political associations of priests such as Pacem in Terris. *KNS*, #327, June 8, 1989, p. 16.

22. Ellis, *Russian Orthodox Church*, pp. 216f.

23. *Ibid.*, p. 482, n. 42.

24. Interview by the author with Father A., Leningrad, December 7, 1987.

25. *Vietnam: "Renovation" (Doi Moi), the Law and Human Rights in the 1980s* (London: Amnesty International, 1990), p. 15. No author given.

26. "Buddhism Becomes the Cambodian State Religion," *Religion in Communist Lands*, Winter 1989, pp. 337ff.

27. *Pulse*, March 23, 1990, p. 6.

28. Quoted by Walter H. Kansteiner, "Zimbabwe's Churches and the New Order," *Wall Street Journal*, January 5, 1988, p. A22. There is an expanded version of this article in "Zimbabwe's New Order: Where do the Churches Fit," *World Perspectives*, August 3, 1988, published by *NNI*.

29. Ellis, *Russian Orthodox Church*, p. 481, n. 28.

30. *Ibid.*, p. 9.

31. *Ibid.*, pp. 58-61.

32. J. S. Conway, *The Nazi Persecution of the Churches* (New York: Basic Books, 1968), Chapter 2.

33. Quoted from *Pravda*, November 11, 1954, in Galter, *Red Book*, p. 27. This should not be taken in any absolute sense. The KGB was killing Christian activists virtually up to the time this is being written in mid-1990.

34. *KNS*, No. 343, February 8, 1990, p. 21.

35. Appendix to U.S. Senate Hearings, Testimony of Rev. Richard Wurmbrand, May 6, 1966, "The Catholic Church and Cuba," p. 27. Translated from the French which was a translation from the Chinese. Issued by the Foreign Language Press of Beijing for use by the Latin American section of Liaison Department of the Chinese Communist Party, 1959.

36. Armando Valladares, *Against All Hope: The Prison Memoirs of Armando Valladares*, trans. Andrew Hurley (New York: Alfred A. Knopf, 1987).

37. Ellis, *Russian Orthodox Church*, p. 9.

38. *Ibid.*, p. 188.

39. *Ibid.*, p. 307.
40. This interview was published in the Soviet magazine *Ogonyok* in December 1988, and translated as "Law and Conscience," *Liberty*, July-August 1989, pp. 2-6. There was much western speculation at the time Kharchev left the CRA that the leadership deprived him of his post because of the *Ogonyok* interview. Kharchev and Nezhny both spoke at the conference of the International Religious Liberty Association in London in July 1989. This group is largely sponsored by the Seventh Day Adventists who also publish *Liberty*. With all the liberalization in the Soviet Union, Soviet spokesmen still protect the sacred name of Lenin from criticism. At the same conference Kharchev had this to say about why the Soviet Union began repressing religion: "I came to understand that the theory of Marxist-Leninism was distorted after Lenin by the bureaucracy, the party, which was created by Stalin. . . . With this new understanding came a crisis of conscience. How could I continue working?" The distortion came *after Lenin*, according to Kharchev, and this bureaucrat blames the bureaucracy, and not specified leaders apart from Stalin. In truth Lenin himself was the blame for the system that led to the repression and was also personally responsible for much of the repression. Kharchev, "Soviet Legislation on Freedom of Conscience," *Church-State Relations and the Freedom of Conscience*, Proceedings of the Third World Congress on Religious Liberty, July 23-26, 1989, p. 22.
41. "Law and Conscience," p. 6.
42. *Ibid.*, p. 3.
43. *KNS*, No. 327, June, 8, 1989, p. 2.
44. Interview with Josef Tson by the author, Chicago, October 12, 1987.

CHAPTER SEVEN: *The American Church on the Defensive*

1. H. Edward Rowe, *The Day They Padlocked the Church* (Shreveport, LA: Huntington House, 1983); Everett Sileven, *The Story of America's First Padlocked Church* (Louisville, NE: Fundamentalist Publications, 1983).
2. Harold Berman, "The Interaction of Law and Religion," *Humanities in Society*, Spring 1979, cited in Carl Horn III, "Taking God to Court," *Christianity Today*, January 2, 1981, pp. 25f.
3. Horn, "Taking God to Court," p. 26.
4. Lynn R. Buzzard and Samuel Ericsson, *The Battle for Religious Liberty* (Elgin, IL: David C. Cook Publishing Co., 1982), pp. 54-57.
5. *Ibid.*, pp. 68-70.
6. Franklin Hamlin Littell, "Religious Freedom in Contemporary America," *Journal of Church and State* (Spring, 1989), p. 222, cited in Ronald B. Flowers, "Church and State in the United States," *Church-State Relations and the Freedom of Conscience*, pp. 10f. Proceedings of the Third World Congress on Religious Liberty, London, July 23-26, 1989, sponsored by the International Religious Liberty Association.
7. Buzzard and Ericsson, *The Battle for Religious Liberty*, pp. 74f.

8. *Ibid.*, p. 60.

9. *Ibid.*, p. 52.

10. Carl H. Esbeck, "Toward a General Theory of Church-State Relations and the First Amendment," *Public Law Forum* (St. Louis University School of Law), Vol. 4, No. 2, 1985, pp. 325-354.

11. Quoted in Buzzard and Ericsson, *The Battle for Religious Liberty*, p. 156.

12. *Ibid.*, pp. 141f.

13. *National and International Religion Report*, February 26, 1990, pp. 3f.

14. Nancy Milito, "Christian Parents Charged with Child Abuse for Ordinary Spanking," *Religious Freedom Alert*, May 1990, p. 3.

15. Buzzard and Ericsson, *Battle for Religious Liberty*, pp. 242f.

16. "Labor Department Bureaucrats Launch Attack on Salvation Army," *Religious Freedom Alert*, October 1990, p. 3.

17. *Twin Cities Christian*, June 18, 1987, pp. 12-14.

18. Quoted in *National and International Religion Report*, June 18, 1990, p. 1.

19. Buzzard and Ericsson, *The Battle for Religious Liberty*, pp. 220f.

20. Roland N. Stromberg, *An Intellectual History of Modern Europe* (New York: Appleton-Century-Crofts, 1966), p. 268; Carlton J. H. Hayes, *A Generation of Materialism: 1871-1900* (New York: Harper and Brothers, 1941), p. 118; for a general interpretation of modern humanism in Christian perspective see Herbert Schlossberg, *Idols for Destruction: Christian Faith and Its Confrontation With American Society* (Washington, D.C.: Regnery Gateway, 1990 [1983]), Chapter 2.

21. Buzzard and Ericsson, *The Battle for Religious Liberty*, pp. 13f.

22. Albert Boiter, "Law and Religion in the Soviet Union," *The American Journal of Comparative Law*, Winter 1987, pp. 97-126.

23. For a defense of positivist law see, H. L. A. Hart, "Positivism and the Separation of Law and Morals," *Harvard Law Review*, Vol. 71, No. 4, February, 1958, pp. 593-629; a response to Hart showing the weaknesses of positivist law may be found in Lon L. Fuller, "Positivism and Fidelity to Law—A Reply to Professor Hart," *ibid.*, pp. 630-672.

24. Harold J. Berman, *Law and Revolution: The Formation of the Western Legal Tradition* (Cambridge, MA: Harvard University Press, 1983), p. 39.

25. Robert F. Drinan, quoted in William A. Donohue, *The Politics of the American Civil Liberties Union* (New Brunswick, NJ: Transaction Books, 1985), p. 310. Here is Donohue's conclusion on the ACLU position toward religion: "From the Union's perspective, separation between church and state means erecting an iron curtain between the two institutions. It is skeptical, if not distrustful, of the ambitions of the clergy. Freedom is won by relegating religion to a purely private sphere remote from the body politic. In fact, the establishment of a free society is predicated on the idea that religion must be surgically removed from culture. Freedom to worship must be protected but a free people will guard against the untoward consequences that religious influence might bring.

Therefore a cultural vivisection is in order: remove religion and immunize society (via the legislature and judiciary) against its reoccurrence" (p. 14).

26. Jonathan Chao, "Church and State in Socialist China, 1949-1988," *Transformation*, Vol. 6, No. 3, July-September 1989, pp. 6f.

27. Daniel Patrick Moynihan says that democratic governance "has become a process that . . . deliberately seeks to effect such outcomes as who *thinks* what, who *acts* when, who *lives* where, who *feels* how. That this description no more than defines a totalitarian society is obvious enough. But it has come to characterize democratic government as well. *I do not resist this development.*" Moynihan, *Maximum Feasible Misunderstanding: Community Action in the War on Poverty* (New York: Free Press, 1969), p. xiii. Emphasis added to the final sentence only.

28. Richard John Neuhaus, *The Naked Public Square: Religion and Democracy in America* (Grand Rapids: William B. Eerdmans Publishing Company, 1984), p. vii.

29. *Ibid.*, p. 21.

30. *Ibid.*, p. 86.

31. Carl F. H. Henry, "Christianity in a Troubled World," *Ministry* (Reformed Theological Seminary), Spring 1990, pp. 3f.

32. Jerry Bergman, *The Criterion: Religious Discrimination in America* (Richfield, MN: Onesimus Publishing, 1984). Bergman lost his job in a state university for holding creationist views, which he did not express in the classroom, even though he had published more scholarly work than the rest of his department combined and was acknowledged to be an effective teacher.

33. *The Religious Freedom Alert*, June 1990, pp. 1-15. The ruling has drawn hot dissent from the American Jewish Congress, Americans United for Separation of Church and State and the Baptist Joint Committee on Public Affairs. These groups and many more, including a number of mainline Protestant denominations, together with fifty-five constitutional law scholars, have asked the Court to reconsider this case. The Court has not done this since 1960, when it reaffirmed its original decision. The National Council of Churches' long-time spokesman on these issues, Dean M. Kelley, spoke strongly against the decision: "There is a shell of the free exercise clause left, but the heart and guts are cut out." Kelley predicted that the court would eventually reverse itself.

34. Bryce Christensen, "School Prayers in the Literature Class," Appendix B of Paul C. Vitz, *Censorship: Evidence of Bias in Our Children's Textbooks* (Ann Arbor, MI: Servant Books, 1986), p. 123.

35. C. S. Lewis, *God in the Dock*, ed. Walter Hooper (Grand Rapids, MI: Eerdmans, 1970), p. 314. On this issue see Schlossberg, *Idols for Destruction*, Chapter 5.

CHAPTER EIGHT: *A Theological Understanding of the Persecution of the Church*

1. *Pulse*, December 22, 1989, p. 5.

2. Quoted in Niels C. Nielsen, Jr., *Solzhenitsyn's Religion* (Nashville:

Thomas Nelson, 1975), p. 151, in Brother Andrew, *Is Life So Dear?: When Being Wrong Is Right* (Nashville: Thomas Nelson, 1985), p. 99.

3. Josef Tson, "A Theology of Martyrdom," typescript, address at Southampton, England, October 1988, pp. 5f.

4. Elizabeth Odio Benito [Special Rapporteur], *Elimination of All Forms of Intolerance and Discrimination Based on Religion or Belief*, United Nations Commission on Human Rights, August 31, 1986, p. 40.

5. Glenn Frankel, "Freed Hostage Tells of Loneliness, Fear and Friends Still Captive," *Minneapolis Star Tribune*, August 31, 1990, p. 4A.

6. Irina Ratushinskaya, *Grey Is the Color of Hope*, trans. Alyona Kojevnikov (New York: Alfred A. Knopf, 1988), p. 322.

7. For example, G. W. H. Lampe, "Martyrdom and Inspiration," *Suffering and Martyrdom in the New Testament*, ed. William Horbury and Brian McNeil (Cambridge, MA: Cambridge University Press, 1981), pp. 118-125.

8. Josef Tson, *A Theology of Martyrdom*, a leaflet of the Romanian Missionary Society, pp. 2ff. Tson's reference is to Matthew 16:25: "For whoever would save his life will lose it, and whoever loses his life for my sake will find it."

9. Quoted in Bill McGurn, "France: The New Voice of Notre Dame," *Wall Street Journal*, March 12, 1986, p. 35.

10. Interview with Josef Tson by the author, Chicago, October 12, 1987.

11. This is the thesis of John S. Pobee, *Persecution and Martyrdom in the Theology of Paul* (Sheffield, England: JSOT Press, 1985).

12. E. Gordon Rupp, *Principalities and Powers: Studies in the Christian Conflict in History* (London: The Epworth Press, 1952), p. 11.

13. Carl. F. H. Henry, "Christianity in a Troubled World," *Ministry* (Reformed Theological Seminary), Spring 1990, p. 5.

14. Jane Ellis, *The Russian Orthodox Church* (Bloomington, IN: Indiana University Press, 1986), pp. 333f.

15. *Ibid.*, pp. 369-373.

16. *Ibid*, p. 396. There is an excellent treatment of both groups on pp. 381-397.

17. Author's interview with Tatiana Goricheva, Paris, August 25, 1987.

18. Author's interview with Alexander Ogorodnikov, Moscow, December 14, 1987.

19. This is taken from *37*, No. 17 (1979), quoted in Ellis, *The Russian Orthodox Church*, p. 395.

20. Tson, "A Theology of Martyrdom," p. 4.

21. Brother Andrew, *Building in a Broken World* (Wheaton, IL: Tyndale House, 1981), pp. 13f.

22. See, for example, Brother Andrew, *Is Life So Dear?*, Chapter 9.

23 Goh Keat-Peng, "Church and State in Malaysia," *Transformation*, July-September 1989, p.17.

24. Daniel Kyanda, "A Theology of Persecution: The Development of a

Biblical Strategy for the Church Based on First Peter with Case Studies from Ethiopia, Uganda, Burundi and Mozambique," M.A. thesis, Nairobi International School of Theology, 1988, p. 34.

25. *Ibid.,* p. 17.

26. *Ibid.,* p. 18. The attack on 160 evangelicals in Mexico on February 2, 1990, resulted in unprecedented unity among the groups represented by the victims. Also unprecedented is the fact that the evangelical leadership has been able to meet with high government officials. *Pulse,* June 22, 1990, p. 1.

27. Author's interview with Jonathan Chao, Newport Beach, CA, July 16, 1987.

28. Jan Pit, *Persecution: It Will Never Happen Here?* (Santa Ana, CA: Open Doors, 1981), pp. 95f.

29. Rupp, *Principalities and Powers,* p. 94.

CHAPTER NINE: *The Church Reacts to Its Tormentors*

1. Quoted in Jane Ellis, *The Russian Orthodox Church: A Contemporary History* (Bloomington, IN: Indiana University Press, 1986), p. 209. This section of the book carries similar statements from members of the hierarchy.

2. *European Background Brief* (Open Doors), June-July 1989, No. 57, pp. 1f.

3. Ellis, *The Russian Orthodox Church,* p. 275.

4. Author's interview with Viktor K., Leningrad, December 8, 1987.

5. Alexander Ogorodnikov, "Religion and 'Perestroika' in the Soviet Union," translated letter dated January 12, 1988, and circulated informally. Ogorodnikov prepared this letter for delivery to the conference on religion in the Soviet Union meeting at that time in Monterey, CA. A Russian Orthodox archbishop was present at the meeting along with several other church officials, but they left long before the end of the conference. Evidently the content of some of the papers made things a bit hot for them, although everyone treated them with courtesy and even deference, and they expressed their views freely.

6. *Religion in Communist Lands,* Winter 1989, p. 365. The date of the Synod's communication is March 30, 1989.

7. Richard Wurmbrand, *Tortured for Christ* (n.p.: Hayfield Publishing Co., 1967), p. 7.

8. "Church Life in Romania," *Religion in Communist Lands,* Winter 1989, p. 357.

9. *KNS,* #350, May 17, 1990, p. 9. Keston College commented on the unexplained disappearance in June 1989 of Bulgarian priest Fr. Hristofor Subev, president of the unrecognized Independent Committee for the Defense of Religious Rights: "Fr. Subev's activities have recently incurred the displeasure, not only of the state authorities, but also of the Holy Synod of the Bulgarian Orthodox Church." *Ibid.,* #329, July 6, 1989. The

officially recognized Committee for Human Rights in Bulgaria apparently could not provide any information on Subev.

10. *Ibid.*, #328, June 22, 1989, pp. 2f.

11. Ellis, *Russian Orthodox Church*, pp. 287ff.

12. Daniel Kyanda, "A Theology of Persecution: The Development of a Biblical Strategy for the Church Based on First Peter with Case Studies from Ethiopia, Uganda, Burundi and Mozambique," M.A. thesis, Nairobi International School of Theology, 1988, p. 39.

13. *Ibid.*, p. 17.

14. Phu Xuan Ho, "Church-State Relations in Vietnam," *Transformation*, July-September 1989, p. 24.

15. Shawky F. Karas, *The Copts Since the Arab Invasion: Strangers in Their Own Land* (Jersey City, NJ: American, Canadian, and Australian Coptic Associations, 1985), pp. 193f. Less happily, Karas also reports that the opposition to Shenouda included Coptic prelates who were jealous of their leader's popularity.

16. Puebla Institute, *Nepal: Religious Repression in the Hindu Kingdom* (Washington, D.C., 1990), p. 6. No author given.

17. Ellis, *Russian Orthodox Church*, pp. 294f., 304.

18. *Ibid.*, p. 305.

19. *Ibid.*, pp. 309-315.

20. *Ibid.*, pp. 60f. An interesting example of this phenomenon occurred in late seventeenth-century France when Louis XIV revoked the Edict of Nantes and in effect made Protestantism illegal. The executive order forbade the Protestant (Huguenot) laity from leaving the country, while it ordered the pastors into exile. Although both of these orders were obeyed only imperfectly, the Huguenot masses did remain in France without their pastors and persisted under the persecution for several generations until the religious disabilities under which they lived were revoked. Protestant theology, emphasizing the doctrine of the priesthood of all believers, seems tailor-made for its ability to carry on without clergy, but examples in the sacerdotal churches suggest that lay leadership can be vital and effective any place there is a Christian church.

21. Ogorodnikov, "Religion and 'Perestroika' in the Soviet Union."

22. Ho, "Church-State Relations in Vietnam," p. 24.

23. Author's interview with a Soviet pastor, West Germany, August 27, 1987.

24. Ellis, *Russian Orthodox Church*, p. 264.

25. Wurmbrand, *Tortured for Christ*, p. 45.

26. Ron MacMillan, "Heresy: The Soft Underbelly of the Chinese Revival," *Special Report*, News Network International, August 6, 1990, pp. 1-8.

27. Istvan Tokes, "The Ex-lex Situation in the Reformed Church of Transylvania," a letter that reached the West in August 1988. *Religion in Communist Lands*, Winter 1989.

28. Ellis, *Russian Orthodox Church*, p. 489.

29. Robert Conquest, *Tyrants and Typewriters: Communiques from the Struggle for Truth* (Lexington, MA: Lexington Books, 1989), p. xi.

30. M. P. Kulakov, "Response to Kharchev," *Church-State Relations and the Freedom of Conscience*, Proceedings of the Third World Congress on Religious Liberty, July 23-26, 1989, p. 27.

31. Author's interview with a recent Soviet emigrant in West Germany, August 28, 1987.

32. Author's interview with Father A., Leningrad, December 7, 1987.

33. Kun Sam Lee, *The Christian Confrontation with Shinto Nationalism: A Historical and Critical Study of the Conflict of Christianity and Shinto in Japan in the Period Between the Meiji Restoration and the End of World War II (1868-1945)* (Amsterdam: Van Soest, 1962), pp. 185-192. Surprisingly Christian influence over Japanese culture has been remarkably strong, even though Christian missions have been far less successful in attracting converts than in many other countries. A Japanese study done in 1930 revealed that most educated Japanese regarded Christianity as having had an indispensable influence with regard to such areas of Japanese life as anti-prostitution, temperance, welfare, education, and the status of women—and that Buddhists have been affected to about the same extent as Christians. Soichi Saito, *A Study of the Influence of Christianity Upon Japanese Culture* (Tokyo: The Japan Council of the Institute of Pacific Relations, 1931), p. 2.

34. Author's interview with a newly emigrated pastor, West Germany, August 27, 1987.

35. Chris Marantika, "The Church in the Islamic Context," unpublished paper, 1988.

36. Myroslaw Tataryn, "Russian Orthodox Attitudes Towards the Ukrainian Catholic Church," *Religion in Communist Lands*, Winter 1989, pp. 313-331.

37. Kyanda, "A Theology of Persecution," p. 25.

38. Kraig Meyer, *A Clash of Swords: The Sword of the Spirit vs. the Sword of Islam in the Land of Turkey* (Grand Junction, CO: Friends of Turkey, 1986), p. 84.

39. Nadia Ramsis Farah, *Religious Strife in Egypt: Crisis and Ideological Conflict in the Seventies* (New York: Gordon and Breach Science Publishers, 1986), *passim*, especially pp. 36, 51ff. This is not to endorse the bias of this book, which in general is deaf to specifically religious arguments and places its reliance wholly on social analysis, a weak reed for the weighty conclusions it reaches.

40. *KNS*, #343, February 8, 1990, p. 4.

41. "The Christian in a Muslim Society" (no author given), *International Reformed Bulletin*, 1979, p. 17.

42. *KNS*, #326, May 25, 1989, pp. 9ff.

43. Karas, *The Copts Since the Arab Invasion*, pp. 190-203. Samuel was the

Bishop of Public Relations and Social Services—in other words a flack and social worker, not a pastoral leader.

44. *Ibid.*, p. 212; Rodney Clapp *et. al.*, "The Church in Egypt," *Christianity Today*, June 17, 1988, pp. 34, 39.

45. *KNS*, #343, February 8, 1990, p. 21.

46. Goh Keat-Peng, "Church and State in Malaysia," *Transformation*, July-September 1989, p. 20. There is another description of this Federation in *Pulse*, July 15, 1989, p. 5. *Berita NECF* (National Evangelical Christian Fellowship of Malaysia) October-November 1988, p. 8.

47. Kyanda, "A Theology of Persecution," p. 18.

48. *Ibid.*

49. Anne Dexter, *View the Land* (South Plainfield, NJ: Bridge Publishing, 1986), pp. 88f.

50. This argument is stated most forcefully in Hannah Arendt, *The Origins of Totalitarianism*, new ed. (New York: Harcourt, Brace, and World, 1966), pp. 323f. and *passim*.

51. Li Wei Han Document, *The Catholic Church and Cuba*, in U.S. Senate Judiciary Committee hearings, May 6, 1966, appendix, p. 30.

52. Ellis, *Russian Orthodox Church*, p. 119. This conclusion is based on an internal CRA memorandum that has come to light.

53. *Ibid.*, pp. 369-373.

54. Vishal Mangalwadi, *Truth and Social Reform* (New Delhi: Nivedit Good Books Distributors, 1986), p. 17.

55. "Law and Conscience," *Liberty*, July-August 1989, pp. 5f.

56. Tatiana Goricheva, *Talking About God Is Dangerous: The Diary of a Russian Dissident* (New York: Crossroad Publishing, 1987).

57. Ellis, *Russian Orthodox Church*, pp. 322-325.

58. *U.S.S.R. Reformatorisch Dagblad*, July 28, 1989, quoted in Open Doors, *European Background Brief*, August-September 1989, p. 4.

59. Author's interview with a Baptist layman, Leningrad, December 8, 1987.

60. *NNI Special Report* by Ron MacMillan, February 15, 1990.

61. Sharon E. Mumper, "Hong Kong Church in Future Shock in the Wake of the Beijing Massacre," *Pulse*, December 22, 1989, p. 2.

62. Harold O. J. Brown, in *The Religion and Society Report*, September 1989, pp. 7f. This comes from the Zurich doctoral dissertation of former East German pastor Juergen Seidel. Given this background it's remarkable to see the role played by the churches in effecting the peaceful overturning of the East German communist state, showing that in an inhospitable regime a church with many problems can still accomplish things. The church has been given credit by many observers for both bringing about the peaceful revolution that toppled the communist regime in 1989, and for keeping it peaceful when many sought revenge. See Janice A. Broun, "The Role of the Church in East Germany," *Freedom at Issue*, May-June 1990, pp. 15-17. Charles Colson writes that Christian believers were the catalyst of the liberation movements of east Europe. He calls the general

adulation of the Soviet leader *Gorbyphoria*, and derides the assumption that his policies have brought about the changes. Rather, Colson believes that "deep-rooted spiritual forces" are what have made the difference. In East Germany, where church attendance is minimal, the dissident movement grew out of Monday evening services at St. Nikolai church in Leipzig. Colson quotes the British forces' commander in Berlin: "The role of the church in providing a beacon of hope and decency and human courage has been of incalculable importance." The overturn of the Ceausescu regime in Romania came out of the resistance of reformed pastor Laszlo Tokes. In Poland the seeds of the revolution lay in the determined resistance almost three decades earlier when the people of Krakow—whose bishop later became Pope—kept replacing an outdoor cross as often as the communist regime tore it town. Even in the U.S.S.R., Colson quotes Irina Ratushinskaya as saying there were more young people who are Christians than are communists. Charles Colson, "The Shadow of the Cross," *Jubilee*, April 1990, p. 7.

63 . Phu Xuan Ho, "Church-State Relations in Vietnam," p. 21.

64. Quoted by Ron MacMillan, *NNI*, July 10, 1989, p. 3.

65. Tony Lambert, "China a Placid Volcano Waiting to Erupt," *Pulse*, June 8, 1990, p. 4.

66. Author's interview with Fr. A., Leningrad, December 7, 1987.

67. Clapp, "Church in Egypt," p. 40.

68. Author's interview with Alexander Ogorodnikov, Moscow, December 14, 1987.

CHAPTER TEN: *The Church Strikes Back: The Practice of Resistance*

1. *Pulse*, July 15, 1989, p. 5.

2. Daniel Kyanda, "A Theology of Persecution: The Development of a Biblical Strategy for the Church Based on First Peter with Case Studies from Ethiopia, Uganda, Burundi and Mozambique," M.A. thesis, Nairobi International School of Theology, 1988, p. 34.

3. Art Moore, "Ugandan Church Leader Urges African Christians to Prepare for Persecution," *Pulse*, March 9, 1990, p. 4.

4. Bat Ye'or, *The Dhimmi: Jews and Christians Under Islam*, rev. ed., trans. David Maisel and Paul Fenton (Rutherford, NJ: Fairleigh Dickinson University Press, 1985), p. 141.

5. Author's interview with Viktor K., Leningrad, December 10, 1987.

6. Author's interview with a well-traveled Arab Christian with personal knowledge of the house churches in North Africa, Minneapolis, April 1989.

7. Author's interviews with recent emigrants from the Soviet Union, West Germany, August 27-28, 1987.

8. Letter of 1988 from Shaanxi province, China, in a newsletter of the Overseas Missionary Fellowship, July-August 1989, p. 4.

9. Jane Ellis, *The Russian Orthodox Church: A Contemporary History* (Bloomington, IN: Indiana University Press, 1976), pp. 295ff.

10. Author's interview with emigrant, West Germany, August 27, 1987.

11. Ellis, *Russian Orthodox Church*, pp. 431ff.

12. Author's interview with Ogorodnikov, Moscow, December 14, 1987.

13. Ellis, *Russian Orthodox Church*, pp. 374ff.

14. News Release, Committee for Religious Freedom, Palisade Colorado, April 15, 1988.

15. Barbara G. Baker, "Believers in Turkey Claim Their Legal Rights," *Christianity Today*, April 7, 1989, p. 44.

16 "The World Reacts: International Opinion to ISA [Internal Security Act] Detentions," *Aliran*, January 1988, pp. 9-12.

17. Author's interview with Josef Tson, Chicago, October 12, 1987.

18. Ellis, *Russian Orthodox Church*, p. 307.

19. *NNI*, December 13, 1989, pp. 16f.

20. Author's interview with Josef Tson, Chicago, October 12, 1987.

21. Goh Keat-Peng, "Church and State in Malaysia," *Transformation*, July-September 1989, pp. 19f.

22. Kraig Meyer, *A Clash of Swords: The Sword of the Spirit vs. The Sword of Islam in the Land of Turkey* (Grand Junction, CO: Friends of Turkey, 1986), p. 86.

23. Interview with a recent emigrant from the Soviet Union, West Germany, August 28, 1987.

24. Author's interview with an emigrant from the Soviet Union, West Germany, August 27, 1987.

25. Phu Xuan Ho, "Church-State Relations in Vietnam," *Transformation*, July-September 1989, p. 24.

26 Quoted in Josef Tson, *Marxism: The Faded Dream* (Basingstoke, Hants, England: Marshalls, 1985 [1976]), pp. 51f.

27. There is an excellent account of this in Oxana Antic, *Fifteen Years of the 'Khristianin' Publishing House*, Radio Liberty Research RL 120/87, March 23, 1987.

28. W. S. Nelson, "Pan-Islamism in Turkey," *Islam and Missions*, ed. E. M. Wherry, *et. al.* (New York: Fleming H. Revell, 1911), p. 49.

29. Jan Pit, *Persecution: It Will Never Happen Here?* (Santa Ana, CA: Open Doors, 1981), pp. 73f.

30. Konstantin Kharchev, "Soviet Legislation on Freedom of Conscience," *Church-State Relations and the Freedom of Conscience*, Proceedings of the Third World Congress on Religious Liberty, London, July 23-26, 1989, p. 22.

31. Reuven Brenner, "Don't Frighten the East Bloc Bureaucrats," *Wall Street Journal*, December 26, 1989, p. A7.

32. Ellis, *Russian Orthodox Church*, p. 258; *News Bulletin* (Vietnam Ministries), Fall Quarter 1989, p. 2.

33. That story is well told by Anita Deyneka, *A Song in Siberia: The True*

Story of a Russian Church That Could Not be Silenced (Elgin, IL: David C. Cook, 1977). The book is based on interviews with residents of Barnaul after their emigration to West Germany.

34. *Sparks* (Wheaton, IL: 1979) Vol. 4, No. 3, p. 16, quoted in Charles Dokmo, "Geography of Dissent in the U.S.S.R.," unpublished paper, p. 61.

35. *Ibid.*, p. 436.

36. Author's interview with Josef Tson, Chicago, October 12, 1987.

37. Author's interview with Soviet emigrant, West Germany, August 28, 1987. This lower officer used to shake with fear when entering the church, evidently because he suspected he might be acting against the interests of the God his ideology told him did not exist. Whenever he came in, the members would pray or sing hymns to increase the pressure on him.

38. Bertram Schlossberg interview with Baruch Maoz, Jerusalem, February 1989. A Jewish Christian in Jerusalem told me that when he got to know the rabbi who was organizing the opposition to the church, the man was so taken with him he offered him a scholarship in his school!

39. Author's interview with emigrant from the Soviet Union, West Germany, August 27, 1987.

40. Author's interview with an emigrant from the Soviet Union, West Germany, August 29, 1987.

41. Wurmbrand, *Tortured for Christ*, p. 60.

42. Author's interview with Viktor K., Leningrad, December 8, 1987.

43. Author's notes from the meeting, Moscow, December 14, 1987.

44. *Christianity Today*, July 10, 1987, p. 43.

45. For an excellent recent study on the implications of high and low time preferences, see T. Alexander Smith, *Time and Public Policy* (Knoxville, TN: University of Tennessee Press, 1988).

CHAPTER ELEVEN: *Resistance and Accommodation*

1. That is the position, for example, of Jane Ellis, *The Russian Orthodox Church: A Contemporary History* (Bloomington, IN: Indiana University Press, 1986), p. 261, who endorses the opinion of another expert on the Russian Orthodox Church, William Fletcher. Ellis describes the position as one of "total subservience," and she is fully aware of the extent to which this prevents the church from carrying out its responsibilities. She also describes in great detail the suffering of many of its members at the hands of the regime and the inability of the subservient hierarchy to help them (pp. 262 and *passim*).

2. Daniel Kyanda, "A Theology of Persecution: The Development of a Biblical Strategy for the Church Based on First Peter with Case Studies from Ethiopia, Uganda, Burundi and Mozambique," M.A. thesis, Nairobi International School of Theology, 1988, pp. 12f. Kyanda also points out that a Frelimo sympathizer was bishop in the north (pp. 26f.).

3. *Ibid.*, p. 40. Kyanda emphasizes distinguishing "between the critical and

the peripheral, the crucial and the marginal. Lack of sound judgment in polarized situations can turn crisis into tragedy."

4. Ellis, *The Russian Orthodox Church*, p. 162.

5. Iosif Ton, "The Present Situation of the Baptist Church in Romania," *Religion in Communist Lands*, Supplementary Paper, No. 1, November 1973, pp. 9f., 16f.

6. Vishal Mangalwadi, *Truth and Social Reform* (New Delhi: Nivedit Good Books Distributors, 1986), pp. 50f.

7. Mangalwadi has written an account of his experiences which appears in Herbert Schlossberg, *Called to Suffer, Called to Triumph* (Portland: Multnomah Press, 1990).

8. *National and International Religion Report*, July 18, 1988, p. 7.

9. The democratic revolution in Nepal in 1990 was a case in point. And the leader of the National Democratic Party of Soviet Georgia spoke of the April 9, 1989 army repression that killed twenty-three people in a square of Tblisi, the capital of Georgia: "It was a big mistake by the Kremlin, because people saw with their own eyes that [the Soviets] are an occupation force." The killing "has united people. It is like a mystical force." Quoted in Peter Gumbel, "Secessionist Fever Spreads in Soviet Union," *Wall Street Journal*, March 28, 1990, p. A8.

10. Sergiu Grossu, *The Church in Today's Catacombs*, trans. Janet L. Johnson (New Rochelle, NY: Arlington House, 1975), pp. 123f. Ilie Tsundrea, Baptist pastor in Bucharest, reports that after the revolution in Romania numerous soldiers, including officers, came in to say they had been believers all along. *National and International Religion Report*, January 15, 1990, p. 2.

11. *Islam's Clandestine Operations*, #6 in the Project File Series, February 1989, no pagination. Banbury, Oxon, England.

12. Author's interview with a well-traveled Arab Christian who had just returned from North Africa, Minneapolis, April 1989.

13. *Pulse*, April 13, 1990, p. 3.

14. Quoted in Ellis, *Russian Orthodox Church*, pp. 309ff.

15. *Newswire* (Slavic Gospel Association), February/March 1990, pp. 2f.

16. *KNS*, #343, February 8, 1990, p. 21.

17. *NNI*, February 15, 1990, pp. 7f.

18. Kyanda, "A Theology of Persecution," p. 41.

19. Jan Pit, *Persecution: It Will Never Happen Here?* (Santa Ana, CA: Open Doors, 1981), pp. 73f.

20. Quoted in Trevor Beeson, *Discretion and Valour: Religious Conditions in Russia and Eastern Europe*, rev. ed., (Philadelphia: Fortress Press, 1982), p. 66.

21. Quoted in Grossu, *Church in Today's Catacombs*, pp. 150f. Krasnov-Levitin appears in other sources as Levitin or Levitin-Krasnov.

22. *KNS*, #326, June 8, 1989, p. 18.

23. George Otis, Jr., "Discretion and Valor Revisited," p. 6. Unpublished

paper prepared for the Fieldstead Institute Consultation on the Persecution of the Church, Colorado Springs, Colorado, September 1989.

24. *Ibid.*, p. 3.

25. Newsletter, Overseas Missionary Fellowship, July-August 1989, p. 3.

26. Baruch Maoz interview by Bertram Schlossberg, Jerusalem, February 1989.

27. Spoken in my hearing at a conference in a free country, November 1990.

28. Beeson, *Discretion and Valor*, p. 8.

29. Albert Galter, *The Red Book of the Persecuted Church* (Westminster, MD: The Newman Press, 1957), p. 82.

30. The *Chronicle* is published in English by the Lithuanian R. C. Priests' League of America in Brooklyn, New York. For a fascinating story of a clandestine Lithuanian nun who formed part of the *Chronicle* team see Nijole Sadunaite, *A Radiance in the Gulag: The Catholic Witness of Nijole Sadunaite*, trans. Casimir Pugevicius and Marian Skabeikis (Manassas, VA: Trinity Communications, 1987).

31. This is the thesis of John S. Pobee, *Persecution and Martyrdom in the Theology of Paul* (Sheffield, England: JSOT Press, 1985).

32. G. W. H. Lampe, "Martyrdom and Inspiration," *Suffering and Martyrdom in the New Testament*, eds. William Horbury and Brian McNeil (Cambridge, MA: Cambridge University Press, 1981), p. 125.

33. Brother Andrew, *Is Life so Dear?: When Being Wrong Is Right* (Nashville, Thomas Nelson, 1985), p. viif.

34. *Ibid.*, pp. 22, 32f.

35. *Ibid.*, p. 36.

36. *KNS*, #329, July 6, 1989, pp. 5f. This report comes from Latvia.

37. Cf. Ellis, *Russian Orthodox Church*, p. 210: ". . . there is the strong influence of the history of their church, which has no tradition of opposition to the state, and whose Byzantine theological inheritance does not encourage it to adopt such a position."

38. Marsh Moyle, "The Effects of Persecution on Church and Missions in Central and Eastern Europe," unpublished paper, November 1989, pp. 3-5. An earlier version of this paper was presented at the Fieldstead Institute Consultation on the Persecution of the Church, Colorado Springs, Colorado, September 1989.

39. *Ibid.*, p. 7.

40. Alexander Solzhenitsyn, *The Oak and the Calf: Sketches of Literary Life in the Soviet Union*, trans. Harry Willetts (New York: Harper Colophon Books, 1975), p. 284.

41. *Ibid.*, p. 297.

42. *Ibid.*, pp. 198, 309.

43. Otis, "Discretion and Valor Revisited," p. 2.

44. Janice Broun, *Conscience and Captivity: Religion in Eastern Europe* (Washington, D.C.: Ethics and Public Policy Center, 1988), p. 290.

45. *New York Times*, September 18, 1989.

CHAPTER TWELVE: *Extending a Helping Hand*

1. For an extended discussion of the Biblical critique of religion see Herbert Schlossberg, *Idols for Destruction: Christian Faith and Its Confrontation with American Society* (Washington, D.C.: Regnery Gateway, 1990 [1983]), Chapter 6, "Idols of Religion."

2. Sergiu Grossu, ed., *The Church in Today's Catacombs*, trans. Janet L. Johnson (New Rochelle, NY: Arlington House, 1975), p. 19.

3. *See*, for example, the dissertation of Ludvik Nemec, *Episcopal and Vatican Reaction to the Persecution of the Catholic Church in Czechoslovakia* (Washington, D.C.: The Catholic University of America Press, 1953).

4. Quoted in Basilia Schlink, *The Eve of Persecution* (Carol Stream, IL: Creation House, 1974), p. 31.

5. Joshua Muravchik, "The National Council of Churches and the U.S.S.R.," *This World*, #9, 1984, pp. 30-52. For an excellent overview of NCC politics see K. L. Billingsley, *From Mainline to Sideline: The Social Witness of the National Council of Churches* (Washington, D.C.: Ethics and Public Policy Center, 1990).

6. Kent R. Hill, *The Puzzle of the Soviet Church* (Portland: Multnomah Press, 1989), pp. 160f.

7. "Koreans Reject NCC 'Peace' Plan," *The Presbyterian Layman*, September/October 1989, pp. 1, 6.

8. *Pulse*, March 9, 1990, p. 6.

9. Telephone interview with Marston Speight, NCC specialist on Christian-Muslim relations and adjunct faculty member at Hartford Theological Seminary, August 19, 1988.

10. Telephone interview with Charles Kimball, Islamic specialist at the NCC, August 17, 1988.

11. *NNI*, June 7, 1990, pp. 15-17.

12. Michael Nazir Ali, *Frontiers in Muslim Christian Encounter* (Oxford: Regnum Books, 1987), p. 25.

13. Herbert Schlossberg, "Who'll Help Presbyterians Persecuted in Mexico?," *Mainstream* (Newsletter of Presbyterians for Democracy and Religious Freedom), Fall 1989. This article was based on numerous *NNI* reports and conversations with observers in Mexico and the responsible official of the Presbyterian Church (USA).

14. No author, *Introducing Nepal and the UMN* (United Mission to Nepal Publications Office, 1987), pp. 12f.

15. From *Religion in Communist Lands*, Vol. 4, No. 1, 1976.

16. Jane Ellis, *The Russian Orthodox Church: A Contemporary History* (Bloomington, IN: Indiana University Press, 1986), p. 291.

17. William Branigin, "Philippine Rebels Targeting Rights Groups, Churches," *Washington Post*, October 18, 1986.

18. *National and International Religion Report*, March 26, 1990, p. 7.

19. *First Things*, August-September 1990, p. 74.

20. Allan C. Brownfeld, "Betraying Romania's Christians," *Orange County Register*, March 27, 1988.

21. *Christianity Today*, March 19, 1990, p. 53.

22. *National and International Religion Report*, February 12, 1990, p. 6.

23. J. A. Emerson Vermaat, *The World Council of Churches & Politics: 1975-1986* (New York: Freedom House, 1989), pp. 27-37, 65-76. Vermaat is a Dutch journalist. For a critical overview of the history of the WCC these two books of Ernest W. Lefever are very useful: *Amsterdam to Nairobi: The World Council of Churches and the Third World* (Washington, D.C.: Ethics and Public Policy Center, 1979); and *Nairobi to Vancouver: The World Council of Churches and the World, 1975-87* (Washington, D.C.: Ethics and Public Policy Center, 1987). The theme of this period of the WCC's history might be conveniently summarized by the title of Chapter 10 in this second volume: "A Persistent Double Standard."

24. Olga S. Hruby, in *Religion in Communist Dominated Areas*, Spring 1990, p. 35.

25 Harold O. J. Brown, "A Curious Silence," *The Religion and Society Report*, November 1990, p. 3.

26. Hill, *The Puzzle of the Soviet Church*, pp. 193ff.

27. Valeri Barinov and Danny Smith, *Jailhouse Rock* (London: Hodder and Stoughton, 1990), p. 303.

28. Paul Steeves, "The Soviet Church: How Free Can it Be?," *Christianity and Crisis*, May 28, 1990, pp. 179f. Steeves, attacking a colleague's paper at a historical meeting in Chicago in 1980, defended Lenin as worthy of support by Christians who should have regarded the founder of the Soviet state as a brother. This proposal received some heated responses by shocked participants, including me.

29. Telephone conversation, September 7, 1988.

30. Jean Daujat in *The Church in Today's Catacombs*, ed. Grossu, p. 15.

31. Quoted in P. D. Devanandan, *The Gospel and Renascent Hinduism* (London: SCM Press, 1959), p. 38.

32. Roy C. Amore, *Two Masters, One Message* (Nashville: Abingdon, 1978), p. 177. See another example in the context of interfaith dialogue in the United Kingdom: John Hick, *God Has Many Names: Britain's New Religious Pluralism* (London: The MacMillan Press, 1980).

33. Albert Galter, *The Red Book of the Persecuted Church* (Westminster, MD: The Newman Press, 1957), p. 257.

34. Jacques Ellul, preface to Bat Ye'or, *The Dhimmi: Jews and Christians Under Islam*, rev. ed., trans. David Maisel and Paul Fenton (Rutherford, NJ: Fairleigh Dickinson University Press, 1985), p. 27.

35. *NNI*, October 4, 1988, p. 14.

36. That is the thesis of Norman Daniel, *Islam and the West: The Making of an Image* (Edinburgh: Edinburgh University Press, 1960).

37. Author's interview with Josef Tson, Wheaton, Illinois, July 2, 1987.

38. Elizabeth Odio Benito, *Elimination of All Forms of Intolerance and*

Discrimination Based on Religion or Belief (United Nations Commission on Human Rights, August 31, 1986), pp. 5-7.

39. *Ibid.*, p. 7.

40. Angelo Vidal d'Almeida Ribeiro, *Implementation of the Declaration on the Elimination of All Forms of Intolerance and of Discrimination Based on Religion or Belief* (United Nations Commission on Human Rights, January 6, 1988), p. 26. For a critique of an earlier UN document on religious oppression see Robert F. Drinan, *Cry of the Oppressed: The History & Hope of the Human Rights Revolution* (San Francisco: Harper & Row, 1987), pp. 187-191. Drinan here sees the weaknesses but tries to put a positive face on the UN effort by pointing to the political difficulties of such an effort.

41. Special Briefing on Religious Liberty in the International Community, April 13, 1988.

42. Robert Conquest, *Tyrants and Typewriters: Communiques From the Struggle for Truth*, (Lexington, MA: Lexington Books: 1989), pp. 195ff.

43. Ellis, *The Russian Orthodox Church*, pp. 424f.

44. *Aide Aux Croyants de L'U.R.S.S.*, Winter 1989, p. 3.

45. Anita Deyneka, "God in the Gulag," *Christianity Today*, August 9, 1985, pp. 29f.

46 For her story see Irina Ratushinskaya, *Grey Is the Color of Hope*, trans. Alyona Kojevnikov (New York: Alfred A. Knopf, 1988).

47. Brother Andrew, *Building in a Broken World* (Wheaton, IL: Tyndale House, 1981), p. 69.

48. *Ibid.*, p. 97.

49. George Weigel, *Catholicism and the Renewal of American Democracy* (Mahwah, NJ: Paulist Press, 1989), p. 190.

50. Michael Johnson, "Mission Financial Practices and Church Growth in Yugoslavia," unpublished paper, July 1988.

51. John Goodchild, "How to Deal with the Soviets," *Wall Street Journal*, May 15, 1989, p. A12.

52. *Pulse*, March 9, 1990, p. 5.

53. Quoted in Gary Cox, "Making Mission Possible," *Frontier* (Keston College), July-August, 1990, p. 8.

54. Daniel Kyanda, "A Theology of Persecution: The Development of a Biblical Strategy for the Church Based on First Peter with Case Studies from Ethiopia, Uganda, Burundi and Mozambique," M.A. thesis, Nairobi International School of Theology, 1988, pp. 5f.

55. There is a good treatment of these issues in an anonymous article, "The Christian in a Muslim Society," *International Reformed Bulletin*, Nos. 74-75, 1979, pp. 15-21. This article mentions the first Arab empire under the Omeyads with its capital in Damascus. The Arabs were not capable of administering their realm. They needed the cooperation of the Christians of the empire to help them as administrators. When this need was no longer as pressing, their successors began increasing the pressure

on the Christians. Also when Egyptians rid their land of the Turkish rulers at the end of World War I, Christians and Muslims worked hand-in-hand.

56. This is the argument of Lynn R. Buzzard and Samuel Ericsson, *The Battle for Religious Liberty* (Elgin, IL: David C. Cook Publishing Co., 1982), p. 16.

57. Appeal to the Delegates of the 5th Assembly of the World Council of Churches, Nairobi, Kenya, 1975, *Religion in Communist Lands*, 1976.

58. There are two interesting volumes of papers that are examples of what I mean, although they relate mostly to the issue of persecution in countries where human rights are relatively well respected, the situation dealt with in Chapter 7 of this book. *The Theology of Christian Resistance*, ed. Gary North (Tyler, TX: Geneva Divinity School Press, 1983); *Tactics of Christian Resistance*, ed. Gary North (Tyler, TX: Geneva Divinity School Press, 1983). These are Volumes 2 and 3 of a short-lived series entitled *Christianity and Civilization*.

59. Ellis, *The Russian Orthodox Church*, pp. 431ff.

60. U.S. Department of State, *Country Reports on Human Rights Practices for 1988*, February 1989, p. 1451.

61. Quoted in *Nepal: Religious Repression in the Hindu Kingdom* (Washington, D.C.: Puebla Institute, 1990), p. 29.

62. For example, Richard Wurmbrand attributed his release after fourteen years in a Romanian prison to the influence of American public pressure. Richard Wurmbrand, *Tortured for Christ* (n.p.: Hayfield Publishing Co., 1967), pp. 30f.

63. Midge Conner, "Ishmael's Chinese Companions," *China Prayer Letter and Ministry Report*, April 1990, pp. 1-6.

64. "When reading most of the literature devoted to Islam in Algeria, we notice the permanence of disputes between religious groups on the one hand and the central power on the other. A main characteristic, then, is the lasting opposition to central administration either based almost directly on religious arguments, or using Islam at least as a means of a channel to contest the legitimacy of governmental authorities." Jean-Claude Vatin, "Religious Resistance and State Power in Algeria," *Islam and Power*, eds. Alexander S. Cudsi and Ali E. Hillal Dessouki (Baltimore: The Johns Hopkins University Press, 1981), pp. 122f.

65. Jubilee Campaign press release, May 16, 1986.

66. I received this information from an informed source who works on behalf of the persecuted church.

67. Frank R. Wolf, "Change in Romania: Can the U.S. Help?," *World*, August 1, 1988, p. 16. Wolf says the whole idea of a maverick stance toward the Soviet Union was a carefully crafted deception, which worked. Also Frank R. Wolf, "Can the U.S. Foster Change in Romania's Human Rights Practices?" *World Perspectives*, July 14, 1988. On Funderburk see *Christianity Today*, July 10, 1987, p. 37.

68. *The Church in Today's Catacombs*, ed. Grossu, p. 15.

69. John Calvin, *Institutes of the Christian Religion*, Preface to King Francis I, I, 2.

GENERAL INDEX